T0301680

Environmental Taxation in China and Asia-Pacific

CRITICAL ISSUES IN ENVIRONMENTAL TAXATION

Series Editors: Larry Kreiser, *Cleveland State University, USA*, Julsuchada Sirisom, *Mahasarakham University, Thailand*, Hope Ashiabor, *Macquarie University, Australia* and Janet E. Milne, *Vermont Law School, USA*

The *Critical Issues in Environmental Taxation* series provides insights and analysis on environmental taxation issues on an international basis and explores detailed theories for achieving environmental goals through fiscal policy. Each book in the series contains pioneering and thought-provoking contributions by the world's leading environmental tax scholars who respond to the diverse challenges posed by environmental sustainability.

Previous volumes in the series:

Original book published by CCH Incorporated

Volumes I–IV published by Richmond Law Publishers

Volumes V–VIII published by Oxford University Press

Titles in the series published by Edward Elgar:

Volume IX   Environmental Taxation in China and Asia-Pacific
            Achieving Environmental Sustainability through Fiscal Policy
            Edited by Larry Kreiser, Julsuchada Sirisom, Hope Ashiabor and Janet E. Milne

Volume X   Environmental Taxation and Climate Change
            Achieving Environmental Sustainability through Fiscal Policy
            Edited by Larry Kreiser, Julsuchada Sirisom, Hope Ashiabor and Janet E. Milne

Environmental Taxation in China and Asia-Pacific

Achieving Environmental Sustainability through Fiscal Policy

Edited by

Larry Kreiser

Professor Emeritus of Accounting, Cleveland State University, USA

Julsuchada Sirisom

Lecturer of Accountancy, Mahasarakham University, Thailand

Hope Ashiabor

Associate Professor of Law, Macquarie University, Australia

Janet E. Milne

Professor of Law, Vermont Law School, USA

CRITICAL ISSUES IN ENVIRONMENTAL TAXATION, VOLUME IX

Edward Elgar

Cheltenham, UK • Northampton, MA, USA

Published by
Edward Elgar Publishing Limited
The Lypiatts
15 Lansdown Road
Cheltenham
Glos GL50 2JA
UK

Edward Elgar Publishing, Inc.
William Pratt House
9 Dewey Court
Northampton
Massachusetts 01060
USA

A catalogue record for this book is available from the British Library

Library of Congress Control Number: 2011926268

MIX
Paper from
responsible sources
FSC® C018575

ISBN 978 0 85793 775 9

Typeset by Columns Design XML Ltd, Reading
Printed and bound by MPG Books Group, UK

Contents

Figures

Tables

Editorial review board

The 14 chapters in this book have been brought to publication with the help of an editorial review board dedicated to peer review. The four members of the board are committed to the field of environmental taxation and are active participants in environmental taxation events around the world.

Lead Editor

Larry Kreiser
Cleveland State University, USA

Co-Editors

Julsuchada Sirisom
Mahasarakham University, Thailand

Hope Ashiabor
Macquarie University, Australia

Janet E. Milne
Vermont Law School, USA

Contributors

Ashiabor, Hope, Associate Professor of Law, Department of Business Law, Macquarie University, Sydney, Australia.

Bachus, Kris, Research Manager, Policy Research Centre for Sustainable Development and at the University of Leuven, Belgium.

Butcher, Bill, Associate Head of School, The Australian School of Taxation and Business Law, Australian School of Business, University of New South Wales, Australia.

Cao, Jing, Assistant Professor. School of Economics and Management of Tsinghua University in Beijing, China.

Cottrell, Jacqueline, Freelance environmental consultant and manager of Green Budget Europe (GBE), a European expert platform that promotes market-based instruments for the environment, Germany.

Gao, Shuting, Chinese Academy for Environmental Planning, China.

Ge, Chazhong, Chinese Academy for Environmental Planning, China.

Liu, Xianbing, Kansai Research Centre, Institute for Global Environmental Strategies, Japan.

Long, Feng, Chinese Academy for Environmental Planning, China.

Lu, Yuzhu, Lingnan University, Hong Kong.

Mortimore, Anna, Lecturer in Taxation Law at Griffith University and Ph.D. student, Faculty of Business and Economics, Macquarie University, Australia.

Nel, Rudie, University of Stellenbosch, South Africa.

Nienaber, Gerhard, University of Pretoria, South Africa.

Ogisu, Kazunori, Institute for Global Environmental Strategies, Japan.

Pearce, Prafula, Curtin University, Australia.

Ren, Yajuan, Chinese Academy for Environmental Planning, China.

Saccasan, Moira, Associate Lecturer, University of Western Sydney, Sydney, Australia.

Shishime, Tomohiro, Institute for Global Environmental Strategies, Japan.

Suk, Sunhee, Institute for Global Environmental Strategies, Japan.

Sun, Guili, Chinese Academy for Environmental Planning, China.

Tan, Seck L., National University of Singapore, Singapore.

Thampapillai, Dodo J., National University of Singapore, Singapore.

Trang, Le Nguyen Thuy, Faculty of Environmental Sciences, University of Natural Science, Vietnam National University, Ho Chi Minh City, Vietnam.

Wang, Jinnan, Chinese Academy for Environmental Planning, China.

Wang, Walter, Adjunct Professor of Law at the University of San Diego School of Law, USA.

Yen, Nguyen Thi Hai, Faculty of Environmental Sciences, University of Natural Science, Vietnam National University, Ho Chi Minh City, Vietnam.

Foreword

Climate change is a consequence of burning fossil fuel without paying the ecological costs of carbon emissions. The root cause of climate change is our current economic system, which depends on cheap fossil fuel. Therefore, the ultimate solution to climate change has to be a fundamental economic system change from an economy that takes ecological services such as a stable climate as free goods to an economy that recognizes the right price for ecological services and resources we are consuming.

Economic system change is easy to say but politically difficult to implement. Policy makers, businesses and consumers fear that paying the ecological price of fossil fuel will increase the tax burden on the economy, which could damage and slow down economic growth. This is why climate negotiations for burden sharing are so difficult.

Here lies the historical opportunity for experts working on environmental taxation. Ecological tax reform (ETR) holds the hope of internalizing ecological prices of ecological services and resources into the market price without increasing the tax burden on the entire economy. The double dividend hypothesis of ETR even holds the hope of stimulating economic growth while greening the economy.

Green economy, the main theme of the Rio+20 Summit in 2012, is an economy where investment in ecological services and resources could generate profit, employment and growth rather than economic loss. However, green economy requires an economic system change of shifting from an economy based on market prices that ignore ecological costs of climate change towards an economy that internalizes ecological prices into its price structure.

Though ETR has great potential, it has been tested only among a few European countries. The idea that tax policy can be used for 'greening the economy' for a 'double dividend' is little understood outside of Europe.

Environmental tax experts share a historical mission of providing concrete fiscal policy options that internalize ecological prices into the market price without damaging the economy and possibly stimulating the economy. There is a knowledge gap as to whether ecological fiscal policy can be applied in developing countries and what are the conditions that would make it function properly. It is an important task for ecological tax policy experts to indentify fiscal policy options that can create the conditions for a double dividend from ETR that holds the key to creating a synergy between economic growth, poverty reduction and environmental sustainability.

Traditional development patterns have followed the 'Grow first, Clean up later' approach. Many developing countries are following this pattern. Now is the time for change. Developing countries should be able to leapfrog to a green economy without repeating the same past mistakes of developed countries.

Green economy or green growth that promotes a win-win synergy between the economy and ecological sustainability will not happen automatically in the marketplace. It has to be made to happen. Governments have to jump start the green growth process by closing two gaps, namely the price gap between market price and ecological price and the time gap between short-term cost and long-term benefit.

Policy makers will not risk their political leadership unless they are convinced of the practicality and feasibility of fiscal policy options that promote internalizing ecological costs into the market price while not jeopardizing economic growth and employment. I congratulate the authors of Critical Issues in Environmental Taxation as they clarify and identify policy options necessary to stimulate the synergy between economic growth and ecological sustainability. This volume will encourage policy makers to venture out and jump start the process of greening the economy.

Mr Rae Kwon Chung, Director, Environment and Development Division, United Nations Economic and Social Commission for Asia and the Pacific (Former Climate Change Ambassador, The Republic of South Korea)

Preface

Gandhi once said, 'We must become the change we want to see.' If we want to have a safe environment, we must promote environmental sustainability.

Volume IX of Critical Issues in Environmental Taxation contains 14 chapters that provide insights and analysis for achieving environmental sustainability through tax policy. The main emphasis of Volume IX is on environmental taxation in China and Asia-Pacific.

The chapters are written by environmental taxation scholars from around the world. We hope you find their ideas to be interesting, thought-provoking, and worthy of serious consideration by policy makers.

Larry Kreiser, Lead Editor

Julsuchada Sirisom, Co-Editor

Hope Ashiabor, Co-Editor

Janet E. Milne, Co-Editor

September 2011

Acknowledgements

Chapter 2—Other contributors to the chapter are Zhao Yue, Yu Fang, Jiang Hong-qiang (Chinese Academy for Environmental Planning), Sun Gang (Fiscal Sciences Institute of Ministry of Finance), Gong Hui-wen, Chen Li (Taxation Sciences Institute of State Taxation Administration), and Zhang De-yon (Institute of Finance and Commerce of Chinese Academy of Social Sciences).

Jacqueline Cottrell (Chapter 6)—Thanks to Rebekka Frank for kindly editing and commenting on this chapter and bringing it into line with Edward Elgar requirements for publication.

Abbreviations

ACEA	Association of European Car Manufacturers
ATC	Australian Transport Council
BAU	Business as usual
CCS	Carbon capture and storage
CDM	Clean development mechanism
CER	Certified emission reduction
CGE	Computable general equilibrium
CIF price	Cost, insurance and freight price
CO_2	Carbon dioxide
COD	Chemical oxygen demand
CPRS	Carbon pollution reduction scheme
CSD	Committee for Sustainable Development (United Nations)
ERD	Economic demonstrated reserve
EFR	Environmental fiscal reform
EHS	Environmentally harmful subsidies
EIT	Enterprise Income Tax Law (China)
EPB	Environmental planning bureau
EPHC	Environment Protection and Heritage Council (Australia)
ERC	Energy Research Centre (United Kingdom)
ETR	Environmental tax reform
EU	European Union
EU-27	The 27 member states of the European Union
FBT	Fringe benefits tax
FCAI	Federal Chamber of Automotive Industry (Australia)
FRT	First registration tax (vehicles) (Hong Kong)
GBE	Green Budget Europe
GDP	Gross domestic product
GHG	Greenhouse gas

GST	Goods and services tax
HC	Hydrocarbon
HFC	Hydrofluorocarbon
IEA	International Energy Agency
IPCC	Intergovernmental Panel on Climate Change
JAMA	Japan Automobile Manufacturers Association
JPOI	Johannesburg Plan of Implementation
KAMA	Korean Automobile Manufacturers Association
LCV	Light commercial vehicle
LCT	Luxury car tax
LPG	Liquefied petroleum gas
LTBR	Long-term bond rate
MGD	Millennium Development Goal
MRRT	Minerals resource rent tax (Australia)
N_2O	Nitrous oxide
NO_x	Nitrogen oxides
NACE	National average carbon emissions
NAFC	National average fuel consumption
NDRC	National Development and Reform Commission (China)
NERI	National Environmental Reasearch Institute, University of Aarhus
NTC	National Transport Commission (Australia)
OECD	Organisation for Economic Co-operation and Development
PEI	Poverty-Environment Initiative (United Nations Environment Programme)
PES	Payment for environmental services
PFC	Perfluorocarbon
POP	Persistent organic pollutant
PRC	People's Republic of China
PPP	Purchasing power parity
PRRT	Petroleum resource rent tax (Australia)
PTG	Policy Transition Group (Australia)
RSPT	Resources super profits tax (Australia)
SARS	South African Revenue Service

TPES	Total primary energy supply
UNDP	United Nations Development Programme
UNEP	United Nations Environment Programme
UWWTP	Urban wastewater treatment plant
VAT	Value added tax
VLF	Vehicle licence fee

PART I

Environmental Taxation Strategies in China

1. Greening the dragon: energy tax policy in China

Walter Wang

INTRODUCTION

Due to the tremendous growth China has experienced in recent years, China surpassed the United States in 2009 as the world's largest energy consumer.[1] In 2006, coal accounted for 70 per cent of the total energy consumption in China.[2] China's energy demand continues to grow alongside its economy. In June 2010, China consumed 8.98 million barrels of oil per day, 10 per cent higher than one year before.[3] The International Energy Agency projects China's emissions of energy-related greenhouse gases will exceed the rest of the world's combined emissions by 2020.[4] The World Bank has reported that 16 of the 20 most polluted cities in the world are in China.[5] These figures support the fact that the Chinese government faces a daunting task to craft policies that address the externalities such growth has caused. China must somehow strike a balance between economic growth, urbanization, energy consumption, pollution, a rising consumer class, and the health and welfare of its citizens.

Tax policy is used by many nations to drive innovation, stimulate capital investment, and alter consumer behavior. China is no different in this respect, though the magnitude of the problems the country faces may be greater than any other country in the world. This chapter will discuss the broad energy goals set forth by the Chinese government and how tax policy has supported the achievement of these goals.

POLICIES DESIGNED TO PROMOTE GREEN INVESTMENT

China has developed a number of general laws that support the development and implementation of clean transportation, energy efficiency, and renewable energy. These laws provide a framework within which more detailed regulations may be enacted. Below is a brief discussion of the core laws enacted by the People's Republic of China (PRC) that are invaluable to a discussion about clean transportation, energy efficiency, and renewable energy. Each law is broad in scope, but all view taxation as an important mechanism both to stimulate growth in the clean energy area and to influence behavior. While funding from financial institutions and direct government spending may, in reality, constitute the lion's share of incentives, taxation remains an important part of the equation.

Renewable Energies Law

Originally adopted by the National People's Congress on 28 February 2005, the Renewable Energies Law was revised by the National People's Congress on 26 December 2009, effective 1 April 2010.[6] The purpose of the Renewable Energies Law is to promote the development and use of renewable energy to increase energy supply, improve energy structure, and ensure energy security.[7] Under Article 14 of the law, the purchase of all power generated from renewable energy sources is guaranteed,[8] and electricity grid enterprises are required to expand the reach of electricity grids,[9] thus resulting in an increase in renewable energy projects. The price for power generated from renewable resources is to be fixed by the relevant department under the State Council,[10] and when the fixed price is more than the price of electricity from conventional sources, the electricity grid provider will be compensated by the government for the difference.[11] The funds used to compensate the electricity grid provider will be derived from a renewable energy development fund, which will include amounts from the national annual financial budget and certain renewable energy fees.[12] The fund will also be used to support scientific and technological research, development of renewable energies, renewable energy projects in rural areas, and the promotion of local manufacturing of equipment for the development and utilization of renewable energies.[13]

The Renewable Energies Law directs financial institutions and tax authorities to implement regulations that support renewable energy projects. It also directs financial institutions to issue discounted loans for renewable energy development and utilization projects,[14] and directs the State Council to formulate tax incentives for projects that are listed in the renewable energy industry development guidance catalogue.[15]

Circular Economy Promotions Law

In addition to promoting the development and utilization of renewable energy, China has enacted laws promoting the 'circular economy,'[16] which generally refers to an economy focused on a reduction in resource consumption and waste generation, and promotion of recycling and resource recovery.[17] One key principle of the Circular Economy Promotions Law is to improve the industrialization process in a manner 'conducive to resource saving' and environmental protection.[18] The law also requires the government to provide tax preferences for industrial activities that promote the circular economy.[19] Additionally, various tax policies must encourage the importation of technology, equipment, and products designed to save energy, water, and materials.[20] China has also directed its financial institutions to provide credit and other financial support to companies and projects governed by the Circular Economy Promotions Law.[21]

Energy Conservation Law

China's Energy Conservation Law was revised in 2007 and became effective 1 April 2008.[22] This law is directed at promoting energy conservation in manufacturing, building, consumer products, and transportation. National and industrial building standards are to be formulated by the administrative department of construction under the State Council, and shall apply to existing buildings.[23] To ensure that the rules are enforced, projects that do not meet such standards will not be approved and existing construction will be suspended until the project design meets the applicable standards.[24] The law also contains provisions requiring the government to become more energy efficient not only in the construction and retrofitting of buildings, but also in its energy procurement strategy.[25]

In addition to promoting energy efficient buildings, the law seeks to make the transportation sector cleaner and more efficient. The Energy Conservation Law directs the State to encourage development and production of energy saving methods of transportation, and the use of clean fuels. To stimulate investment and development in these areas, the government must enact tax policies to encourage energy resource conservation and the importation of advanced energy conservation technologies and equipment.[26]

MOVING THE TRANSPORTATION SECTOR FORWARD

One of the many areas in which domestic tax policy can influence energy consumption is the transportation sector. Within this sector, two key areas provide opportunity for governments to alter behavior, namely the auto industry and the fuels industry. As previously discussed, the encouragement of the development, production, and use of environmentally friendly automobiles and clean fuels is one of the stated goals of the Energy Conservation Law.

The Chinese auto industry is the most unique of these two areas, having been declared a pillar industry by the government,[27] and having attracted a massive amount of foreign investment. In 2009, there were approximately 13.64 million vehicles sold in the Chinese domestic market.[28] By 2015, it is anticipated that the Chinese auto industry will have a manufacturing capacity of approximately 31.24 million vehicles, six times the US manufacturing capacity in 2007.[29] While the average urban salary of 29 229 Yuan (2008)[30] remains low by global standards, there are growing middle and upper classes that desire the freedom of car ownership. Unfortunately, rising car ownership has increased pollution and traffic, as illustrated by the 60-mile traffic jam stretching from the outskirts of Beijing toward the border of Inner Mongolia in August 2010.[31]

In response to the recent global financial crisis and requirements set forth by both the Central Committee of the Communist Party of China and the State Council regarding sustainable growth, the Chinese government formulated a plan to restructure the auto industry.[32] In formulating this plan, the government recognized 'the restraints on the automobile industry in terms of energy, environmental protection and urban traffic.'[33] Among other goals, the plan calls for the innovation, development and popularization of energy-saving and environmentally friendly autos.[34] The plan also calls for the build-up of infrastructure to support the growth of electric cars, and the production of 500 000 purely electric, plug-in electric and hybrid autos, such that they account for 5 per cent of total sales volume.[35] Finally, the plan calls for an increase in the market share for smaller cars.[36] A majority of the funding for these mandates is in the form of direct government spending. However, in an effort to provide an immediate stimulus to the auto market at the small car end, the government temporarily reduced the vehicle purchase tax from 10 per cent to 5 per cent for passenger cars with 1.6 l or lower displacement between 20 January 2009 and 31 December 2009.[37,38] When the temporary reduction in the vehicle purchase tax expired, it rose to 7.5 per cent, rather than 10 per cent, to account for the rebound in the economy.[39]

Adjustment of the vehicle purchase tax was not the only measure taken by the government. While the main goal of the reduction of the tax was to stimulate auto sales, it only applied to smaller vehicles, suggesting another goal of the tax reduction was to reduce the increase in pollution and consumption of oil that might occur from the purchase of larger vehicles. This theory corresponds with the manner in which the government has reshaped the consumption tax related to automobiles. Specifically, in 2006, the consumption tax for vehicles was progressive. For example, the consumption tax for a vehicle with an engine displacement of 1.5 l or less was 3 per cent, while the tax for a vehicle with more than 4.0 l of displacement increased to 20 per cent.[40] While such a rate schedule inherently supports the development and production of smaller vehicles, these rates did not penalize larger cars. However, in 2008 when the State Council reduced the rate for cars with an engine displacement of 1 l or less to 1 per cent, it also increased the consumption tax rate for vehicles with an engine displacement of more than 4 l to 40 per cent.[41] These rates became effective as of 1 January 2009. The increased consumption tax for larger vehicles suggests a motivation on the part of the government to create an incentive for smaller vehicles and a disincentive for larger ones.

Chinese fiscal policies are clearly at a crossroads. The government is attempting to stimulate its auto industry, but must also provide for a more sustainable environment. While revisions to both the vehicle purchase tax and the consumption tax have achieved the goal of stimulating the auto industry in a time of global economic downturn, these policies may not adequately achieve broader environmental goals. Smaller cars have better fuel economy and cause less pollution, but increasing the cars in an already crowded environment is not the best solution from either an environmental or an energy security standpoint.

The government has long recognized that a fuels tax could be an effective instrument to reduce oil consumption and ultimately reduce the nation's reliance on foreign sources of oil.[42] A fuels tax was initially proposed in 1994, but little action was taken until 1999, when the National People's Congress replaced the 1997 Highway Law with a fuel tax.[43] Even then, no action was taken to actually implement the law. As former Premier, Zhu Rongji pointed out at a speech given at Tsinghua University in 2001, the imposition of the fuel tax would increase gasoline prices, and coupled with other costs, could make driving prohibitively expensive.[44] Zhu Rongji's statement highlights the conflict among policy makers when instituting energy fiscal policies. The government desires economic growth, but has realized that environmental and energy security problems must play a greater long-term role in policy implementation.

For example, if the purpose of a fuels tax is to alter behavior, thus reducing oil consumption, the implementation of such a fuels tax needs to be sufficient to curb consumption. If the rate is too low, it will not cause behavior alteration, and other fees and or taxes such as tolls will be necessary to alter behavior. If, rather than behavior modification, the goal is to replace tolls and other road charges, then the rate need only be sufficient to raise the necessary revenue to replace the revenue previously received from the other tolls and charges. However, if the goals of these policies are not sufficiently broad, they may not further the goals as set forth in the Energy Conservation Law and other laws as previously discussed.

The Chinese government finally implemented a fuels tax in 2008, which became effective 1 January 2009. The tax is set at 1.0 Yuan/l for gasoline, and 0.08 Yuan/l for diesel.[45] The fuels tax replaced six categories of tolls for road maintenance and management.[46] It also replaced the commodity tax on fuels (0.2 Yuan/l for gasoline and 0.1 Yuan/l for diesel).[47] On a comparative basis, although China's fuels tax is significantly higher than the US federal gas tax, currently 18.4 cents per gallon, it is significantly lower than the UK where the tax is over $3.36[48] per gallon. The combination of a low tax rate and the elimination of other fees will likely have very little effect in terms of overall consumption, thus failing to support China's push for reducing energy consumption.[49]

At the municipal level, Shanghai has utilized a unique method to limit the rise of private automobile ownership. While not a tax per se, the system effectively is a tax intended to alter behavior. Since 1994, Shanghai has had a new license plate quota to control auto ownership.[50] Under this system, auctions are held once a month for new license plates. In August 2010, only 9000 plates were auctioned, with an expected average price of around $5905,[51] thus significantly increasing the cost of a new vehicle.[52] Revenues from the auctions fund road maintenance and construction, and public transportation.[53] Due to the perceived success in reducing the number of registered vehicles in Shanghai, this system has served as a model for other areas such as Shaanxi Province.[54] Although the auction appears successful when one compares the number of registered cars in Shanghai (720 000) with the number in Beijing (2.48 million),[55] many Shanghai residents have bypassed the auction process by merely securing licenses from other jurisdictions, thus reducing the efficacy of the auctions.[56] While cars with licenses from other jurisdictions are not permitted to drive on the city's elevated roads during certain rush hour times,[57] many people are willing to violate this law, as the fine for a violation (200 Yuan) is nominal relative to the cost of purchasing a Shanghai license plate at auction.[58]

GREEN BUILDINGS AND RENEWABLE ENERGY

The energy consumption of buildings accounts for 25 per cent of the total primary energy consumption in China.[59] China's Ministry of Housing and Urban-Rural Development has developed its own green rating for buildings, similar in some respects to Energy Star[60] or LEED[61] ratings.

Compliance with energy and building codes in China is relatively poor,[62] thus any internal standard may not provide accurate data, and reliance on international standards may be more reliable until domestic compliance increases. In addition to developing a green rating system for buildings, China is moving rapidly to generate renewable energy. Total investment in clean energy in 2009 reached nearly $35 billion, almost double the amount spent by the US government.[63] In 1999, China made just 1 per cent of the world's solar panels; by 2008, it was the world's leading producer with a 32 per cent market share.[64] Much of the investment in energy efficiency and renewable energy technology, manufacturing, and adoption is funded directly by the government or through favorable lending practices. However, as previously noted, the government has directed tax policy to be used as a mechanism to achieve national goals.

Preferential Tax Rates for New Energy and Energy Conservation Technology Ventures

China ushered in a new era of business taxation when the National People's Congress approved the new Enterprise Income Tax Law (EIT) on 16 March 2007, effective 1 January 2008. The previous regime provided a two-track system which provided preferential treatment to foreign invested enterprises at the expense of domestic enterprises. The EIT, however, provides for a uniform tax rate for both domestic and foreign invested enterprises, thus leveling the playing field for domestic companies. Additionally, the EIT supports certain government-designated industries. Under the EIT, the standard tax rate for all enterprises, except certain non-tax resident enterprises, is 25 per cent.[65] According to Article 25 of the EIT, preferential tax treatment is to be granted to industries and projects that the government supports or the development of which it encourages.[66] Among the industries and projects subject to preferential treatment are projects in the areas of environmental protection, energy conservation, water conservation, and certain technology transfers, effectively reducing the tax rate from 25 per cent to 15 per cent.[67,68] Additional tax preferences are granted to enterprises that either derive revenue from the sale of certain energy saving equipment or invest in such equipment and will be discussed later in this chapter.[69]

Enterprises engaged in new energy and energy conservation technology ventures qualify for preferential treatment under this regime, provided the enterprise or its services and products: (1) is a tax-resident enterprise that is registered in China for at least one year,[70] (2) owns the self-controlled intellectual property rights used in the core technology of its principal products,[71] (3) falls within the scope of hi-tech sectors supported by the state,[72] (4) has employees with university degrees accounting for 30 per cent of the staff, with 10 per cent of such employees working in research and development,[73] (5) meets strict requirements on minimum research and development expenditures, and (6) has minimum sales revenue targets from its high technology products and/or services.[74] Since this regime was initiated, nearly 20 000 companies have been certified, though according to anecdotal evidence, nearly 50 per cent of the companies obtained certification based on falsified information.[75] The government has declared that preferential status will be cancelled for five years if the company submits a false application or commits other violations such as tax evasion,[76] although it is uncertain whether the government will enforce these penalties for fraud. While clearly attempting to support the goals set forth in broader laws, the implementing regulations may require further refinement to make the policy effective and prevent such fraud at the outset. Despite potential abuses, municipalities such as Shanghai support enterprises such as new energy automobile companies and new energy enterprises in their efforts to qualify for preferential tax treatment under the EIT.[77]

Tax Holidays and Reduced Tax Rates for Certain Energy-Related Enterprises

Another method of encouraging investment in clean energy is through the combination of tax holidays and reduced tax rates for certain companies. Enterprises engaged in environmental protection, energy conservation and water conservation projects, including those that develop and utilize energy conservation and emissions reducing technologies, enjoy a tax holiday for the first three years and a 50 per cent reduction in the tax rate for the following three years.[78]

Benefits for Energy Service Companies

Companies that qualify as energy service companies have been specifically identified by the Chinese authorities as eligible for the combination of the three-year tax holiday and 50 per cent reduction in the EIT for the following three years. In Circular 166, issued in 2009, the government clarified requirements for energy service companies to qualify for preferential treatment, and mandated that energy service companies be engaged in technology upgrades for energy savings and emission reductions in order to qualify for preferential treatment.[79] These companies are often contracted to reduce a customer's energy consumption in return for a share of the customer's expense savings.[80] In addition to qualifying for the EIT benefits, energy service companies will also be exempt from business tax and value added tax (VAT), according to the State Council.[81] As an additional incentive, the transfer of energy-saving equipment to the customer will not cause attribution of deemed income to the company.[82] Energy service company customers fully amortize or depreciate the transfer of equipment, and can also currently deduct payments made to the energy service company.[83]

Encouragement of Investment in Energy-Efficient Products

The EIT provides additional preferences for capital investment in energy-efficient products. Here, separate preferences are available to the manufacturer and the purchaser, but both highlight the fact that China's tax policy is not strictly aimed at research and development and manufacturing. Under Article 34 of the EIT, companies that derive revenue from the production and sale of certain energy-efficient equipment can exclude 10 per cent of the revenue for purposes of determining their EIT liability.[84] Equipment that qualifies includes certain electric motors, ventilators, air conditioning equipment, heat exchangers, cooling towers and power-saving equipment.[85] Similarly, enterprises that purchase such equipment can claim a 10 per cent credit against the EIT.[86] In the event such amount exceeds the tax liability owing, the excess may be carried forward for five years.[87]

The Kyoto Protocol and Certified Emission Reductions

The Kyoto Protocol has intensified the energy efficiency and renewable energy push in China. Under Article 12 of the Protocol, Annex I countries (developed countries) may invest in greenhouse gas emission reduction projects in non-Annex I countries (developing countries) and claim the resulting certified emission reductions (CERs) to meet their commitments under the Protocol.[88] As a non-Annex I country, to capitalize on clean development projects, the Chinese government formulated its own goals and procedures for approval and development of such projects. The government concluded that projects related to energy efficiency, development and utilization of new and renewable energy and recovery and utilization of coal-bed methane were priorities,[89] and that such projects should promote the transfer of technology to China.[90]

According to the Chinese Ministry of Finance, CERs generated from these projects belong to both the government and the project company,[91] resulting in the government collecting a certain percentage of the revenue generated from the transfer of CERs to the Annex I country. This percentage ranges from 65 per cent for hydrofluorocarbons (HFCs) and perfluorocarbons (PFCs) projects,[92] to 30 per cent for nitrous oxide (N_2O) projects.[93]

However, for priority projects such as those noted above, the government's share of the revenue is only 2 per cent.[94] Because the government claims so much of the revenue from the transfer of CERs, retroactive guidance provides that for purposes of the EIT, the government's share of the revenues is currently deductible.[95]

The government has also specified that project companies engaged in HFC, PFC, and N_2O projects qualify for the three-year tax holiday and 50 per cent reduction in the EIT for the following three years.[96] One justification for these tax benefits may be that, for example, HFC projects are relatively inexpensive to initiate and generate a significant amount of revenue, which may be used to expand plant operations, increase employment, and paradoxically increase emissions of HFC and other contaminants.[97] Although the guidance related to the preferential tax treatment granted to clean development mechanism (CDM) projects is of recent vintage (2009), it is unclear whether such treatment will directly foster the creation of additional CDM projects. China accounts for a substantial majority of clean development projects and domestically has approved a total of 2685 projects;[98] however, such projects appear to be stalling, given the policy uncertainties that will arise when phase one of the Kyoto Protocol ends in 2012.[99]

The preferential tax policies identified above highlight a mix of preferences for manufacturing, research and development, and utilization of new energy and energy conservation/efficient measures. Although there are concerns about fraudulent applications in the case of the high and new technology policies, the tax policies enacted attempt to carry out the goals set forth in the general laws.

TAX MEASURES TARGETED SPECIFICALLY AT THE WIND ENERGY SECTOR

The preferential treatment granted to enterprises under the EIT is one method used to spur innovation and utilization of renewable energy and energy efficient products. Similarly, China has implemented specific measures for the wind industry to allow it to flourish. Although China imposes VAT upon the sale of most goods within the country, due to the recognition that wind energy carried great potential, the Ministry of Finance and the State Administration of Taxation reduced the VAT payable upon the sale of wind energy from 17 per cent to 8.5 per cent in 2001.[100] In certain provincial areas such as Hebei, Liaoning, Jilin, and Guangdong, the VAT for wind power is as low as 6 per cent.[101] Moreover, enterprises can obtain a refund for import duties and import VAT related to the purchase of key components and raw materials for developing or manufacturing wind turbines.[102] The purported rationale for these policies was to accelerate domestic manufacturing of wind turbines. Therefore, refunds received by the enterprises must be earmarked for research, production of new products, and the enhancement of innovation within the company.[103] Additionally, the enterprise must be capable of manufacturing wind turbines with a minimum power capacity of 1.2MW.[104] As a complement to the import VAT refund, the government also canceled the import tax exemption on wind turbines with a maximum power capacity of 2.5MW,[105] thereby providing further encouragement for domestic production of such turbines.

CONCLUSION

The need for a more sustainable China is evident. As one commentator has said, '[i]t is a practical discussion on health and wealth.'[106] China is trying to become sustainable through a mixture of direct funding, favorable bank lending policies, and preferential tax policies. The preferential tax policies aimed at the small car market, combined with penalties for larger cars, may help increase efficiency and reduce growth in overall consumption of oil. However, this policy is counterintuitive as it increases demand for the purchase of smaller cars, rather than the use of public transportation or bicycles. Preferential tax treatment for energy efficiency and renewable energy projects is better tailored to support the goals of the state. While such policies originally focused on research, development and manufacturing, once competency in this area increased, utilization has become a great focus. With these advancements in technology as well as the improvement of the relevant policies, one cannot doubt that China's tax policies have helped stimulate growth in efficient transportation, energy efficient building, and renewable energy technologies.

NOTES

1. Institute for Energy Research (2010), 'China: world's largest energy consumer; surpasses the US', available at: www.instituteforenergyresearch.org/2010/08/06/china-world%E2%80%99s-largest-energy-consumer-surpasses-the-u-s/#_edn1 (accessed 30 September 2010).
2. US Energy Information Administration, available at: www.eia.gov/emeu/cabs/China/Coal.html (accessed 30 September 2010).
3. Institute for Energy Research, *supra* note 1.
4. Bradsher, K. (2010), 'China fears warming effects of a rising consumer class', *The New York Times*, 5 July, sec. A, p. 1.

5. Walsh, B. (2007), 'The World's Most Polluted Places', *Time.com*, available at: www.time.com/time/specials/2007/article/0,28804,1661031_1661028_1661016,00.html (accessed 30 September 2010).

6. Law of the People's Republic of China on Renewable Energies (2009 Revision), 26 December 2009, *2009 China Law LEXIS 671*. For the purposes of this law, 'renewable energies' is defined as 'non-fossil' energies such as wind, solar, hydro, bioenergy, geothermal and ocean energy (See Article 2).

7. *Ibid.*, Article 1.

8. *Ibid.*, Article 14.

9. *Ibid.*, Article 14.

10. *Ibid.*, Article 19.

11. *Ibid.*, Article 20.

12. *Ibid.*, Article 24.

13. *Ibid.* See also Interim Measures for Special Fund Management for the Development of Renewable Energies, Cai Jian (2006) No. 237, 16 June 2006, *2006 China Law LEXIS 7663*.

14. *Ibid.*, Article 25.

15. *Ibid.*, Article 26.

16. Circular Economy Promotion Law of the People's Republic of China, 29 August 2008, *2009 China Law LEXIS 193*.

17. *Ibid.*, Article 2.

18. Several Opinions of the State Council on Speeding up the Development of Circular Economy, Guo Fa (2005) No. 22, 2 July 2005, *2005 China Law LEXIS 13417*.

19. Circular Economy Promotion Law of the People's Republic of China, *supra* note 16, Article 44.

20. *Ibid.*

21. Circular on the Investment and Financing Policies, Measures and Opinions for Supporting the Development of Circular Economy, Fa Gai Huan Zi (2010) No. 801, 19 April 2010, *2010 China Law LEXIS 151*, Articles 3–4. Relevant projects include projects that save energy, water or materials or would realise comprehensive utilisation, cleaner production, seawater desalinization or zero emission, recycling of scrapped auto parts, engineering machinery and waste treatment.

22. Energy Conservation Law of the People's Republic of China, Order of the President (2007) No. 77, 28 October 2007, *2008 China Law LEXIS 2223*.

23. *Ibid.*, Articles 14 and 34.

24. *Ibid.*, Article 35.

25. *Ibid.*, Articles 47 and 51.

26. *Ibid.*, Articles 62 and 63.

27. Restructuring and Rejuvenation Program of the Automobile Industry, General Office of the State Council, 20 March 2009, *China Law LEXIS 327*.

28. Schmitt, B. (2010), 'China's government worried about unbridled auto industry growth', available at: www.thetruthaboutcars.com/china%E2%80%99s-government-worried-aboaut-unbridled-auto-industry-growth/ (accessed 23 September 2010).

29. *Ibid.*

30. Zhu, J. (2010), 'China's wage proportion decreases for 22 years', *China Daily*, available at: www.chinadaily.com.cn/china/2010–05/13/content_9842411.htm (accessed 23 September 2010).

31. Oster, S. (2010), 'China's traffic jam could last weeks', *The Wall Street Journal*, available at: http://online.wsj.com/article/SB100014240527487041256045754491739 89748704.html (accessed 23 September 2010).

32. Restructuring and Rejuvenation Program of the Automobile Industry, *supra* note 27.

33. *Ibid.*, Article 1.

34. *Ibid.*, Article 2.

35. *Ibid.*, Article 2(3).

36. *Ibid.*

37. *Ibid.*, Article 4(1).
38. *Ibid.*
39. State Administration of Taxation (2010), 'A brief analysis of national tax revenue from January to April 2010', available at: www.chinatax.gov.cn/n6669073/n6669118/9746541.html (accessed 23 September 2010).
40. Circular of Ministry of Finance and State Administration of Taxation on Adjusting and Perfecting Consumption Tax Policies, Cai Shui No. 33, 20 March 2006, The Ministry of Finance and the State Administration of Taxation, *2006 China Law LEXIS 7936*.
41. PRC Tentative Regulations on Consumption Tax (Revised), 5 January 2009, *China Law & Practice*.
42. Kong, B. (2009). 'China's energy decision-making: becoming more like the United States', *Journal of Contemporary China*, **18** (62), 793.
43. *Ibid.*, at 791–2.
44. *Ibid.*, at 793–4. See also Yan, X. and R. Crookes (2009), 'Reduction potentials of energy demand and GHG emissions in China's road transport sector', *Energy Policy*, **37**, 658 at 664, where the authors note that the fuels tax has been debated and postponed on numerous occasions since it would lead to a 'politically sensitive increase in gasoline and diesel prices'.
45. Jing, F. (2008), 'Fuel tax reform an energy milestone', *China Daily*, available at: www.chinadaily.com.cn/bizchina/2008–12/29/content_7349014.htm (accessed 27 September 2010). See also Announcement of the National Development and Reform Commission, the Ministry of Finance, the Ministry of Transport and the State Administration of Taxation on Soliciting Public Opinions on Refines Oil Tax Reform Program, 5 December 2008, *2009 China Law LEXIS 200*, Article 2(2).
46. *Ibid.*
47. Jia, H. (2009), 'China bites the bullet on fuel tax', *Chemistry World*, available at: www.rsc.org/chemistryworld/Issues/2009/January/ChinaBitesTheBulletOnFuelTax.asp (accessed 27 September 2010).
48. This figure has been converted from the British pound.
49. *Ibid.*, citing Ni Weidou, an energy expert at Tsinghua University who believed the rate was too low to curb consumption.
50. Wang, R. (2010) 'Shaping urban transport policies in China: will copying foreign policies work?', *Transport Policy*, **17**, 147 at 149.
51. 'Car license plate auction prices to remain high' (2010), *Global Times*, available at: www.globaltimes.cn/www/english/features/metroshanghai/business/2010–08/562703.html (accessed 27 September 2010).
52. Wang, *supra* note 50.
53. Asia-Pacific Environmental Innovation Strategies, 'Emission Control Measures in Shanghai, China', available at: http://enviroscope.iges.or.jp/contents/APEIS/RISPO/inventory/db/pdf/0031.pdf (accessed 27 September 2010).
54. *Supra* note 51.
55. Wang, *supra* note 50.
56. *Ibid.*
57. Xi, X. (2010), 'Plate, pride and prejudice', *Global Times*, available at: www.globaltimes.cn/www/english/features/metroshanghai/community/2010–06/540248.html (accessed 27 September 2010).
58. *Ibid.*
59. Ernest Orlando Lawrence Berkeley National Laboratory (2010), 'Assessment of China's energy saving and emission reduction accomplishments and opportunities during the 11th five year plan', available at: http://china.lbl.gov/sites/china.lbl.gov/files/LBNL-3385E.Ace_Study_Report_FINAL.Rev_.pdf (accessed 28 September 2010), at 26.
60. Energy Star is a joint program of the US Environmental Protection Agency and the US Department of Energy.

61. LEED, or Leadership in Energy and Environmental Design, is an internationally recognized green building certification system. LEED was developed by the US Green Building Council.
62. China Green Building Blog (2009), 'Two Pronged Approach: Top Down', http://chinagreenbuildings.blogspot.com/2009/04/two-pronged-approach-top-down.html (accessed 26 September 2010).
63. Usher, B. (2010), 'Red China, green China', *The New York Times*, 7 May, sec. A, p. 27.
64. *Ibid.*
65. PRC Enterprise Income Tax Law, 16 March 2007, *China Law & Practice*, April 2007, Article 4.
66. *Ibid.*, Article 25.
67. *Ibid.*, Article 27.
68. *Ibid.*, Article 28.
69. *Ibid.*, Article 33 and 34.
70. Measures for the Administration of the Recognition of Hi-Tech Enterprises, Ministry of Science and Technology, Ministry of Finance, and State Administration of Taxation, Guo Ke Fa Huo No. 172, 14 April 2008, *China Law & Practice*, May 2008, Article 2.
71. *Ibid.*, Article 10(1).
72. *Ibid.*, Article 10(2).
73. *Ibid.*, Article 10(3).
74. *Ibid.*, Article 10(4) and (5).
75. Zhou, Q. and A. Yang (2010), 'Fabricated high-tech boom', *Caixin Online*, available at: www.marketwatch.com/story/chinas-high-tech-subsidies-boosts-paper-pushers-2010-08-10 (accessed 29 September 2010).
76. Stender, N., F. Ye, and C. Gong (2008), 'Tax preference guideline provides scrutiny for high/new-tech enterprises', *China Law & Practice*, October.
77. Circular of the General Office of Shanghai Municipal People's Government on Transmitting the Policies and Provisions on Promoting the Development of Shanghai New Energy Automobile Industry Formulated by the Municipal Development and Reform Commission and the Municipal Economic Information Commission, The General Office of Shanghai Municipal People's Government, Hu Fu Ban Fa No. 55, 7 December 2009, *2009 China Law LEXIS 733*, Article 9. See also, Hu Fu Ban Fa No. 54, 7 December 2009, *2009 China Law LEXIS 738*, at III(4).
78. Implementing Regulations for PRC Enterprise Income Tax Law, 6 December 2007, *China Law & Practice*, February 2008, Article 88.
79. Stender, N. and F. Ye (2010), 'China makes a renewed commitment to clean energy', *China Law & Practice*, February.
80. Stender, N. and F. Ye (2010), 'Rewarding green efforts', *China Law & Practice*, June. Energy service companies are required to have a minimum registered capital of RMB 1 million and meet certain technical requirements.
81. *Ibid.*, citing State Council's Opinion on Accelerating the Implementation of Energy Management Contracting to Promote the Development of Energy Saving Service Industry, Guo Ban Fa No. 25, 2 April 2010.
82. *Ibid.*
83. *Ibid.*
84. Implementing Regulations, *supra* note 70, Article 99.
85. Circular of the Ministry of Finance, State Administration of Taxation and the State Commission of Development and Reform on the Issuance of the Catalogue of Income Tax Preferences to Enterprises Manufacturing Special Energy and Water Saving Equipment and the Catalogue of Income Tax Preferences for Enterprises Manufacturing Special Environmental Protection Equipment, Cai Shui No. 115, 20 August 2008, *2008 China Law LEXIS 2043*.
86. Implementing Regulations, *supra* note 70, Article 100.

87.   *Ibid.* See also Circular of the Ministry of Finance and the State Administration of Taxation on Issues Concerning Implementing the Catalogue of Enterprise Income Tax Preference for Environmental Protection Special Equipment, the Catalogue of Enterprise Income Tax Preference for Energy-saving and Water-saving Special Equipment and the Catalogue of Enterprise Income Tax Preference for Safe Production Special Equipment, Cai Shui No. 48, 23 September 2008, *2008 China Law LEXIS 2694.*

88.   Zang, D. (2009), 'Green from above: climate change, new developmental strategy, and regulatory choice in China', **45** *Tex. Int'l L.J.* 201 at 205.

89.   Measures for the Operation and Management of Clean Development Mechanism Projects, Ministry of Finance, 12 October 2005, *2005 China Law LEXIS 13059*, Article 4.

90.   *Ibid.*, Article 10.

91.   *Ibid.*, Article 24.

92.   *Ibid.*, Article 24(1).

93.   *Ibid.*, Article 24(2).

94.   *Ibid.*, Article 24(3).

95.   Wang, K. (2009), 'China introduces tax incentives for clean development Projects', 2009 *WTD* 66–4.

96.   *Ibid.*

97.   Sauter, J. (2009), 'The Clean Development Mechanism in China: Assessing the Tension Between Development and Curbing Anthropogenic Climate Change', *Va. Envtl L.J.*, **27**, 91 at 103–104.

98.   National Development and Reform Commission (2010), 'Projects approved by DNA of China (up to 7 September 2010)', available at: http://cdm.ccchina.gov.cn/WebSite/CDM/UpFile/File2509.pdf (accessed 28 September 2010).

99.   Fogarty, D. (2010), 'China renewables to power ahead without CDM', *Reuters*, available at: www.reuters.com/article/idUSTRE67J14620100820 (accessed 28 September 2010).

100.   Circular of the Ministry of Finance and the State Administration of Taxation on the Comprehensive Utilization of Some Resources and Value-added Tax Policy on Other Products, Cai Shui No. 198, 1 December 2001, *2001 China Law LEXIS 2084.*

101.   Liao, C., J. Eberhard, Y. Zhang, *et al.* (2010), 'Wind power development and policies in China', *Renewable Energy*, **35**, 1879 at 1885.

102.   Circular of the Ministry of Finance on Adjusting the Tax Policy on the Import of High Power Wind Generating Sets and Its Key Components and Parts and Raw Materials, Cai Guan Shui No. 36, 14 April 2008, *2008 China Law LEXIS 1940*, Article 1.

103.   *Ibid.*

104.   *Ibid.*, Article 2.

105.   *Ibid.*, Article 5.

106.   Friedman, T. (2010), 'Aren't we clever?', *The New York Times*, 19 September, sec. W.K., p. 9, quoting Peggy Liu, chairwoman of the Joint US-China Collaboration on Clean Energy.

2. Policy design of environmental tax in China[1]

Jinnan Wang, Chazhong Ge, Shuting Gao and Yajuan Ren

Environmental tax policy is used as a kind of economic means to regulate pollution and to protect the environment. In a broad sense, it includes establishing environmental tax, fiscal and preferential policies related to the environment and natural resources, as well as eliminating subsidies and environmental charge policies which are harmful for environmental protection. From this point of view, many countries have environmental tax policies. In a narrow sense, environmental tax means to collect or cut taxes from enterprises or individuals, which are engaged in developing, protecting or utilizing environmental resources, according to the degree of exploitation, pollution, destruction or protection of the environmental resources. Therefore, few countries regard environmental tax as one of categories of general taxation.

With the establishment and improvement of Chinese market economy system and the rise of requirement for environmental management, new means of management are urgently needed for China's environmental protection. As a kind of new management method, environmental tax arouses the interest of relevant government departments, scholars and experts. On the other hand, environmental protection needs a large amount of government investment for it to be successful, and environmental tax can raise fiscal revenue for governments. Although the environmental tax revenue belongs to public financial funds, it could also be used as special-purpose funds for environmental protection. Through investigation and practice in some countries, it is shown that environmental tax can not only change the polluter's behavior, but can also be used to protect the environment and improve the taxation structure with three winners – the environment, the economy and society. Therefore establishing and implementing environmental tax policy is an important means of the construction of an environment-friendly and resources-economic society.

What we should admit is that it is a hard task to set up an environmental tax, for three reasons. First, tax reform takes a long time to introduce, and is a very complicated procedure. Second, regarding environmental tax as an individual tax category, the relationship with other tax categories needs to be established. Third, detailed investigation should be carried out of the collection and management of environmental tax. The specialized technical requirements of environmental tax collection mean that taxation authorities need special training for their staff before they entrust environmental agencies with tasks of environmental tax collection.

Now the Chinese government is pushing forward with the research of environmental taxation and has made a lot of progress. Based on the research results of the study on the framework of the environmental tax policy and its implementation strategy (Jinnan Wang *et al.*, 2006 and 2009), which belongs to one of the tasks in the 15th National Key Technologies R&D Program, this report put forwards the framework of environmental tax policy in China, and proposes several environmental tax plans, and the corresponding implementation strategies as well.

2.1 FRAMEWORK OF ENVIRONMENTAL TAX POLICY

Environmental tax policy is broadly defined as a series of tax policies with the goal of achieving environmental protection, including environmental tax categories and environmental charges, eliminating subsidy policies and tax preference policies which are adverse to environmental protection, establishing preferential tax and supplementary policies which are helpful for the construction of a environment friendly society. In this report, it mainly focuses on the design on the framework of the environmental tax policy, and especially puts forward three kinds of plans which are independent environmental tax plan, integrated environmental tax plan and environmental taxation and charge plan.

2.2 DESIGN OF ENVIRONMENTAL TAX OPTIONS

According to the relationship between the environmental tax and the current tax system in China and its development prospect, environmental tax plans can be divided into four categories, that is independent environmental tax plan, integrated environmental tax plan, environmental taxation and charge plan and environmental tax expenditure plan.

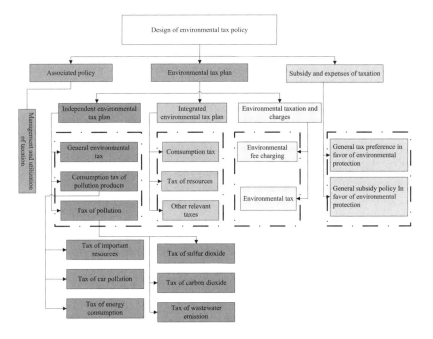

Figure 2.1 Framework of environmental tax policy in China

2.2.1   Independent Environmental Tax Plan

2.2.1.1   General environmental tax

The general environmental tax is based on income with the goal of collecting money for environmental protection. In another words, by keeping the existing charges for pollutants emission and using natural resources, general environmental tax is introduced to raise finances for environmental protection. Since a good ecological environment can be regarded as a kind of public product, and the benefits from pollution control and environmental protection are prevalent, so the government can levy taxes on beneficiaries according to the beneficiary-pays principle. The income goes to the public budget system for overall management, and should mainly be used for infrastructure construction for environmental quality improvement and ecological protection and for environmental management, as outlined in Box 2.1.

BOX 2.1 DESIGN OF GENERAL ENVIRONMENTAL TAX SYSTEM

Taxpayer: All impersonal entities or individuals who pay value added tax, consumption tax and sales tax (three taxes, for short) are taxpayers for general environmental tax, according to fair-play doctrine and the beneficiary-pays principle. Foreign companies will pay the general environmental tax as well.

Tax base: General environmental tax is based on the quantity being paid for the three taxes by the taxpayer, excluding the surcharge for overdue tax payment and fines, etc. which are imposed by the tax authorities.

Tax rate: The tax rate of general environmental tax is intended to be 1–4 per cent of that of the three taxes.

Regulation of tax concession: Tax concession is not allowed in environmental tax. So taxpayers should pay the general environmental tax on the basis of the quantity of tax to be paid for the three taxes, even if a taxpayer avoids paying the three taxes because of preferential taxation policy. However, general environmental tax will be exempted when there is a custom levy circulating tax on import goods.

2.2.1.2 Direct pollution tax

Under the polluter-pays principle, direct pollution tax is based on the quantity of pollutants discharged, with a stimulation function for abatement. With the purpose of encouraging environmentally friendly behavior and restricting discharge of pollutants directly, the direct pollution tax is in accordance with the theoretical principle of environmental tax. Whereas this kind of pollution tax is of direct correlation with the quantity of pollutants, it could be called direct pollution tax or pollution discharge tax.

The key to designing direct pollution tax is to set the tax base directly over the quantity of pollutants discharged by polluters, and the tax rate should be high enough to create a stimulation function, by which polluters will take measures actively to reduce the quantity of pollutants emitted. Because of the stimulation function of this kind of environmental tax, the tax revenue will decrease with time, at least for a specified polluter. Otherwise, it will lose its stimulation function, and then it will no longer be a stimulating tax. The directly discharged pollutants mainly consist of various exhaust gases, wastewater and solid wastes. Now the government can consider changing the charge for sulfur dioxide emission and nitrogen oxides emission into taxation. More directly discharged pollutants will be phased in when conditions permit. See Boxes 2.2 and 2.3 and Table 2.1 for details.

BOX 2.2 DESIGN OF SULFUR DIOXIDE TAX SYSTEM

Object of taxation: The control of sulfur dioxide emission.

Taxpayer: Those liable for sulfur dioxide tax are polluters that discharge sulfur dioxide into the atmosphere, including industrial enterprises, institutions, business companies, service companies and other entities. In order to reduce operating costs, the tax should be concentrated on the major coal and petroleum users; administrative operations and residents could be exempted from sulfur dioxide tax temporarily.

Tax base: Sulfur dioxide tax is based on the real emission quantity of sulfur dioxide. If there is monitoring data, the sulfur dioxide tax should be levied according to the actual amount discharged. For those emission sources producing a large quantity with a wide coverage, which is small scale and hard to monitor, sulfur dioxide tax could be based on the sulfur content of fuels used or by the degree of corresponding measures adapted. If the emission quantity is hard to establish, the tax could be based on calculated emission quantity according to the production capability of the taxpayer's plant and the real output.

Tax rate: The tax rate for sulfur dioxide of coal is shown in Table 2.1, with reference to a study on setting environmental tax policy (Wang *et al.*, 2006).

Collection: Local taxation departments have the right to collect sulfur dioxide tax.

Table 2.1 Sulfur dioxide tax rate of coal (Yuan/ton coal)

Low-sulfur coal		Medium-sulfur coal	
Sulfur content (%)	Tax rate	Sulfur content (%)	Tax rate
0.4	8.4	1.2	25.0
0.6	12.6	1.4	29.0
0.8	16.6	1.6	33.4
1.0	20.85	1.8	37.6

BOX 2.3 DESIGN OF NITROGEN OXIDES TAX SYSTEM

Taxpayer: Major taxpayers of nitrogen oxides are end users of coal-fired boilers and owners of motor vehicles.

Tax base: Nitrogen oxides tax is based on the real emission quantity of nitrogen oxides. The source of nitrogen oxides is somewhat different from other pollutants, as part comes from fuels and raw materials and a larger part is produced by the chemical combination of nitrogen and oxygen during the burning process, i.e. from the combustion source. The combustion source is classi-fied into mobile combustion sources and stationary combustion sources. The mobile combustion source mainly consists of vehi-cles, airplanes, etc., and the stationary combustion source mainly includes boilers and other facilities.

Tax rate: 1200 RMB/ton according to the sulfur dioxide tax rate and the charging standards for nitrogen oxides emissions established by the Chinese Academy of Environmental Sciences in 1997 (Yang and Wang, 1998).

Collection: Local taxation departments have the right to collect nitrogen oxides tax.

2.2.1.3 Environmental tax of water resource

Although there is no close relationship between the production of water pollutants and consumption of water resources, the control of water resource consumption can encourage the reduction of water pollutants to some extent because water is the carrier of water pollutants. Therefore the environmental tax of water resources can be determined according to the scarcity of water resources and the cost for water pollution control. See Box 2.4 for details.

BOX 2.4 DESIGN OF WATER RESOURCES TAX SYSTEM

Object of taxation: Water used as raw material or for or for living purposes.

Taxpayer: Enterprises, institutions and individuals who use water resources.

Tax base: The quantity of water consumed, or the real quantity of water supplied.

Tax rate: 20–30 per cent of the water rate temporarily, which will be changed to a differential tax rate according to the scarcity of water resources and water pollution conditions.

Collection: State taxation departments have the right to collect water resource tax. Waterworks can withhold water resources tax according the specified tax rate.

2.2.1.4   Polluting products tax

Polluting products tax is another environmental tax category based on stimulation, with the user-pays principle. The subjects of polluting products tax are products with the potential to cause pollution, and so it is called a pollution products tax. It will stimulate consumers to reduce their consumption of products that may cause pollution, or encourage consumers to select products that generate no or less pollution.

The major products which can cause pollution are energy fuel, ozone spoilage substances, chemical fertilizers, pesticides, phosphoric detergents, batteries containing mercury and cadmium, etc. A range of pollution products taxes should be levied upon such products, for example, special polluting products tax and fuel environmental tax. See Boxes 2.5 and 2.6 for further details.

BOX 2.5 DESIGN OF SPECIAL POLLUTING PRODUCTS TAX SYSTEM

Object of taxation: All types of products and consumer goods that can cause environmental pollution, including chemical fertilizers, pesticides, phosphoric detergents, disposable wooden tableware, batteries with mercury and cadmium, etc.

Taxpayer: Consumers or users of these types of product.

Tax base: The quantity of consumption and value of the pollution products.

Tax rate: The government should categorize taxable items according to the pollution they produce, and implement differential rate of 1–3 per cent.

Collection: State taxation departments have the right to collect the special polluting products tax at a link in the consumption chain.

BOX 2.6 DESIGN OF CARBON AND FUEL ENVIRONMENTAL TAX SYSTEM

Imposition object: Fuels such as carbon and oil fuel (oil fuel mainly consists of gasoline and diesel oil).

Taxpayer: Enterprises, units and individuals who use coal and oil fuel.

Tax base: This tax is based on the quantity of usage of carbon and oil fuel. For enterprises using carbon as fuels, it is based on the real quantity of carbon consumed; for individuals using carbon as fuels, it is based on the real quantity of carbon purchased; for oil fuel, it is based on the real quantity of oil fuels purchased by taxpayer.

Tax rate: The tax rate of carbon environmental tax is 20 RMB per ton of carbon according to the sulfur dioxide tax rate; the tax rate for oil fuel is 0.20 RMB/l and for gasoline is 0.15 RMB/l.

Collection: State taxation departments have the right to collect. By selecting carbon distribution links, the taxation authorities can entrust sales agencies with the task of withholding carbon environmental tax. Sales agencies should be installed with tax control instruments.

2.2.2 Integrated Environmental Tax Plan

Although there are no independent environmental taxes in the Chinese environmental taxation system, integrated environmental tax is functioning by the reform and improvement of current tax categories and cooperation with the environmental charge system.

2.2.2.1 Consumption tax

For environmental protection purposes, the government adjusts the taxation of petroleum products and their substitute products, which accounts for the lower proportion of energy consumption in current consumer tax. However, carbon, which accounts for higher proportion in energy consumption, and other consumer goods which cause higher levels of environmental pollution, are all excluded from the taxation. As the result, environmental protection has been made ineffective. A change in consumption tax is urgently needed. A proposal for adjusting consumption tax is given in Box 2.7.

BOX 2.7 PROPOSAL FOR CHANGES IN CONSUMPTION TAX

New tax items: (1) New tax categories for products causing heavy pollution and with large resources consumption to be added, such as phosphate detergents, batteries containing mercury and cadmium, disposable tableware and plastic bags, etc. Their tax rates could be referred to that of the special polluting products tax of the independent environmental tax. (2) Differential tax rates should be implemented for tax categories of carbon and clean energy. Environmental cost should be considered in a carbon consumption tax, while the taxation of clean energy should be at a low differential rate.

Adjusting tax rate: (1) To increase the consumption tax rate of gasoline and diesel oil, meanwhile considering the environmental cost. (2) For cars with the same exhaust volume, differential rates should be applied according to whether an exhaust gas purifier is installed. (3) The tax rate of clean vehicles is at the low differential tax rate or exempted.

2.2.2.2 Resource tax

The current resource tax is a tax category to grade income and to promote rational exploitation and utilization of natural resources, but has little effect on saving resources and protecting the eco-environment. Therefore some changes should be made to the current resource tax to achieve the objective of protecting resources and the eco-environment in China. See Box 2.8 for details.

BOX 2.8 PROPOSAL FOR CHANGES IN RESOURCES TAX

New tax items: (1) The tax category of freshwater resources to include the development and utilization of ground water and surface water. The rate of freshwater resource tax should be set with thorough consideration of the scarcity of water resources and ecological compensation. (2) A tax category of forest resources, which means to levy a tax on deforestation. (3) A tax category of grassland resources is added to levy tax on grassland development and utilization, but natural grazing land will be exempted from this tax item.

Adjusting tax rate: The government should adjust the tax rates of natural resources according to the scarcity of those resources and the costs of ecological compensation.

2.2.2.3 Enterprise income tax

Some preferential tax policies should be stated and given to enterprises which operate in the environmental protection industry and those that take active measures to cut pollutants emission. To some extent, the scope of preferential policies should be limited. Environmental protection administrations should play the leading role in identifying the qualification for applying these preferential policies.

2.2.2.4 Other relevant tax categories

There is some advice on reform of city maintenance construction tax, farmland use tax and vehicle and vessel usage tax, as shown in Box 2.9.

BOX 2.9 PRIMARY ADVICE ON ADJUSTMENT OF OTHER RELEVANT TAX CATEGORIES

City maintenance construction tax

New tax item: City maintenance construction tax to be levied in the countryside.

Adjusting tax rate: To increase tax rate for environmental protection needs only.

Farmland use tax

New tax item: Farmland use tax will be levied upon wetland use. Non-agricultural land in the countryside is also listed under the scope of farmland use tax, which is levied at a low rate.

Adjusting tax rate: To increase the rate of farmland use tax to a greater extent; the tax rate of wetland use tax is high and the tax rate of non-agricultural land is low.

Vehicle and vessel usage tax

Adjusting tax rate: To increase tax rate and to set different tax rates according to the quantity of exhaust volume

---

2.2.3 Environmental Tax and Charge

This refers to the problem of how to handle the relationship between tax and charge in the above discussion on the independent environmental tax plan. Under the current environmental charge system, many independent environmental tax categories overlap with environmental charges, and both have the same functional mechanism. But the standard of environmental charge is far lower than the average marginal disposal cost. Thus coexistence of environmental tax and environmental charge can increase the degree of the stimulation function. When designing environmental tax policy, we should consider how to set a reasonable framework for environmental tax and environmental charge: see Box 2.10.

BOX 2.10 KEY POINTS OF ENVIRONMENTAL TAX AND CHARGE

The functional mechanism of environmental tax and environmental charge is the same, which affects the production and consumption behaviors of polluters by changing price.

There are some problems with the implementation of the environmental charge, such as lower standards and incomplete scope, which provides an opportunity to introduce environmental tax. The combined function will provide stronger stimulation.

The environmental charge and environmental tax will coexist for a long time in China, so the government should consider their different impacts on polluting enterprises, consumers and local authorities. Several important items in environmental charge could be changed to environmental tax, such as the charge for sewage disposal and sulfur dioxide emissions, etc. However, it is unnecessarily hasty to change all environmental charge into environmental tax.

Maintaining the current environmental charge system and introducing new environmental tax should become the highest priority of the Chinese government in establishing an environmental tax policy, with the emphasis on setting up coal tax and ecological tax.

2.2.4   Environmental Tax Expenditure Policy

The government could regulate some preferential treatments in the tax system to encourage environmental protection, such as the reduction and exemption of value added tax, consumption tax and enterprise income tax. By including similar regulations in an independent environmental tax, all of these tax preferential treatments would be called environmental tax expenditure policies. At present there are many problems with the environmental tax expenditure policy, such as being too general in principle without special clarification in practice; being vague and without clear statement; having fewer preferential categories means relevance and feasibility are lacking; and narrow benefit coverage. All of these lead to ineffective and unexpected implementing effects. Corresponding environmental tax expenditure policies should be established or supplemented on time, and preferential approaches should be enriched in order truly to promote the improvement of environmental protection. Detailed measures suggested for improving Chinese environmental tax expenditure policy are as follows.

2.2.4.1 To clarify the policy coverage to strengthen its pertinence
First, set up the environmental protection technology criteria to give tax incentives for research and development and the transfer, introduction and use of high technology which is beneficial to environmental protection, for example, imposing sales tax with a lower rate for technology transfer revenue. Secondly, make it a priority to set up policies which will encourage the development of the environmental protection industry, for example, environmental protection enterprises are bestowed with a certain tax preference treatment, such as reduction and exemption of income tax, lower value added tax rate for environmental protection equipment and accelerated depreciation of environmental protection equipment. Environmental protection investment (including foreign capital) should be encouraged by means of investment tax credit or tax reimbursement; meanwhile, the government should not allow foreign projects which cause high pollution to be transferred into China. Thirdly, develop a circular economy and study on tax policy for the reclaimable resources industry. Finally, give tax preference to resource-saving behavior as well as environmentally friendly behavior.

2.2.4.2 To adjust means and forms of preferential tax policy
Apart from maintaining reduction and exemption of taxes and zero tax, accelerated depreciation, investment tax credit and cost price deduction can be applied for different objects to encourage enterprises to take measures to cut pollution.

2.2.4.3 To determine the preferential degree of environmental tax expenditure policy
The preferential degree should be moderate for environmental tax preference functioning. But it is not easy to implement, and requires analysis and evaluation of preferential policies according to the actual situation.

2.2.4.4 To establish comprehensive preferential policies
Tax expenditure policy includes not only environmental preferential policy, but also industry and regional preferential measures. Therefore the government should take other preferential policies into account when setting up environmental preferential tax policies so that all these policies act in harmony. If not, their functions will cancel each other out and reduce to

zero when conflict occurs. The government should also take account of the goal of environmental protection when establishing other preferential policies.

It should be regarded as a part of the environmental tax expenditure policy to eliminate subsidies which are harmful for environmental protection, or to adjust the subsidy structures to benefit environmental protection.

2.3 IMPLEMENTATION STRATEGY

2.3.1 Step-By-Step Approach

The step-by-step principle can be summarized by three phrases: 'easy first, hard later', 'old first, new later' and 'integrated first, independent later'. The first step is to eliminate subsidies and preferential tax policies which are harmful to environmental protection. The second step is to undertake a comprehensive review of environmental tax and environmental charge. The third step is to set up an integrated environmental tax plan. The last step is to introduce an independent environmental tax.

2.3.1.1 To eliminate subsidies and tax preference policy harmful to environmental protection

Some subsidies have a negative effect on the environment. There are some tax preference policies which indirectly encourage enterprises to utilize resources and to destroy the environment. The government should revise those subsidy and tax preference policies, and consider the overall effects on the economy, society and environment when setting up new subsidy policies and preferential policies.

2.3.1.2 To undertake a comprehensive review of environmental tax and charges

The functioning mechanisms of environmental tax and environmental charge are virtually the same in that both force enterprises and individuals to cut pollutant emission by changing pricing signals. The government should consider the overlapping functions and try to apply either exclusively to avoid the tax and charge being higher than the pollution control cost.

2.3.1.3 To carry out integrated environmental tax plan

According to the integrated environmental tax plan, relevant tax categories, such as consumption tax, resources tax, etc., would be reformed for environmental protection. The tax system structure needs no change and only the tax items of relevant tax categories need to be adjusted, which could be implemented by approval of the State Council. Therefore reform of the current tax system by using the integrated environmental tax plan would be a relatively easy undertaking.

2.3.1.4 To introduce an independent environmental tax plan

The final step is the independent environmental tax plan, which needs to change China's taxation system and the reform which should be finally sanctioned by the Chinese Government and the Chinese Communist Party Central Committee. The objective of an independent environmental tax plan is clear, with a definite tax base and stronger stimulation function. Although it is hard to implement, it should be the ultimate goal for efforts in pollution reduction and control.

2.3.2 Piloting Program Ahead

China is undergoing a reform of its environmental tax system, so it is necessary to select some key projects that offer several environmental effects and are easy to operate in important areas.

2.3.2.1 Polluting products tax

According to the current taxation system, it is feasible to add polluting product tax to consumption tax. There is a lot of common ground between the two.

2.3.2.1 Coal consumption tax

Coal combustion is the major source of air pollution in China, and coal exploitation results in ecological destruction (Crompton and Wu), so the government should add a coal resource consumption tax where appropriate in the long run. The base of consumption tax is the consumption quantity of coal.

2.3.2.1 Taking water resource into resource tax

Water shortage is starting to restrict economic development in China. The government should also emphasize collection of a water resource tax in its tax policy, and add a water resource tax to the resources tax.

2.3.3 The Collection and Management of Environmental Tax

The collection and management of environmental tax is more complicated than that of traditional tax. Some environmental taxes are based on quantity, others on the price. Therefore technical support is needed for the collection of an environmental tax. Technical issues could be resolved through training or by entrusting other agencies with the task of tax collection. The management structure should be clearly specified to improve its capability of collecting environmental tax.

2.3.3.1 Public awareness of environmental tax

Environmental tax is a completely new concept in China, and needs public support. The government should utilize all media channels to publicize the significance, function and necessity of the introduction of environmental tax. Based on investigations, more than 90 per cent of the public support the imposition of an environmental tax.

2.3.3.2 To strengthen the fundamental work of environmental tax

Environmental tax is based on production and pollutant emissions data, some of which needs to be obtained by monitoring. Therefore it is necessary to set up an accurate and reliable pollutants emission monitoring and declaration system. The capabilities of relevant agencies should be strengthened with significant investment and the installation of facilities and measuring instruments.

2.3.3.3 To carry out further study on environmental tax

Further investigations on environmental tax should be carried out, such as how to determine the tax rate and taxation coverage. An empirical study should be undertaken, with its emphasis on analysis of the effect of environmental tax on government finance, polluters and beneficiaries, on international trade of relevant industries, on environmental public finance and also on the national economy.

NOTE

[1.] The paper is based on a project funded by the National Key Researches Program of the Chinese government.

REFERENCES

Crompton, Paul and Wu Y. (2005), 'Energy consumption in China: past trends and future directions', *Energy Economics*, **27**(1), 195–208.
Jinnan Wang, Chazhong, Ge, Shuting Gao, *et al.* (2009), 'Framework design of the separated environmental tax for China' [in Chinese], *China Population, Resource and Environment*, **19**(2), 69–72.

Ming, Su (2004), 'Research of fiscal and taxation policy for environmental protection in China' (in Chinese), *Environmental Economics*, **7**(7), 33–5.
Wang J., C. Ge, S. Gao, *et al.* (2006), *Environmental Tax Policy and Policy Implementation Strategies*, Beijing, China Environmental Science Press.
Yang, J. and Jinnan Wang (1998), *Design for the Reform of Pollution Levy System in China*, Beijing, China Environmental Sciences Press.

3. Lagging behind or catching up? A comparison of Chinese and European environmentally related taxes

Kris Bachus and Jing Cao

3.1 INTRODUCTION

In the past 15 years, much has been written on the environmentally related tax systems of European countries. Environmental tax reforms in Sweden, Denmark, Norway, Finland, the Netherlands, the United Kingdom and Germany are considered to be the most important cases (National Environmental Research Institute, University of Aarhus (NERI) 2007), hence they are the subject of many publications on both academic and policy oriented levels. On the other hand, publications on environmental tax reform in China are still relatively scarce. This is partly due to the fact that the policy debate in China on environmentally related taxes has started only recently.

Belgium is another country that is rarely selected for comparative studies on environmentally related taxes, since it has never implemented a green tax reform and its federal political model is very complex. Still, the policy debate on environmental tax reform has come to the forefront several times, a number of environmentally related taxes have a long history and some features of its tax system are definitely interesting to study.

In this chapter, we make a comparative analysis of the Chinese and Belgian environmental tax systems and their history and political economy. China is mainly compared with Belgium, but part of the comparison also includes other European countries. One environmental tax, the transport fuel tax (diesel and gasoline) is selected for a more in-depth analysis. With this comparison we aim to find out whether China is catching up with the European Union (EU) as far as environmentally related taxation is concerned. We will also provide an analysis of what can be expected in the future in both regions.

Note that in all tax rates given in this chapter VAT is excluded, since it is generally treated as not relevant for environmentally related taxation (Organisation for Economic Co-operation and Development (OECD) 2001, p. 70).

3.2   GENERAL COMPARATIVE ELEMENTS

It is not hard to imagine that China and Belgium are two countries with more differences than similarities. In order to put the following comparative analysis into perspective, Table 3.1 provides an overview of some economic and environmental features of China, Belgium and the 27 member states of the EU (EU-27).

Table 3.1 General comparative issues for China and Belgium

	China	Belgium	EU-27
Population (million)	1325.64	10.74	498.73
GDP (year 2000 US$)/cap	1963	25 088	19 870
GDP based on PPP per cap GDP (year 2000 US$/cap)	8150	30 562	25 150
Total tax revenue, including social security contributions (% of GDP)	21.8	44.3	39.3
TPES/cap	1.6	5.47	3.51
Electricity consumption/cap (kWh/cap)	2453	8523	6384
CO_2 emissions/cap (ton)	4.91	10.36	7.72
CO_2 emissions/GDP (kg/year 2000 US$)	2.5	0.41	0.39
CO_2 emissions/GDP PPP (kg/year 2000 US$)	0.6	0.34	0.31
% of world GHG emissions	22.3	0.38	13.1

Note: cap: capita; GDP: gross domestic product; GHG: greenhouse gas; PPP: purchasing power parity; TPES: total primary energy supply, a measure for total primary energy consumption.

Source: OECD/International Energy Agency (IEA) statistics database (2010) and IEA Key World Energy Statistics (2010).

In 2008, China's GDP, energy consumption and CO_2 emissions were still significantly lower than the EU's. Belgium's figures are clearly above this European average. However, China's carbon intensity, measured by the CO_2 emissions per unit of (nominal) GDP, is about six times the European average. When adjusted by PPP, China's carbon intensity is lower, but still double the European average which suggests that China's energy and carbon efficiency are far behind the Belgian and average European levels.

3.3   ENVIRONMENTALLY RELATED TAXATION IN CHINA, BELGIUM AND THE EU

Most international publications on environmentally related taxes use an indicator based on government revenues to obtain an indication of the degree of application of environmental taxes in different countries. Although these revenue-based indicators are a far from ideal measure (Bachus *et al.* 2006), they have the advantage of easy international comparison. Therefore, we choose to use them in our analysis. Figure 3.1 shows the revenues from environmentally related taxes as a percentage of total tax revenues.

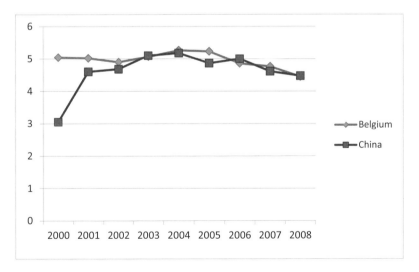

Source: European Commission (2010b); Chinese Statistical Yearbook (2010).

Figure 3.1 Revenues from environmentally related taxes as a percentage of total taxation, Belgium and China

Unexpectedly, the two curves show a high degree of similarity. However, we cannot conclude from this that both countries' tax systems have similar environmental accents. This becomes clear by examining the other classical greening indicator, the government revenues from environmentally related taxes as a percentage of GDP, which is shown in Figure 3.2.

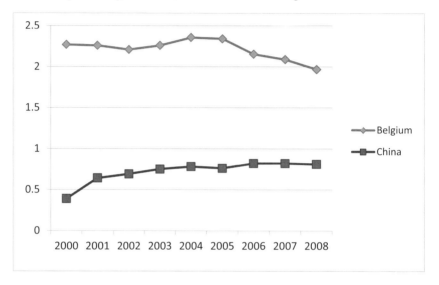

Source: European Commission (2010b); Chinese Statistical Yearbook (2010).

Figure 3.2 Revenues from environmentally related taxes as a percentage of GDP, Belgium and China

This figure shows a totally different picture: Belgium's revenue from environmentally related taxes as a percentage of GDP is much higher than China's, although the difference has been reducing in recent years. The difference between the two curves is explained by the generally lower tax revenues and rates in China: total tax revenues are 17.3% of GDP in China, compared with 44.3% in Belgium (in 2008).

Still, both indicators fail to express the greening of the tax system adequately, since the revenue-based indicators include both the tax rates and the tax base, whereas a shift in the tax base should not lead to the conclusion of a shift in the tax system. Consequently, it is necessary to put forward an indicator that is solely based on the tax rates. The *implicit tax rate on energy* is such an indicator. This indicator is incomplete, since it only includes energy, but since energy taxation is responsible for the majority of all environmentally related taxation revenues,[1] it is still an interesting measure.

Figure 3.3 shows that Belgium has comparatively low taxes on energy products. Only Greece and five new member states have a lower energy tax burden, resulting in a tax rate which is 40% lower than the EU-27 average. Compared with its neighboring countries France, the Netherlands, the UK, Germany and even Luxemburg, the difference is even larger and more pronounced.

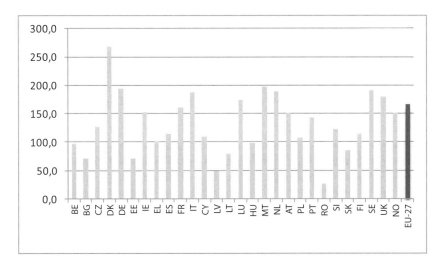

Source: European Commission (2010b).

Figure 3.3 Implicit tax rate on energy for the EU-27 countries in 2008 (in year 2000 €/tons of oil equivalent)

The low figure is because Belgium taxes most energy products at a low level: transport fuel excises are low (see section 3.6.2), but non-transport energy taxes such as heavy heating oil, natural gas and electricity are even lower. Nonetheless, the figure is probably slightly underestimated. The Belgian implicit tax rate on energy is rather volatile, which – according to the European Commission (2010b, p. 400) – can be explained by 'timing differences that arise because of lags in tax payments and business-cycle effects'. Indeed, in 2007, the difference from the EU average was smaller. On the other hand, the difference from the five neighboring countries was still very significant.

In China, the current fuel and energy taxes are very low compared with the European standard. Most of the energy-related taxes are imposed in the category of 'resource tax'. For instance, coal is taxed at 0.3–5 yuan/ton (XinJiang province adopts a new tax regime at 5% ad-valorem), crude oil is taxed at 14–30 yuan/ton (XinJiang province adopts a new tax regime at 5% ad-valorem) and natural gas is taxed at 7–15 yuan/1000 cubic metres. Compared with the European case in Figure 3.3, such natural resource taxes are very low. In 2009, a new fuel tax was charged for transport-related fuels such as gasoline and diesel; the current level for China is 1.4 yuan/litre on leaded gasoline, 1.0 yuan/litre on unleaded gasoline and 0.8 yuan/litre on diesel and kerosene.

3.4   HISTORY OF ENVIRONMENTALLY RELATED TAXATION IN BELGIUM AND CHINA

3.4.1   EU and Belgium

Taxation has always been a matter on which EU policy has had little influence. Tax policy decisions on an EU-level are not impossible, but they have to be unanimously agreed upon by all member states (Cnossen 2002, p. 25; Joumard 2001, p. 9), making their use very unlikely in practice. Nevertheless, a European carbon tax was on the agenda in the early days of European climate policy, even before emissions trading. However, the 1992 proposal of the European Commission[2] was never adopted, for two reasons (Ellerman *et al.* 2010; Bollen *et al.* 2006). The first was the view of some member states that the power of taxation is so central to the management of an economy that it is not to be relinquished, even if the environment would benefit. The second argument was the competitiveness issue: despite the mitigating and compensating measures to limit the economic impact for energy-intensive and export-oriented industries, these sectors still lobbied heavily against the proposal, both at the member state and the EU levels. The debate led to a number of adjustments, but the opposition proved too strong and the proposal was formally withdrawn in 1997. It continued on a less ambitious level and resulted eventually, in 2003, in a directive imposing a minimum level of fuel taxes on all member states.[3]

Hence, implementation of environmentally related taxation may only be expected on a member state level. Most progressive member states have at some point in the past 20 years introduced an ecological tax reform, but Belgium has not. However, its history on environmentally related taxes dates back to 1972, when the excises on transport fuels were introduced. Since then, a significant number of environmentally relevant taxes have been introduced. Most of them had no environmental or regulatory objectives, but were aimed at raising government revenue. Taxes on electricity and gas were introduced in 1993; coal has always been taxed at a very low level (€11/1000 kg). In the 1990s, the use of environmental levies became a popular part of environmental policy, with taxes on packaging, environmentally harmful products such as batteries, waste landfill and incineration, wastewater,[4] groundwater, manure, surface water use, natural resources extraction, deforestation and disposable products (including plastic bags)[5] (Anon. 2010). Although the number of taxes in this 'pollution-resource tax' group is comparable to the number of energy and transport taxes, these environmentally aimed taxes and levies are much less significant if measured in government revenues: only 7.5% of the revenues of all environmentally related taxes in Belgium are in this group, compared with 63.4% for energy taxes and 29.1% for transport taxes (European Commission 2010b).

3.4.2   China

Currently China does not have an independent environmental tax, although a pollution levy system was established about thirty years ago. The current environmental tax reform in China focuses on how to convert the current levy system into a tax system, and how revenue collected from pollution taxes or energy taxes can be better fitted into the fiscal system or recycled with other taxes.

   Starting from 2006, when drafting the 11th Five Year Plan, the State Council of China recognized the need to design an environmental tax reform (ETR) in China, and noted clearly in the plan that it would 'consider environmental protection needs in further reform of resource tax, consumption tax, import/export tariff, and explore environmental tax reform'. In 2007, the State Council of China announced a 'Work Plan on Energy Saving and Pollution Reduction', declaring that the Chinese government would implement an environmental tax policy in the near future, and in May 2010, the State Council (via the National Development and Reform Commission (NDRC)) announced it would 'plan on resource tax reform, ... finalize consumption tax reform, and study detailed plans for environmental tax reform'. Recently, a draft of the ETR plan was passed by the Ministry of Finance, State Administration of Taxation and Ministry of Environmental Protection, and was submitted to the State Council. The new ETR plans to impose a tax on sulphur dioxide emissions, wastewater, noise and solid waste, and is expected to phase out the old pollution levy system as an independent tax category. The initial tax level is likely to be similar to the current levy rate level; however, it should be noted that in

China the effective levy rate is much lower than the official nominal levy rate because of incomplete implementation. As well as the tax on conventional pollutions, due to China's new 40–45% carbon intensity target for 2020 and the 12th Five Year Plan to strengthen the energy intensity target, it is also likely that China may impose a separate carbon tax. Both the environmental tax on conventional pollutions and the carbon tax are presently under consideration and the detailed plan next needs to be submitted to the People's Congress for approval. According to China's legislation, imposing new taxes or changing existing ones has to be approved by the People's Congress. This regulatory process may take a long time, hence implementation should not be expected in the near future.

3.5 COMPOSITION OF THE TAX REVENUES

Belgium is a country with relatively high labor taxes and relatively low environmentally related taxes: its ranked position in the EU-27 on both types of revenue is fourth and 23rd respectively (European Commission 2010b). This position can be fully attributed to the low energy taxes (ranked 26th out of 27). In comparison, transport taxes and pollution/resource taxes are clearly higher (ranked 12th and seventh respectively).

To compare the policy choices that are behind the composition of the tax system, we compare both countries' tax revenues in Figure 3.4.

The contrast between the two countries' tax systems is striking, particularly the relative proportion of revenues from labor taxes, capital taxes and VAT. Just like other European countries, Belgium has a very high labor tax, while in China the labor tax revenue only accounts for 6.6%, while enterprises contribute 42.6% and domestic VAT tax accounts for 31% (in 2009). The policy lessons that can be drawn from this comparison is that both countries have a margin for an environmental tax reform, but not in the same sense. Both countries have low environment (and energy) taxes, which gives them a margin to increase. However, the implications of revenue recycling would be drastically different for the two countries, that is, what pre-existing tax should be cut to offset the imposition of environmental taxes to keep the government revenue neutral? Belgium has a clear opportunity to reduce labor taxes, while China has no margin. Instead, China has more room to reduce its capital taxes or VAT.[6] We add to this that our analysis is based on the presumption that a revenue-neutral tax reform is pursued.

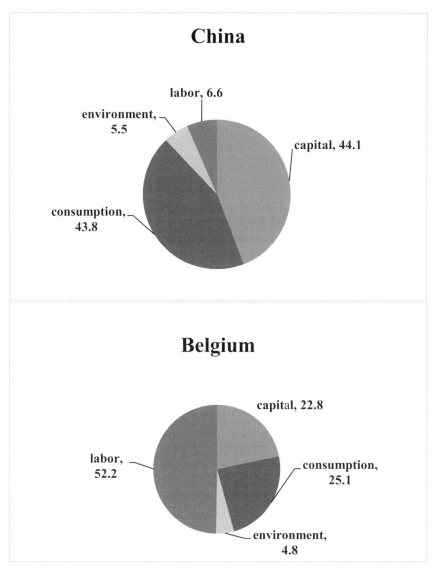

Source: Chinese Statistical Yearbook (2010, 2009) for China, European Commission, 2010b for Belgium.

Figure 3.4 Composition of the tax revenues in China and Belgium

3.6 FUEL TAX RATES IN BELGIUM AND CHINA

3.6.1 History

Excise taxes are an interesting form of tax from a government perspective. The taxed goods are usually very easy to tax, tend to have a rather solid tax base and are therefore very popular with policy makers to feed the budget. Moreover, according to Cnossen (1977), the first excise taxes in history were imposed in China, during the Han dynasty (BC 206–AD 220), where goods like tea, alcohol, fish and reeds for fuel and thatching were subject to a tax.

However, China's recent history of using transport fuel taxes as a policy instrument is rather limited. The tax was introduced in 1983, with a uniform rate for gasoline and diesel. In the subsequent 26 years, the tax rate of 0.2 yuan/litre remained unchanged, until the fuel tax reform in 2009.

In Belgium, by contrast, the tax rate has undergone a large number of adjustments since its introduction in 1971.

3.6.2 Belgian Transport Fuel Taxes from 1971 to 2010

Figure 3.5 shows the evolution of the diesel and gasoline tax rates in China and Belgium in real terms.

A drop in real prices occurred in Belgium over the period 1973–89, mainly because the fuel tax rates did not follow the high overall inflation. Between 1983 and 1989, the tax rates remained fixed, so the real rate dropped as fast as the prices rose. This situation came to an end in 1989, when a period of successive increases set in. In the space of ten years, the real tax rate rose by 45% in real terms for gasoline. The diesel excise tax rate increase was even sharper, but shorter: +88% between 1989 and 1994. In both cases this led to another set-off period, with a new freezing of the rates for gasoline (1996–2002) and diesel (1993–2002), causing a new fall in real rates. In 2004–05, the government imposed a new set of increases. In this period, the excise rates started fluctuating considerably. This was due to a new system of adjustment of the tax rates, called the 'positive cliquet system' (Belgische Petroleumfederatie 2010a). This means that each time the maximum fuel prices go down as a result of the international oil price fluctuations, only half of the price fall is converted into a lower fuel price; the other half is converted into a rise in excise tax rates. The positive cliquet system was (automatically) applied eight times for gasoline and nine times for diesel in 2004 and 2005. In the period 2006–07 an opposite system, the 'negative cliquet system', was introduced. It meant that, beyond a certain threshold of the maximum fuel prices, excise tax rates decreased each time the fuel price increased.

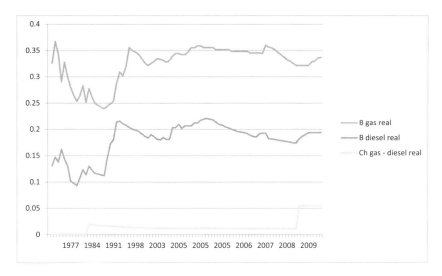

Source: own calculations, based on Belgische Petroleumfederatie (2010c); the Chinese data is collected from the NDRC.

Figure 3.5 Evolution of the gasoline and diesel tax rates in China and Belgium (1971–2009, in 1983 €)

In December 2007, the Belgian government decided to lower the diesel tax further to €0.302/litre, the minimum level allowed by the EU directive from 2003 (see above).

3.6.3   Chinese Fuel Tax Reform since 2009

On January 1, 2009, China launched a fuel tax reform on cars, buses and trucks, initiated under the nation's top economic planner, the NDRC, together with the Ministry of Finance and the Ministry of Transport. This was a big breakthrough after 15 years of discussion and debate on fuel tax reform in China. In 2008, the record low world oil prices offered a rare opportunity for China to push ahead with such a fuel taxation reform. In addition, it also provided some channels to revise the current fuel price mechanism, as well as resource tax reform. Although the fuel tax reform was kick-started by energy security concerns, it will in the long run give the market a larger role in pushing for a better environment and better energy efficiency.

The scheme of the current fuel tax removes six types of pre-existing fees on road and waterway maintenance and management, and raises the fuel consumption tax from 0.2 yuan/litre to 1.0 yuan/litre for (unleaded) gaso-line and 0.8 yuan/litre for diesel. Before the fuel tax reform, the real fuel excise tax rates, unchanged at 0.2 yuan/litre for 26 years, went down to 0.011 yuan/litre in 1983 prices, a 45% drop by 2009. After the fuel tax reform, it was 175% higher in real prices than in 1983, but still considerably lower than in Belgium. Due to the economic crisis in 2008, with the remarkable fall in international gasoline prices, the Chinese government found it a perfect time to impose such a tax reform so the tax increase was barely noticeable to consumers, thus facilitating the tax reform.

However, compared with the Belgian and European gasoline tax abso-lute level, currently the fuel taxes in China are still low, and most of the increase in fuel price is simply offset by replacing pre-existing road mainte-nance fees. In addition, the tax revenue is spent on compensating the losses of the Ministry of Transportation and other fuel users who previously were exempt from the road tolls, such as airlines, the army, etc. Therefore, the tax rates are still very modest at the current stage, and the rate is likely to increase in the future as a useful instrument to curb both carbon emissions from the transport department and combat traffic jams in metropolitan cities in China.

3.6.4   International Comparison

In order to be able to fully evaluate the differences between the Belgian and Chinese tax rates, it is interesting to include some more countries in the analysis. Figure 3.6 shows the excise tax rates for six EU countries (neigh-boring countries of Belgium), the US and China.

Qualifying these rates as 'high' or 'low' is a relative matter and highly dependent on the benchmark. Ley and Boccardo (2010) claim motor fuel taxes should have a Pigouvian component, to account for the environmen-tal external effects (mainly air pollution and climate change), a general Ramsey-type consumption tax component and a reduced congestion feed-back. In their model they calculate each of these values for different countries, including China and Belgium. They conclude that, given their assumptions, China considerably undertaxes its motor fuels (US$0.44/ gallon to US$1.65 for the optimal rate), whereas Belgium overtaxes (US$3.74 to US$2.82 optimal).

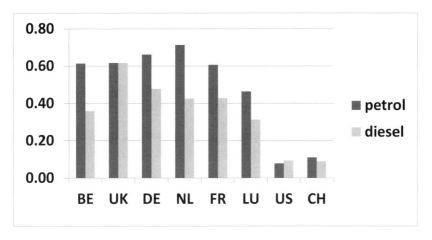

Source: European Commission (2010a), Chinese Ministry of Finance website (www.mof.gov.cn/zhengwuxinxi/caizhengshuju/).

Note: Some of the countries have differentiated rates for low and high sulphur content. For these countries, the arithmetic mean was used.

Figure 3.6 Fuel tax rates for gasoline and diesel in eight countries (EUR, 2010)

3.7   THE INSTITUTIONAL BACKGROUND FOR FEE-TO-TAX AND TAX RATE SETTING

3.7.1   China

China's environmental policy presents a paradox with its good environmental laws and policies but poor environmental performances throughout the whole country. To understand this paradox, one needs to understand China's unique multilevel regulation system as indicated in Figure 3.7. Vertically, the major territorial levels are: the central government (State Council), the provincial government, the city administrations, the county administrations and the township and village-level administrations. Horizontally, underneath the State Council there are many bureaucratic organs such as the NDRC and various ministries and bureaus. At the provincial level there are also similar ministerial counterparts.

Such vertical and horizontal lines of authority function together on almost all the governmental policies, so the compliance of environmental regulation is faced with 'two bosses', which in many cases leads to an ineffective outcome. For instance, local governments may have strong incentives to expand local employment, attract new investment and boost local economic growth, while local environmental policies are often too complex and long term and sometimes conflict with growth priorities. As a consequence, environmental regulations enforcement is not effective in most cases. For instance, the current effective rate of pollution levy is far below the stated level throughout the country. In addition, the low charge rate gives enterprises incentives to pay the fine instead of reducing emissions. In some cases, the discharge fine only counts for around 50% of the operation cost of reduction facilities, or even less than 10% for some projects (Ye and Wang 2009). For these reasons, in 2008, China's receipt of environmental levies was only about 17.7 billion yuan, less than one-fourth of the annual environmental investment. Of all the levies, about 70% is from the waste gas discharge fee, and the rest is mainly from the wastewater discharge fee. Although the pollution levy system is officially based on the 'polluter pays principle', in practice the levies are collected by the local environmental planning bureau (EPB) to fulfill its compliance requirement, while the local government often provides tax breaks or subsidies to the enterprises to sustain local jobs and income, therefore the incentives to abate pollution are very limited.

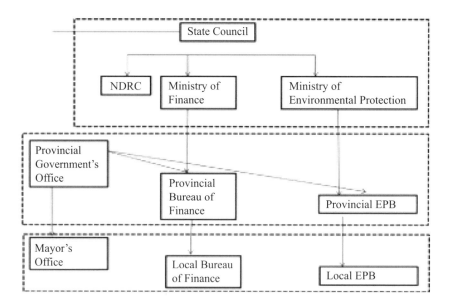

Figure 3.7 China's hierarchy layers of government administration

As a result of the described shortcomings, there is a need to convert the current levy system into a formal environmental tax system, so that the tax will be collected by the fiscal bureau under the new law of environmental tax. The Chinese government is currently reflecting on imposing an independent environmental law on sulphur dioxide, wastewater, solid waste and carbon emissions in order to shift the levy system to a tax system.

For such a new environmental tax reform, a few critical issues need to be addressed. First, how to set the tax rate. Since both the official and the effective levy rates are too low to provide incentives for reducing emissions, the tax rates need to be calculated based on the valuation of actual environmental damages, rather than the abatement costs. Second, the question whether the environmental tax should belong to the national or the local fiscal system is also under debate in China. The national fiscal system is already receiving more revenues from the levies than the local level, but if the (new) tax revenue is allocated to the local level, local governments may still have distorted priorities for growth, which may erode the effectiveness of the ETR. Third, for certain existing taxes such as the resource tax and the fuel tax, not only are the tax rates affecting the commodity price, but also the national price-setting mechanism, which is a competence of the NDRC. Both the market-based tax instrument and the plan-based pricing instrument need to be considered to impose an optimal tax rate on pollution, instead of undershooting or overshooting the policy target. An example of such a policy intervention would be to adjust the tax rate to the international oil price: if the oil price reaches a very low level, an automatic tax increase could be built in, and vice versa.

3.7.2 Belgium

As was indicated in section 3.6.2, the Belgian fuel prices are regulated by a 'maximum price',[7] which is calculated by a formula taking into account the following price components (Anon., 2006):

- cost, insurance and freight price (CIF price) – this is the international oil price;[8]
- storage costs for the national strategic oil stock;
- distribution margin for the petroleum company;
- excise taxes;
- other energy taxes;[9] and
- VAT.

As of 2010, the values of the different components are as shown in Figure 3.8.

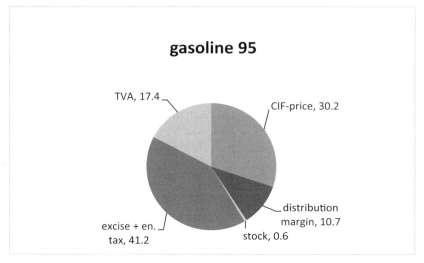

gasoline 95

TVA, 17.4

CIF-price, 30.2

distribution margin, 10.7

stock, 0.6

excise + en. tax, 41.2

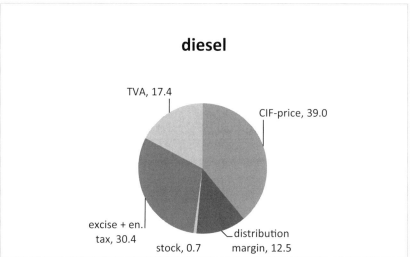

diesel

TVA, 17.4

CIF-price, 39.0

excise + en. tax, 30.4

stock, 0.7

distribution margin, 12.5

Source: Belgische Petroleumfederatie (2010b).

Figure 3.8 Composition of the maximum price for gasoline 95 and diesel in Belgium (%), Dec. 7, 2010

In Belgium, the tax rate for diesel is 36% lower than for gasoline; this results in a price difference of 13%.[10] This difference is higher in Belgium than for the average EU country. The differentiation is as old as the excise tax itself (1971, see Figure 3.5). It is a support measure for the transport sector. However, nowadays diesel is a competitive fuel technically even for small, private cars. In Belgium, this technological change, together with the beneficial fiscal treatment, has led to a gradual but rapid increase of the number of diesel-driven (private) cars, from 29% of the car fleet in 1992 to 57% in 2008 (FOD Mobiliteit en Vervoer 2010).

3.7.3   Responsiveness to the International Oil Price

The Belgian price-setting mechanism is more closely linked to the international oil price than the Chinese one: in 2009, the prices of both diesel and gasoline were automatically adjusted to the oil price as much as 35 times each, compared with 20 times for China under the NDRC price adjustment process since March 2005. See Figure 3.9.

In the past ten years, Chinese fuel prices have increased more rapidly than those in Belgium. The jump in 2008 may be explained by the series of Belgian excise tax rate drops at that time (a 10% drop in real terms between October 2007 and September 2008).

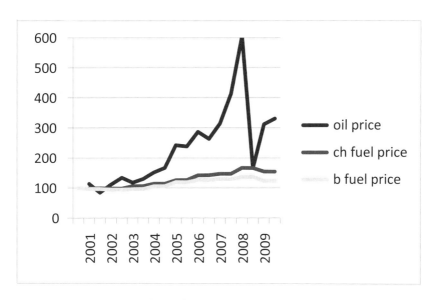

Source: IEA Statistics (www.iea.org/stats/surveys/mps.xls), Belgische Petroleumfederatie (2010c), NDRC.

Figure 3.9 Responsiveness of the Belgian and Chinese fuel price mechanisms to the international oil price

3.8   CONCLUSION AND FUTURE PROSPECTS

This chapter provides a comparative study on China's ongoing environmental tax reform and Belgium's experiences of ETR. On first glance at the absolute numbers, it seems that China falls behind Belgium rather substantially – for instance, environmentally related tax revenue in China is only 0.8% of GDP, while Belgium reaches 2% – but when looking at the relative share in the overall fiscal income, China and Belgium have a similar share of environmental revenue. Facing rapidly increasing vehicle emissions, China launched a new fuel tax reform by raising the consumption tax on gasoline and diesel in 2009. Moreover, experiments are being conducted in Xinjiang and Shanxi provinces with the new resource tax reform in 2010, and three major bureaus are examining the potential policy options to impose a tax on carbon and convert current pollution levy charges into a formal environmental tax. Although the current fuel tax rate is still very low compared with Belgium and other European countries, the recent number of fiscal reforms in China has been significant.

Belgium's progress towards ETR has been limited in recent years. Although it has one of the highest overall tax burdens, the environmental tax burden may be higher than China's, but it is still significantly lower than that of its neighboring countries and even the EU-27 average. In recent years, the revenue from environmental taxation has gone down, mainly due to low energy taxes. However, new increases in (diesel) excise tax rates have already been announced, and although a full ETR is not on the policy agenda yet, some energy tax rises can be expected because of the 2010 fiscal consolidation need in Belgium and many other EU countries.

We conclude that China is indeed catching up, and the current focus of the Chinese government is on how to shift the existing levy system toward a formal fiscal system, and transit from road restriction systems, technology mandates and NDRC energy/carbon target planning tools toward more market based instruments. Still, the current bottleneck to achieve a successful and effective ETR may lie in its coordination across the horizontal and vertical hierarchy layers of government administration.

NOTES

1.   Seventy-two per cent for the EU-27 in 2008.
2.   European Commission (1992), 226 final, Brussels, 30 June 1992, *Proposal for a Council Directive introducing a tax on carbon dioxide emissions and energy.*
3.   Council Directive 2003/96/EC of 27 October 2003 'restructuring the Community framework for the taxation of energy products and electricity'.
4.   The wastewater tax dates from the early 1970s.

5. The tax on disposable products was introduced in 2007.
6. According to European Commission (2010c), taxes on labor and capital are more distortionary than taxes on consumption and the environment. Based on this argument, China might prefer a reduction in its capital taxes rather than its consumption taxes.
7. Gas stations are allowed to sell at a lower price, but not a higher one. In practice, most gas stations sell at the maximum price or give a rebate of up to 10%.
8. CIF price stands for cost, insurance and freight price. It is the price of a good delivered at the frontier of the importing country, including any insurance and freight charges incurred up to that point, or the price of a service delivered to a resident, before the payment of any import duties or other taxes on imports or trade and transport margins within the country (definition taken from OECD Glossary of statistical terms, available at http://stats.oecd.org/glossary/detail.asp?ID=332 (accessed Dec. 6, 2010)).
9. Two minor 'contributions': one for a fund financing soil sanitation costs for gas stations and one for a fund financing subsidies to financially deprived people who use heavy fuel oil for heating their houses.
10. On Dec. 7, 2010, the maximum price was €1.498/litre for gasoline 95 RON, €1.298/litre for diesel, €1.523/litre for gasoline 98 and €0.732/litre for liquefied petroleum gas (LPG).

REFERENCES

Anon. (2010), *Milieuheffingen en -subsidies.* 2010–11 edn, Mechelen, Wolters Kluwer Belgium.

Anon. (2006), *Technische bijlage bij de programma-overeenkomst betreffende de regeling van de maximum verkoopprijzen der olieproducten,* Brussels, Belgian Federal Government.

Bachus, Kris, Luc Van Ootegem and Bart Defloor (2006), 'Signs of a greening tax system in Flanders?', in Alberto Cavaliere, Hope Ashiabor, Kurt Deketelaere, *et al.* (eds), *Critical Issues in Environmental Taxation. International and Comparative Perspectives,* III edn, Richmond, Richmond Law & Tax Ltd, pp. 429–46.

Belgische Petroleumfederatie (2010a), *Accijnzen op motorbrandstoffen: Wat houdt het 'kliksysteem' precies in?,* available at www.petrolfed.be/dutch/factsheets/fs_kliksysteem.htm (accessed Dec. 6, 2010).

Belgische Petroleumfederatie (2010b), *Samenstelling van de maximumprijs van motorbrandstoffen,* available at www.petrolfed.be/dutch/cijfers/maximumprijs_voornaamste_petroleumproducten.htm (accessed Dec. 7, 2010).

Belgische Petroleumfederatie (2010c), *Evolutie accijnzen (incl. energiebijdrage) op de petroleumproducten,* available at www.petrolfed.be/dutch/docs/Evolutie_accijnzen_petroleumproducten_sinds_1971.01.01.xls (accessed Dec. 10, 2010).

Bollen A., W. De Clerq, M. Tas, *et al.* (2006), *Kyoto: van beleidskader tot bedrijfsstrategie,* Mechelen, Kluwer.

Cnossen, S. (2002), 'Tax policy in the European Union: a review of issues and options', CESifo Working Paper No. 758, p. 25.

Cnossen, S. (1977), Excise systems a global study of the selective taxation of goods and services, Baltimore, Johns Hopkins University Press.

Ellerman A.D., F.J. Convery and C. de Perthuis (2010), *Pricing Carbon. The European Union Emissions Trading Scheme,* New York, Cambridge University Press.

European Commission (2010a), *Excise Duty Tables. Part II. Energy Products and Electricity*, p. 64, available at: http://ec.europa.eu/taxation_customs/index_en.htm.

European Commission (2010b), *Taxation trends in the EU*, available at: http://ec.europa.eu/taxation_customs/taxation/gen_info/economic_analysis/tax_structures/index_en.htm.

European Commission (2010c), 'Monitoring tax revenues and tax reforms in EU Member States 2010. Tax policy after the crisis', Taxation working paper No. 24.

Eurostat (2010), *Statistics Database*, available at: http://epp.eurostat.ec.europa.eu/portal/page/portal/statistics/search_database (accessed Dec. 7, 2010).

FOD Mobiliteit en Vervoer, 2010, *Statistiekentabel*, available at: www.mobilit.fgov.be/data/div/stat/Q3N1011.pdf (accessed Dec. 7, 2010).

Joumard, I. (2001), *Tax Systems in European Union Countries*. OECD Economics Department Working Papers No. 301, p. 9.

Ley Eduardo and Jessica Boccardo (2010), *The Taxation of Motor Fuel: International Comparisan*, Policy Research Working Paper, 5212, The World Bank.

National Bureau of Statistics of China (2010), *China Statistical Yearbook 2010*, China Statistics Press, Beijing.

National Bureau of Statistics of China (2009), *China Statistical Yearbook 2009*, China Statistics Press, Beijing.

NERI (2007), *Competitiveness Effects of Environmental Tax Reforms (COMETR)*, Denmark, Cambridge Econometrics, ESRI, IEEP, PSI and WIIW.

OECD/IEA statistics database (2010), available at www.iea.org/stats/index.asp (accessed Dec. 11, 2010).

OECD/IEA (2010), *Key World Energy Statistics*, Paris, OECD/IEA.

OECD (2001), *Environmentally related taxes in OECD countries*. Issues and Strategies, Paris, OECD.

Ye Ruqiu and Guijuan Wang (2009), 'Roadmap for Improving Environmentally Related Taxation in China', presented at the 10th Global Conference on Environmental Taxation, Sept. 23–25, 2009, Lisbon, Portugal.

4. Assessment of fiscal intervention measures in China: perspectives from environmental macroeconomics

Seck L. Tan and Dodo J. Thampapillai

INTRODUCTION

Macroeconomic policy analysis is invariably conducted without reference to environmental capital (KN) and its depreciation (D_{KN}). Hence policy outcomes from such analysis are inevitably unsustainable. Following the literature in environmental economics (Daly, 1991; Thampapillai, 2006), we define KN as an aggregate measure of the natural endowments at the disposal of an economy – analogous to the concept of capital stock in standard macroeconomics. In this chapter we demonstrate a simple macroeconomic framework into which D_{KN} is internalized. The level of national income (Y) that ensues as a result of such internalization is more sustainable than that elicited from standard macroeconomic policy analysis which excludes D_{KN}. The internalization also permits the basis for discerning the level of extra taxation that is required in the standard analysis to achieve the same income outcome as that displayed in the internalized framework. An estimate of this added tax is an indicator of the extent of the divergence between the unsustainable and quasi-sustainable time paths. As indicated below, the levels of extra taxation required are exceedingly high. We consider a set of nominal levels of extra taxation (2 per cent and 5 per cent) to meet environmental investment. Taxes, when not injected back into the economy properly, can be regressive. Hence the additional taxes need to be reinvested within the confines of fiscal balance (Thampapillai, Wu and Tan, 2010). Then the economy could recoup its resilience following a period of adjustment. Such resilience is matched by sustainability when the investments pertain to KN. We provide illustrations of our claims with reference to China.

The chapter is structured as follows. The following section deals with the explanation of the standard Keynesian income determination framework and the internalization of D_{KN} within such a framework. We label the framework that has the internalization of D_{KN} as the sustainability framework because the application of this framework is likely to prompt outcomes that would be more sustainable than those elicited from the application of the standard framework. The section also provides the definition for the extra level of taxation within the standard framework that would render the outcome of the standard framework synonymous with the outcome of the sustainability framework. The third section contains an empirical illustration with reference to China. The main feature here is the allocation of the extra taxes collected as investments on *KN*. Simulations are carried out – under some assumptions – to show that investments on *KN* can recoup and then maintain the resilience of the economy. The types of environmental capital investments that could reverse the regressive effects of the added taxes are then canvassed in the fourth section.

THE CONCEPTUAL FRAMEWORK

We limit our analysis to a simplified Keynesian framework where aggregate income (Y) is determined by aggregate expenditure. We further confine aggregate expenditure to gross domestic product (GDP) and assume (for reasons of simplicity) that all components of GDP barring consumption (C) and investment (I) are fixed. Hence the sum of government expenditure (G) and net exports (NX) is assumed to be contained in a constant (denoted by Φ) during a given time period. The methodology employed relies on the analytics of point estimates. That is given assumed functional definitions for the components of GDP, the coefficients in these definitions are elicited as point estimates from the data.

The assumed functional definitions of C and I are:

$$C = \alpha + \beta Y(1 - \tau) \qquad (1)$$

$$I = \bar{I} + \delta Y \qquad (2)$$

In (1) α, β and τ represent respectively autonomous consumption, the marginal propensity to consume and the rate of taxation. By assuming $\alpha = 0$, we elicit the point estimate values of β as:

$$\beta = C / (Y - T)$$

In (2) $\bar{I}$ represents fixed investment which we suppose is also contained in Φ such that $\Phi = \bar{I} + G + NX$ and point estimate values of δ (propensity to invest) are defined as:

$$\delta = (I - \bar{I}) / Y$$

A simple definition for the equilibrating value of Y within standard framework which is based on ($Y \equiv GDP$) is given by:

$$Y^* = \Phi / [\, 1 - \beta(1 - \tau) - \delta\,] \tag{3}$$

For the sustainability framework the equilibrium for income determination is redefined as ($Y \equiv GDP - D_{KN}$). If we denote D_{KN} as a simple linear proportion γ of GDP then the equilibrating value of Y will be:

$$Y^{**} = [\, \Phi(1 - \gamma)\,] / \{\, 1 - (1 - \gamma)\,[\,\beta(1 - \tau) + \delta\,]\,\}\,] \tag{4}$$

The level of extra taxation ($\Delta\tau$) that is required in the standard framework for synonymity with the sustainability framework can be determined by adding $\Delta\tau$ to τ in the denominator of (3) and then resolving for $\Delta\tau$ by equating the amended expression of (3) with (4). Thus it follows that:

$$\Delta\tau = [\, \gamma / \beta(1 - \gamma)\,] \tag{5}$$

Consider next a context wherein an economy levies a sequence of extra taxes each year over a period of T years ($1, ..., T$), namely ($\Delta\tau_1, \Delta\tau_2, ..., \Delta\tau_T$). Our contention is that when each $\Delta\tau_i$ is returned as KN investments, then D_{KN} and γ in some subsequent time period, say ($i + t$), would begin to decline permitting the economy to expand and become both resilient as well as sustainable. In this chapter, we set $T = 1, 2, 3$, that is we consider extra taxes for the first three years.

EMPIRICAL ILLUSTRATION

In order to demonstrate the premises advanced above, we will use an example with reference to the Chinese economy. In the first instance we obtain point estimates for Φ, β, δ, τ and γ from time series data. Whilst the estimation of Φ, β, δ and τ is straightforward, the estimation of γ warrants as an explanation. For reasons of illustrative convenience, we confine the analysis of KN to the depreciation of the air-shed in terms of air pollution and the depreciation of agricultural soils in terms of utilizing chemicals including artificial fertilizers. Hence D_{KN} is estimated as the sum of the

costs of abating air pollution and applying chemicals and fertilizers on
agricultural soils. Both air pollution and chemicals and fertilizer application data are drawn from the latest issues of the World Development
Indicators (World Bank, 2010). The air pollution loads are all presented in
CO_2 equivalents and the unit cost of abatement is equated to US\$40 per
ton[1] following World Bank (2007). The cost of chemical and fertilizer usage
is averaged to US\$400 per ton following United States Department of
Agriculture (2010). Hence the definition of γ could be differentiated in
terms of air pollution (*AP*) and soil degradation (*SD*) *as follows:*

$$\gamma_t = \gamma_t^{AP} + \gamma_t^{SD} = \frac{D_{KNt}^{AP}}{GDP_t} + \frac{D_{KNt}^{SD}}{GDP_t} \tag{6}$$

The elicitation of point estimates for Φ, β, δ, τ and γ over the period
1990–2009 permits the development of trend equations for each coefficient.
We then select the observed values Φ, β, δ, τ and γ for 2004 and use the trend
equations to project them up to 2020, which allows the projection of
anticipated time paths for Y^* and Y^{**} over this period. Some key findings are
presented below.

Figure 4.1 shows the comparison of the incomes determined from the
standard framework income (Y^*) and the sustainable framework income
(Y^{**}). The actual GDP incomes (Y_A) observed during the first six years
(2004–09) are also included in the comparison.

The actual income, Y_A = GDP, is marginally in excess of Y^* in the first
three years from 2004 to 2006. This excess becomes more pronounced in the
next three years from 2007 to 2009. An explanation may be that the fiscal
stimulus offered by the Chinese government to avert the adverse effects of
the global financial crisis (GFC) could have intensified the GDP. But such
actions were perhaps unwarranted owing to the excess of Y_A over Y^*. An
observation of significant importance is the clear divergence between the
paths of Y^* and Y^{**}. This confirms China's income (Y^*) from the standard
framework is unsustainable in this projected time path. The clear divergence between Y^* and Y^{**} in Figure 4.1 is further reinforced by the increasing size of $\Delta\tau$. As can be seen in Figure 4.2, the magnitude of additional
taxes needed for sustainability (equations above) starts from 44 per cent in
2004 and extends progressively to 56 per cent in 2020 (based on the trends
developed).

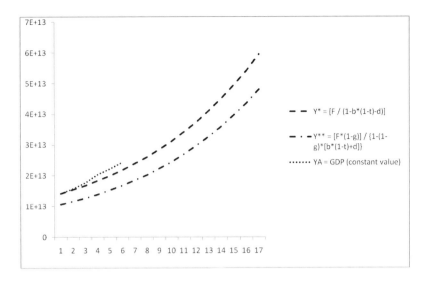

Figure 4.1 Standard framework (Y^*) versus sustainable framework (Y^{**}) versus actual income (Y_A)

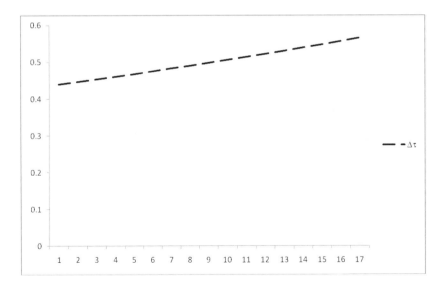

Figure 4.2 Magnitude of extra taxes ($\Delta\tau$)

We consider next the effects of extra taxation and return of these taxes as *KN* investments. As indicated above the extra taxation ($\Delta\tau$) is considered at two levels, namely 2 per cent and 5 per cent. Two types of *KN* investments are considered, namely reforestation (*RF*) and the transformation of existing patterns of farming into organic agriculture (*OA*). Investments in *RF* and *OA* are expected to cause γ_t^{AP} and γ_t^{SD} to decrease respectively following a lag period of six years. We assume that the per hectare cost of *RF* and *OA* are the same because both of these involve income losses in terms of opportunity costs from agriculture. Hence the extent of land area that could be allocated for either *RF* or *OA* can be estimated by dividing $\Delta\tau$ by the per hectare cost of investment. Given the equality of the opportunity cost of *KN* investments, we assume that $\Delta\tau$ in any given year can be divided equally between *RF* and *OA*. Figures 4.3A and 4.3B compare standard income, Y^*, and sustainable income, $Y^{**}(I)$, which incorporates reinvesting taxes towards *KN*. Figure 4.3A is based on $\Delta\tau$ at 2 per cent and Figure 4.3B $\Delta\tau$ at 5 per cent.

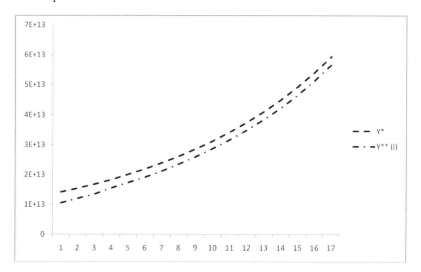

Figure 4.3A Standard framework (Y*) versus sustainable framework (Y**) with 2% extra taxes reinvested in KN

In this context (Figures 4.3A and 4.3B), Y^* has neither tax considerations nor reinvestment whilst $Y^{**}(I)$ has additional taxation for the first three years that leads to reinvestment. The additional taxes collected in a

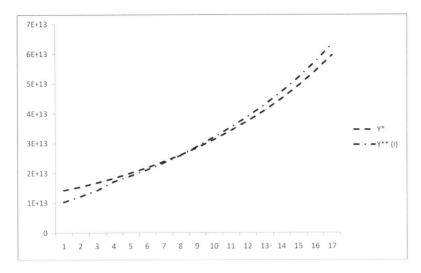

Figure 4.3B Standard framework (Y*) versus sustainable framework (Y**) with 5% extra taxes reinvested in KN

given year are assumed to be reinvested in the subsequent year. Such reinvestment of the taxes has allowed:

- for $Y^* > Y^{**}(I)$, but with strong possibility of convergence at the 2 per cent extra taxation level;

and

- for $Y^{**}(I)$ to exceed Y^* after eight years at the 5 per cent extra taxation level.

However, if the reinvestment of the extra taxes is not included in the accounting process then the path of Y^{**} remains below that of Y^* as shown in Figures 4.4A and 4.4B.

The divergence between Y^* and Y^{**} in Figures 4.4A and 4.4B is less pronounced than that observed in Figure 4.1, where extra taxation is not considered. It is observed from the Figures that there is a marginal narrowing of the divergence when extra taxes are imposed. This is primarily due to the reduction in γ. The reinvestment of taxes goes towards reducing environmental degradation and the buildup of KN stocks.

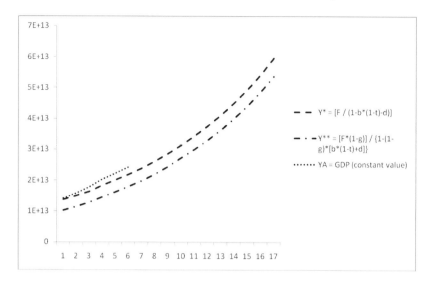

Figure 4.4A Standard framework (Y) versus sustainable framework (Y**) with 2% extra taxes but no reinvestment versus actual income (Y_A)*

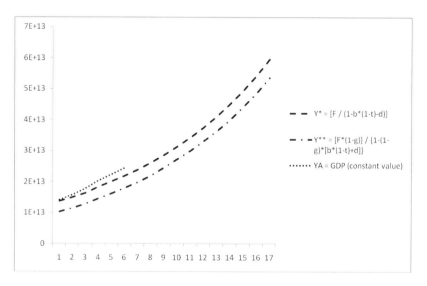

Figure 4.4B Standard framework (Y) versus sustainable framework (Y**) with 5% extra taxes but no reinvestment versus actual income (Y_A)*

CONCLUDING NOTES

The analysis considered thus far highlights the importance of *KN* investments which could be facilitated through a system of marginal taxes. A complete analysis should involve the identification of an exhaustive portfolio of potential *KN* investments. Besides the two actions of reforestation and organic agriculture considered above, potential investments could include: methods of biomimcry (Benyhus, 2002); closed loop systems in sanitation (Ciambrone, 1997; Graedel and Allenby, 2001; GTZ, 2006; McDonough and Braungart, 2002); exploration of renewable energy sources; and low emission bio-fuel from algae (Hartman, 2008). Such investments comply with Hartwick's (1997) strategy for minimising stock pollution.

The analysis considered thus far highlights the importance of *KN* investments that could be facilitated through a system of marginal taxes. A complete analysis should involve the identification of an exhaustive portfolio of potential *KN* investments. Besides the two actions of reforestation and organic agriculture considered above, potential investments could include: methods of biomimcry (Benyhus, 2002); closed loop systems in sanitation (Ciambrone, 1997; Graedel and Allenby, 2001; GTZ, 2006; McDonough and Braungart, 2002); exploration of renewable energy sources; and low emission bio-fuel from algae (Hartman, 2008). Such investments comply with Hartwick's (1997) strategy for minimizing stock pollution.

NOTE

[1.] The abatement of these loads was valued at US$40 per ton of CO_2 equivalent (Year 2000 price).

REFERENCES

Benyhus, J. (2002), *Biomimicry: Innovation Inspired by Nature*, London, Harper Perennial.

Ciambrone, D.F. (1997), *Environmental Life Cycle Analysis*, Boca Raton, FL, CRC Press.

Daly, H.E. (1991), 'Towards an environmental macroeconomics', *Land Economics*, **67**(2), 255–9.

Graedel, T. and B. Allenby (2001), *Industrial Ecology*, 2nd edn, New York, Prentice-Hall Publishers.

GTZ (2006), 'Urine diverting dry toilets project – Kunming, China', Ecosan Projects, 11 October.

Hartman, E. (2008), 'A promising oil alternative: algae energy', *The Washington Post*, 6 January.

Hartwick, J.M. (1997), 'Paying down the environmental debt', *Land Economics*, **73**(94), 508–15.

McDonough, W. and M. Braungart (2002), *Cradle to Cradle: Remaking the Way We Make Things*, New York, North Point Press.

Thampapillai, D.J. (2006), *Environmental Economics – Concepts, Methods and Policies*, South Melbourne, Oxford University Press.

Thampapillai, D.J., X. Wu and S. Tan (2010), 'Fiscal balance: environmental taxes and investments', *Journal of Natural Resources Policy Research*, **2**(2), 137–47.

United States Department of Agriculture, Economic Research Service (2010), *The Economics of Food, Farming, Natural Resources, and Rural America. Data Sets, Fertilizer Prices*, updated 18 May, available at: www.ers.usda.gov/Data/.

World Bank (2007), *World Development Indicators*, Washington, DC, World Bank, available at: www.data.worldbank.org/products/data-books/WDI-2007.

World Bank (2010), *World Development Indicators*, online edition, 2010, available at: www.data.worldbank.org/data-catalog/world-development-indicators/wdi-2010.

APPENDICES

Appendix 1: Definition of Equilibrium in Standard Frameworks in Macroeconomics

In a standard Keynesian framework, stabilization occurs when income equals planned aggregate expenditure ($Y \equiv PAE$); and PAE makes up the gross domestic product (GDP) of the economy. PAE is defined as:

$$PAE = C + I + G + X - M,$$

where C = consumption, I = investment, G = government expenditure, X = exports and M = imports.

I, G, X, and M are assumed constants in this analysis and are denoted by Φ, that is $\Phi = I + G + X - M$.

The assumed functional definition of C is *as follows*.

$$C = \alpha + \beta Y(1 - \tau) \tag{1}$$

In (1) α, β and τ represent respectively autonomous consumption, the marginal propensity to consume and the rate of taxation. By assuming $\alpha = 0$, we elicit the point estimate values of β as:

$$\beta = [\, C \,/\, (Y - T) \,]$$

The assumed functional definition of I is:

$$I = \bar{I} + \delta Y \tag{2}$$

In (2) $\bar{I}$ represents fixed investment which we suppose is also contained in Φ such that $\Phi = \bar{I} + G + NX$ and point estimate values of δ (propensity to invest) are defined as $[(I - \bar{I}) / Y]$.

At equilibrium, aggregate income (Y) is equal to planned aggregate expenditure or GDP, that is $Y \equiv GDP$. Solving for Y, equilibrium income Y^* becomes a function of marginal propensity to consume (β), taxes (τ), and propensity to invest (δ), that is $Y^* = f(\beta, \tau, \delta)$; and is defined as:

$$Y^* = \{ \Phi / [1 - \beta(1 - \tau) - \delta] \} \tag{3}$$

Appendix 2: Definition of Equilibrium in Environmental Macroeconomic Framework

In the environmental macroeconomic framework, KN is internalized and denoted by the depreciation of KN, D_{KN} as a simple linear proportion γ of GDP, that is $D_{KN} = \gamma \, GDP$. At equilibrium, aggregate income (Y) is now equal to planned aggregate expenditure or GDP less depreciation of KN, that is $Y \equiv GDP - D_{KN}$. Solving for Y, equilibrium income Y^{**} becomes a function of marginal propensity to consume (β), taxes (τ), propensity to invest (δ), and proportion of environmental degradation (γ), that is $Y^{**} = f(\beta, \tau, \delta, \gamma)$, and is defined as:

$$Y^{**} = ([\Phi(1 - \gamma)] / \{ 1 - (1 - \gamma)[\beta(1 - \tau) + \delta] \}) \tag{4}$$

To accommodate the effect from taxes, the extra tax $(\Delta\tau)$ is added to τ in the denominator of Y^* (3) to obtain a revised Y^* (5):

$$Y^* = \{ \Phi / [1 - \beta(1 - \tau - \Delta\tau) - \delta] \} \tag{5}$$

An optimal level of extra taxation $(\Delta\tau)$ would have to be levied upon the revised Y^* (5) so as to achieve the same income outcome as in Y^{**} (6). The optimal level of extra taxation can be solved by equating the revised Y^* (5) to Y^{**}:

$$\Phi / [1 - \beta(1 - \tau - \Delta\tau) - \delta] = ([\Phi(1 - \gamma)] / \{1 - (1 - \gamma)[\beta(1 - \tau) + \delta]\}) \tag{6}$$

Thus, solving for $\Delta\tau$, the required level of taxation is: $\Delta\tau = \{ \gamma / [\beta(1 - \gamma)] \}$.

5. Study on the design of wastewater environmental tax in China: from wastewater pollutant discharge fee to environmental tax

Chazhong Ge, Shuting Gao, Yajuan Ren, Guili Sun and Feng Long

INTRODUCTION

A discharge fee policy on water pollutants has been in use for about thirty years in China. This policy has played an important role in reducing water pollution from the industrial enterprises. However, as a result of the reform of the levy and the introduction of new policies on environmental protection, the amount collected from discharged wastewater pollutant is in a downward trend. Compared with the wastewater discharge levy in a form of fee, wastewater environmental tax offers more advantages. Furthermore, there are some critical issues in changing pollutant discharge fee into environmental tax. This chapter gives a brief overview of the policy assessment on the current wastewater pollutant discharge fee system in China and discusses the wastewater environmental tax policy including what is taxed, the tax basis and the tax rate. Based on this, it is concluded that now is not the appropriate time to change the wastewater pollutant discharge fee to wastewater tax.

The research on the Reform of Water Pollutant Discharge Fee Policy is supported by the National Water Pollution Control Technology Major Projects, aims to propose to the Chinese government a policy reform direction for the wastewater pollutant discharge levy. At the same time, there are reports on introducing environmental taxes, and suggesting that the pollutant discharge fee should be converted into an environmental tax in the Chinese media (Xi, 2010; Zhou, 2010; Wang, 2010). For the reasons raised above, it is necessary to consider the relationship between the pollutant discharge fee and environmental tax and investigate whether environmental tax can be used as the reform direction for the wastewater pollutant discharge fee policy.

I. CHINA'S WASTEWATER POLLUTANT DISCHARGE FEE POLICY

At the end of 1970s, China adopted the 'Polluters Pays Principle' PPP) for formulating its national environmental policy to address environmental issues brought about by economic development. By drawing on the experiences of some OECD membership countries in environmental protection, China started to implement a pollutant discharge levy system in 1982 to impose a fee on discharged pollutants from industrial enterprises, the levying categories covers atmospheric pollution, water pollution, solid waste discharge and noise (Yang and Wang, 1998).

The pollutant discharge fee system was regarded as the earliest economic instrument used for environmental protection in China. Since being introduced in 1982, it has helped to encourage polluting enterprises to build up pollution reduction facilities and adapt cleaner technologies on their own initiative to reduce pollution, and resulted in a number of high-polluting and high-energy consumption enterprises to close down, merge with others and upgrade the production technology (Yang and Wang, 1998; Ge *et al.*, 1999). Thus it has made great contributions to the pollution reduction and environmental protection in China.

(i) Current Situation and Trends of Wastewater Pollutant Discharge Fee Policy

According to the *China Environmental Statistics Annual Report 2009*, there were 31 provincial areas in China running a pollutant discharge levy system in 2009. From 2003 the 'Regulation on Pollution Discharge Fees' Collection, Usage and Management officially replaced the 'Provisional Regulation of Pollution Discharge fee's collection' which had been in place for 28 years since 1982. By the end of June 2009, the discharge fee collected in China was 80.78 billion RMB Yuan[1] and the cumulatively collected discharge fees since the policy started in 1982 totaled 147.95 billion RMB Yuan. In terms of regional structure on the levied pollutant discharge fee, eastern China, the more developed area in China took a larger proportion. while the central and western China had a high increasing rate.

So far as environmental categories are concerned, revenue collected from wastewater was the second largest after waste air. However, It can be seen from Figure 5.1 that wastewater pollutant discharge fee has declined over

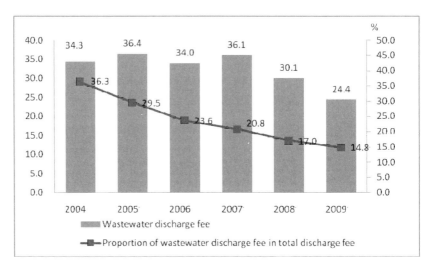

Source: Environmental Statistics Annual Reports 2004–2009.

Figure 5.1 Revenue collected from the water pollution discharge fee (2004–09)

years. dropping from 36.3% of the totally collected in 2004 to 14.8% in 2009,. So far as levied pollution factors are concerned, COD and ammonia nitrogen are the foremost contribution to the wastewater discharge fee. As for the industrial sector distribution of the pollutant discharge fee is concerned, the chemical, iron and steel, cement and paper industries are the largest contributors. enterprises in these industrial sectors are major ones that pay discharge fees.

(ii)   Impact of Water Pollution Control Policy Change on Wastewater Pollutant Discharge Fee

During the 11th Five Year Plan period,[2] China strengthened its environmental protection and energy saving policies by putting forward compulsory goals of 10% reduction of the total load of two key pollutants discharged, namely SO_2 and COD, and 20% reduction of per capita energy consumption. governments at various levels had attached great importance to the pollution reduction and energy saving goals and taken measures to fulfill the goals. As a result, discharge of COD in wastewater had declined. This has contributed to the declining trend of wastewater discharge fee collected.

Also, in order to promote development of the urban wastewater treatment plants (UWWTPs), some cities encouraged industrial polluters to connect to these UWWTPs. There is a policy that an industrial polluter will not pay the fee if it is connected to UWWTP but required to wastewater treatment fee to the UWWTP. Since more and more industrial polluters are connected to UWWTPs, the revenue collected for wastewater discharge has seen declining trend as indicated in Figure 5.1.

(iii) Shortcomings of Pollution Discharge Fee Collection System

The 2003 reform of pollution discharge fee collection system had addressed the issues in the 'Provisional Regulation on the Pollution Discharge fee's Collection'. Currently, the pollution discharge fee has the following characteristics:

- levying on the total amounts of the three top pollutants discharged from one enterprise as against the previous concentration-based levy pattern;
- pollutant equivalent method is used to count the total pollutant equivalents for different pollutants discharged by the enterprise, the base of pollution discharge fee is set on the counted total pollutant equivalents;
- the pollution discharge fee collection and management system changed from the previous three-level pattern to dependency collection and hierarchical management pattern in order to strengthen the supervision and management functions of higher-level environmental protection departments to the lower-level pollutant discharge fee collection; and
- separating managements and use of the revenue from the pollution discharge fee, and the revenue which will be subject to government budgetary management.

Although China's pollutant discharge fee collection and management system is continuously improving, the system itself still has some shortcomings. As a result, grass-roots environmental protection departments encounter difficulties in the actual collection of the discharge fee, specifically:

- The legal basis for the pollution discharge fee system needs to be improved. Despite a series of laws and regulations, such as the 'Environmental Protection Law', the 'Water Pollution Prevention and Control Law' and the 'Regulation on Pollution Discharge Fees'

Collection, Usage and Management', it is not explicitly stipulated that a violation levy should be imposed on a polluter that discharges pollutants at a higher level than the discharge standards and, furthermore, collection of the violation levy conflicts with other environmental management systems such as the Environmental Impact Assessment System and the 'Three Simultaneous' System[3] to some extent as these systems require the compliance of environmental laws and prohibit any violation.

- The pollutant discharge collecting standard is still very low and the list of pollutants which are actually levied is incomplete. The current pollutant discharge charging rate schedule has not been changed since its implementation in 2003 regardless the changes of the commodity price index. In addition, although more than one hundred pollutants are subjected to pollution discharge levy system under the current regulation, only the top three pollutants are charged while the rest of pollutants are not covered. Persistent organic pollutants (POPs) are not charged as they do not normally reach the top three pollutants discharged. Mobile pollution sources and UWWTPs are exempted under the current regulation. Agricultural non-point source pollution, one of the major wastewater pollutant sources, has not been included in the collection categories. Because of low levy rate, some polluters simply choose to pay the discharge levy rather than treat their pollution.

- The levy procedure is complicated and its workload is high. The present pollutant discharge levy policy specifies that a standard levy procedure includes four stages: reporting by polluters, verification by local environmental protection bureau (EPB), decision-making by local EPB and paying the fee by polluters. Since China covers a vast territory and numerous pollution-emitting enterprises and some local EPB' environmental management capacities are weak, total cost of collecting discharge fee is very high compared with that of the tax collected. Sometimes, there are bargaining between a polluter and the local EPB official on the actual amount of fee due, resulting in a much lower payment, so weakening the effectiveness of pollution discharge fee policy.

II. COMPARISON BETWEEN WASTEWATER POLLUTANT DISCHARGE FEE AND ENVIRONMENTAL TAX

Both the wastewater pollutant discharge fee and wastewater environmental tax tool are used to internalize external environmental costs of the polluters in accordance with the 'polluter pays principle' and also they can compel pollution-emitting enterprises to treat pollution on their own initiative. However, it should be noted that the wastewater pollutant discharge fee and wastewater tax have different meanings, especially under the Chinese context.

(i) Differences between the Wastewater Pollutant Discharge Fee and Wastewater Tax

1. The two policies have different roles to play

The most fundamental function of tax is to raise financial revenue while the regulation and control role takes the second place. As one of taxes, the main function of wastewater environmental tax is to raise financial revenue and its secondary role is to regulate and control the polluters' wastewater emission behaviors, while the main function of wastewater discharge charge is to regulate the polluters' wastewater emission behaviors. This means that the tax emphasizes the 'neutral' principle and the charge places more emphasis on 'regulation and control'.

2. The public has a different understanding of the two policies

Tax is part of a country's functioning. The concept of tax has been deeply rooted among the people and the public has established the simple concept of 'paying tax is perfectly justified'. China's charge system came into being at the beginning of the 1980s, originally for the purpose of contributing to the funding of the national administration, promoting the socio-economic development and solving the problem of financial shortage. With the increasing affairs of management in China, however, financial revenue reduced and the public finance burden on the population rose, leading to the present adverse consequence of indiscriminate charging and multiple and repeat charges. As one of the regulatory charges, the public's recognition of the pollutant discharge fee is far lower than for wastewater environmental tax.

3. **The two policy instruments are implemented by different governmental institutions**

As one of taxes, wastewater environmental tax will inevitably be collected and managed by the tax and financial authorities. Pollutant discharge fee has always been collected and managed by environmental protection departments. The taxation administration right of the tax and fiscal competent authorities is granted by China's Taxation Administration Law issued by the National People's Congress and its legal status is relatively higher. The right of environmental protection departments to collect discharge fee is granted by the 'Regulation on Pollution Discharge Fees' Collection, Usage and Management' issued by the State Council and falls under administrative regulation; its legal status is lower than a law and generally the authority of environmental protection departments is also lower than tax authorities.

4. **The two policies use the revenue collected in different ways**

Revenue from pollutant discharge fee is basically used as earmarked funds for special purposes, normally for environmental protection such as pollution control and the continued development of grass-roots environmental protection departments, while revenue from the wastewater tax is completely went into state treasury, becomes an integral part of national financial revenue, directly participates in national budget allotment and is not necessarily used for pollution treatment and environmental protection unless specifically stipulated in the law.

(ii) **Whether Wastewater Tax can Solve the Problems of Low Collection Rate of Wastewater Pollutant Discharge Fee**

China's pollutant discharge fee has some tax nature. In its design, it is basically a scheme conducted in accordance with the taxation system and it can be said that it exercises the function of adjustment by substituting taxes with a form of charging. However, as the discharge fee is impossible to be completely specific tax (mandatory, gratuitous and fixed, in particular mandatory), it is difficult to achieve the effectiveness generated by tax means in practice, and the low collection rate of discharge fee is an important manifestation. The national total SO_2 discharge fee collection rate in 2005 was only 58%. A similar finding was observed in a field investigation in Baotou City and Inner Mongolia automatic regions in China in 2007, the collection rate of the SO_2 and COD discharge fee was only 35%.

The collection rate of the pollutant discharge fee could be increased to some extent if the water pollution discharge fee was changed to wastewater tax, with more mandatory, gratuitous and fixed functions. The tax competent authorities, whose law enforcement deterrence is higher than environmental protection competent departments, would collect the tax. However, it must also be recognized that the collection rate may not be quickly increased to a very high level simply by changing the wastewater pollutant discharge fee to wastewater tax because there are many factors leading to the low collection rate in addition to the insufficient mandate and the low enforcement deterrence of the pollutant discharge fee

III. DESIGN OF WASTEWATER ENVIRONMENTAL TAX

The section will examine considerations in the design of wastewater environmental tax in China, and will discuss generally the issues related to the structure of environmental tax.

(i) Principles

The structure of environmental tax should conform to the basic principles of the tax system, in light of the particularity of environmental tax, special considerations will be needed and its design should meet some other requirements, especially the principles of effectiveness, fairness and operability.

1. Effectiveness
Effectiveness means that implementation of the policy will achieve its targets as far as possible – to improve environmental quality, i.e. reduce the pollution created by taxpaying entities. The effect of environmental policy is also a measure to judge the influence of the policy instrument on environmental quality as this is often the combined effect of several policy instruments.

2. Fairness
Generally, the tax fairness principle requires that the design of environmental tax should be able to meet the basic requirement of a fair tax burden for taxpayers'. Specifically, regarding the same pollutant, the same region and different polluters, equal tax should be paid for emitting an equal quantity of pollutant; for different pollutants, taxes should be paid respectively in accordance with the level of different pollutants; for differently developed

regions, the costs for recovering the same environmental damage are different, so a different level of tax should be paid for emitting the same and equal amount of pollutants for differently developed regions.

3. Operability
No matter how perfect the policy design is, environmental tax needs to be practicable and operable, because non-executable and inoperable tax policies are meaningless. At the same time, excessive higher operation cost or lower management efficiency policies design should be forbidden.

(ii) Detailed Design

1. Collection object
Currently the discharge levy is charged on water pollutants that are released into the water system. Considering China's present environmental supervision and management level, a simplified collection method should be adopted, the collection object is the wastewater discharged from pollution sources. Coefficients should be used to reflect and adjust the different damages of the discharged wastewater: the higher the hazard, the higher the pollution coefficient.

2. Taxpayer definition
Wastewater tax is for the discharge of wastewater. 'Taxpayers' means all those that discharge wastewater into the water body, including industrial enterprises, public institutions, commercial service enterprises, urban wastewater treatment plants and other organizations, but excluding residents.

3. Tax base and its calculation
The tax base for wastewater tax is designed to be wastewater emission quantity. In order to embody the pollution level (different pollutant types and quantities) of wastewater discharged by different industries, the coefficients for industrial sectors are initially calculated based on the industrial sector environmental performance and proposed to reflect actual discharge quantity and industrial pollution intensity factor (Table 5.1). That is to say, wastewater emission quantity for tax calculation is different from actual emission quantity. The calculation formula for payable tax for wastewater is:

Tax amount payable for wastewater = wastewater discharge quantity
× industrial pollution co-efficient factors × unit tax amount

Table 5.1 Some industrial pollution intensity factors

Industry	Pollution coefficient factor
Nonferrous metal alloy manufacturing	0.5
Inorganic base production	0.5
Machine finish paper and paper board production	1.2
Dye production	2.5
Complex fertilizer production	1.0
Beer production	0.5
Hoisting and conveying equipment manufacturing	1.0
Refit vehicle manufacturing	0.8
Entire vehicle manufacturing	0.5
Manufacturing of tracked special purpose vehicles for industries and mines	0.5

The target tax base of the pollution emission tax is set to embody the tax base features of pollution emission. The primary principle for determination of all tax bases is: as long as the enterprises have the emission quantity data by monitoring and being verified by environmental protection departments, the quantity data should be used first as the tax base. And for normal pollution emission enterprises, wastewater quantity is a conventional monitoring and statistical indicator. For the pollution sources that cannot adopt actual monitoring data (small enterprises, the tertiary industry, etc.), depending on the industrial wastewater emission characteristics, water intake quantity or product yield is used for the calculation. The formula is as follows:

Wastewater emission quantity = water intake quantity (product yield)
× wastewater discharge factor

The environmental protection department jointly with the financial and tax authorities appoint experts to determine and adjust the emission factor based on the current industrial pollution emission characteristics, and the enterprises' technology level and scale, etc.

4. Tax rate

In addition to raising revenue, wastewater tax is used mainly to regulate pollution emission and provide an economic incentive mechanism to control pollution. Therefore, the tax rate determination should give consideration both to fundraising and to pollution regulation and control. The tax rate should be set higher than the cost of treatment of the pollution and the enterprises' tax-bearing capacity should be considered. Tax rate design at the preliminary stage can be approximately equivalent to the present discharge levy rate. According to the current pollution emission charging rate standard and assuming normal enterprises applied the standard, the wastewater pollutant discharge levy is 0.07–0.29 RMB Yuan/ton. Therefore, wastewater tax rate is determined to be 0.2 RMB Yuan/ton.

5. Tax preference

Tax is reduced and exempted or partially returned to the enterprises that adopt advanced cleaner technologies and install and operate a wastewater treatment system whose pollutant emission concentration is much lower than the wastewater discharge standard or considerably reduces wastewater discharge.

(iii) Comparison between Wastewater Tax Amount and Discharge Fee Collection amount

Table 5.2 shows the results of an investigation of various enterprises' wastewater discharge amount, water pollutants discharge and the collected discharge fee and compares the discharge levy collected and emission tax expected to be collected for a preliminary analysis of the influence of a fee to tax reform on enterprises.

The enterprises shown in Table 5.2 have an average discharge fee collection rate of 0.09 RMB Yuan/ton and an average wastewater tax of 0.17 RMB Yuan/ton. The total tax collected will be double than that of fee while there are variations between the enterprises.

Table 5.2 Comparison between enterprises' wastewater discharge fee collection amount and wastewater tax amount

Enterprise	Industry	Fresh water consumption (10 000t)	Wastewater discharged (10 000t)	Discharge fee (10 000 RMB Yuan)				Calculation of emission tax payable (10 000 RMB Yuan)
				COD discharged	Ammonia nitrogen discharged	Petroleum discharged	Total discharge fee collected	
		(1)	(2)	(3)	(4)	(5)	(6)	(7)
A	Nonferrous metal alloy manufacturing	271.53	43.41	2.68	0.80	2.48	5.97	4.34
B	Inorganic base production	353.70	2.48	12.10	2.38	0.04	14.53	0.25
C	Machine finish paper and paper board production	156.00	98.00	1.45			1.45	23.52
D	Machine finish paper and paper board production	22.50	10.80	1.08			1.08	2.59
E	Complex fertilizer production	57.30	10.60	0.30			0.30	2.12
F	Beer production	61.35	41.40	1.28	0.01		1.29	4.14
G	Hoisting and conveying equipment manufacturing	10.93	2.73	0.09			0.09	0.55

Enterprise	Industry	Fresh water consumption (10 000t)	Wastewater discharged (10 000t)	Discharge fee (10 000 RMB Yuan)				Calculation of emission tax payable (10 000 RMB Yuan)
				COD discharged	Ammonia nitrogen discharged	Petroleum discharged	Total discharge fee collected	
		(1)	(2)	(3)	(4)	(5)	(6)	(7)
H	Refit vehicle manufacturing	9.86	4.50	0.31		0.04	**0.35**	**0.72**
I	Entire vehicle manufacturing	117.60	82.32	0.72		0.02	**0.74**	**8.23**
J	Manufacturing of tracked special purpose vehicles for industries and mines	3.66	2.93	0.08		0.01	**0.08**	**0.29**
K	Entire vehicle manufacturing	23.38	19.87	0.87		0.50	**1.37**	**1.99**
	Total	1087.82	319.04	20.96	3.20	3.09	**27.24**	**52.88**

Note: this is the simple case assuming COD, ammonia nitrogen and petroleum are the three top pollutants from these enterprises.

Sources: data in columns (1)–(5) are original data from field investigation, data in column (6) are calculated levy function and data in column (7) are estimated tax based on the designed tax function.

IV. ISSUES AFFECTING THE REFORM OF WASTEWATER POLLUTANT DISCHARGE FEE TO WASTEWATER ENVIRONMENTAL TAX

Over the years of development of the water pollution discharge fee has become an important integral part of water environmental management policy. It must be recognized that it is very difficult to shift from fee to tax completely in a short period of time.

(i) Institutional Obstacles

From an institutional aspect, the mindset of the environmental protection departments is not sufficiently prepared. Discharge fee policy is one of the effective means that was employed by the environmental protection departments to strengthen the supervision and management of polluters. However, if the fee to tax reform scheme weakened the relation between environmental protection departments and polluting enterprises and thus deduced the deterrence of environmental protection departments to the polluters, the reform scheme would hardly proceed. In other words, abandoning the existing pollutant discharge fee system will cause waste to the existing related resources of the environmental protection departments. At the same time, as the fund shortage of many local environmental protection departments has not yet been effectively resolved, the capacity building and operation of some grassroots environmental protection departments will encounter difficulties in funding. Therefore, the fee to tax reform poses some challenges to environmental protection departments.

Secondly, due to socio-economic development imbalance in China, there are regional and industrial differences in water environmental management and the wastewater pollutant discharge fee collection rates across China, small, medium and large cities and east, central and west regions have different discharge fee collection rates and revenues collected patterns. Thus a smooth transition from fee to tax reform, given the different stages of development in different areas, will also be problematic.

In addition, with economic development, a relatively developed urban wastewater pipe network has been built up in developed regions. In accordance with related laws and regulations, the discharge fee for industrial enterprises will not be charged once their wastewater enters the wastewater pipe network. and wastewater treatment plants do not need to pay the discharge fee after their effluents are treated to comply with the pollutants discharge standard, which means that both the industrial enterprises and wastewater treatment plants will not pay for the final discharge behavior, which is against the 'polluter pays principle'. In the rapid construction process of the urban wastewater pipe network, further consideration on how to adjust the contradictions and conflicts between laws, regulations, sectors and systems is needed.

(ii) Technical Obstacles

Due to lack of experience, reform of the water pollution discharge fee to the wastewater tax is problematic and a technical bottleneck exists. Some details in the fee to tax reform scheme need careful consideration.

First, it is difficult to convert the present discharge fee rate to a nationally unified wastewater tax rate. At present the discharge fee applied varies across China and is related not only to the collection capabilities of the various environmental protection departments but also to the priority given by local governments, enterprises' recognition and the monitoring capability of the environmental protection departments.

Secondly, the tax base for wastewater tax is difficult to set. It is also very difficult to relate pollution discharge to the tax base. Pollutants discharged by enterprises is not constant and will vary with raw materials in use and the environmental management level of the enterprises, while the levy base of pollutant discharge is determined by a sampling survey method, applicable to the calculation scheme of the administrative fee but not applicable to the tax system. If enterprises' yield is used as tax base, it must be under the condition that the amount of pollutant discharged by enterprises is positively correlated to yield. But the fact is that often enterprises with high production may not discharge a large quantity of pollutants, and it is also related to an enterprise's energy consumption structure and its technological, management and pollution treatment levels. A basic feature of the tax base is that it can be easily collected by tax authorities and verified by tax auxiliaries or related institutions. Discharge fee rate is difficult to be scaled according to the tax base standard and cannot be verified by the appropriate institutions, which is also a fundamental obstacle for the fee to tax reform.

(iii) Policy Coordination

The reform from fee to tax for wastewater discharge also requires interdepartmental collaboration and policy coordination. An environmental tax will inevitably increase enterprises' costs and it is necessary to deal accurately with the tax's relationship with the current value-added tax, consumption tax, resource tax, customs dues and income tax, and to give consideration to the overall tax burden in order to enhance taxpayers' acceptance. On the other hand, the emission fee to tax reform is closely related to the position of local governments' fiscal income and expenses and involves further adjustment of the central and local fiscal distribution, thus its combination with a reform of the fiscal system must be considered. Furthermore, from a fairness point of view, it is necessary to coordinate and balance the distribution of income and cost between different interest groups, different regions. Otherwise, the management of tax will become more difficult and tax efficiency and fairness will be affected. The biggest difference between tax and a regulatory fee is that tax emphasizes a 'neutral' principle and the fee emphasizes 'regulation and control'; funds from the fee are basically used as special funds while tax is national financial revenue and is for budget allotment. If the fee is converted to tax, the role of the discharge fee as a national regulation and control fund for environmental protection will be lost and it would then be necessary to consider how to ensure a fund for environmental protection investment through financial policies.

1. Setting of preferential tax policy

An incentive-based approach would be more effective than a punitive approach to a new environmental tax. Use of incentives can not only reduce the burden on enterprises and increase their competitive power but can also enhance their ability to pay, effectively regulate the primary distribution proportion and support people's livelihoods. To convert a fee to a tax, a series of tax regulation measures need to be formulated, such as:

- granting tax deductions and exemptions to low energy consumption and pollution-free production and consumption;
- implementing differential tax rates for enterprises at different pollution risk levels;
- deducting VAT and implementing accelerated depreciation for a proportion of environmental protection equipment;
- providing reduction and exemption of income tax for investment in environmental protection projects;
- granting favorable income tax policies to enterprises that produce or use renewable resources;
- encouraging social funds to flow to ecological environmental protection; and
- encouraging environment-friendly enterprises actively to develop and adopt new pollution control and energy-saving technology and new methods to increase resource utilization rate, thus enhancing the whole society's sustainable development capability.

V. CONCLUSION

Although wastewater tax has some advantages, there are problems in converting the pollutant discharge fee to an environmental tax. By simplifying the tax basis, the operability of wastewater tax can be improved but the tax collection accuracy would be reduced. Considering the costs of tax collection and management, we conclude that it would be inappropriate to convert the wastewater pollutant discharge fee to a wastewater tax in the near future.

(i)   Compared with a Fee, a Tax has some Advantages

In economic instrument and mechanism of action, fee and tax collection are essentially not different and both can internalize the external cost of environmental pollution. But from an efficiency point of view, tax collection is generally higher than fee collection; a tax is more compulsory, fixed and gratuitous than a fee. Tax collection to some extent can overcome randomness of the fee's charging behavior, deduce the arrears and refusal to pay; and also, combining wastewater tax with other taxes can reduce collection costs.

(ii)   Some Issues Existed in Converting Discharge Fee to Wastewater Environmental Tax

Collecting an environmental tax would be a complicated work. In addition to the collection effectiveness and influence on the national economy should be emphasized, a series of technical difficulties exist in collection and management, such as tax basis and tax rate determination. China's present supervision and management level is relatively low, especially in the western, poverty-stricken and less developed regions, and unreasonable design would cause the unfairness. moreover, in the 11th -Five Year Plan period COD is the key control pollutant for water pollution control and ammonia nitrogen will be added to the key control pollutants in the 12th-Five Year Plan period. Water pollution prevention and control work will be carried out to fulfill the total emission amount control of these two pollutants. If wastewater tax had wastewater discharge quantity as its tax base, the challenge to water pollution prevention and control would be increased. Furthermore, although the discharge of some pollutants such as heavy metals is small, their impact on and hazard to the eco-environment and human health are high and should be monitored and controlled.

(iii) It is Inappropriate to Convert the Wastewater Pollutant Discharge Fee to Wastewater Tax in the near Future

Water pollutant discharge tax is technically complex and the tax authorities would have some difficulties in collection and management. On the other hand, the present tax collection and management environment is not ideal – tax arrears exist to different extents across China – and a fee to tax reform may not increase the collection rate greatly. Therefore, we conclude that it is not appropriate to convert the wastewater discharge fee to wastewater tax in the near future.

NOTES

1. 1 RMB Yuan equals approximately US$ 0.15 at the end of 2010.
2. The 11th-Five Year Plan period refers to the period from 2006 to 2010. China makes national development plan as well as an environmental protection plan every five years.
3. It requires that environmental protection facilities of a construction project must be designed, built and put into use simultaneously with the main project. Construction projects must meet environmental protection requirements before they can be approved.

REFERENCES

Ge C.Z., Yang J.T. and Wang J.N. (1999), 'The Use of Revenue from Pollution Levy in China', in Grzegorz Peszko (ed.) (2002), *Budgetary Management in Innovative Mechanisms to Manage Public Environmental Expenditure in the Countries Undergoing Transition to Market Economy* (CEE, NIS, China), Paris, OECD Environment Directorate.

Liu L. and Si Y.W. (2009), 'Rational thinking for environmental levy to tax reform', *Northern Economy*, 7, 89–91.

Liu S. (2010), 'The necessity: from pollution charge to pollution tax', *Legal System and Society*, 2, 274–5.

Su M. (2005), *Research of Fiscal and Taxation Policy for Environmental Protection in China*, Beijing, Institute of Fiscal Science of Ministry of Finance.

Sun G. (2008), 'Some suggestions to overcome the difficulties in levying environmental tax in China', *Tax Research*, 8, 45–7.

Wang J.N., Ge C.Z , Gao S.T., *et al.* (2006), *Environmental Tax Policy and Policy Implementation Strategies*, Beijing, China Environmental Science Press.

Wang T. (2010), 'Environmental tax scheme has been approved by three ministries such as Ministry of Finance', *Economic Reference News*, 7 December 2010.

Xi S. (2010), 'Controversial environmental tax with 43 RMB per tone of coal', *Economic Observation News*, 4 September.

Yang J. T. (1998), *Design for the Reform of Pollution Levy System in China*, Beijing, China Environmental Sciences Press.

Zhou H.B. (2010), 'Environmental tax is the selection for 12th five year plan', *China Economic Weekly*, 1 November.

PART II

Environmental Taxation Strategies in Asia

6. Selling climate change mitigation measures: the co-benefits of environmental fiscal reform

Jacqueline Cottrell

1. INTRODUCTION

1.1. Setting the Scene: Trends in Greenhouse Gas (GHG) Emissions

The Intergovernmental Panel on Climate Change (IPCC) has predicted that significant emissions reductions are required to ensure that the average increase in global temperatures does not exceed 2°C. Under most equity interpretations, countries listed in Annex 1 of the United Nations Framework Convention on Climate Change (UNFCCC), which was drawn up during the Earth Summit at Rio de Janeiro in 1992 and entered into force in 1994, will have to reduce their greenhouse gas (GHG) emissions by 40–95 per cent below 1990 levels by 2050 to stabilise concentrations at 450–550 ppm (IPCC 2007c:90). However, GHG emissions are on a rapidly upward trajectory in many countries not listed in Annex 1. Rapidly industrialising economies are accounting for an ever-increasing share of total GHG emissions (from 46 per cent in 1990 to 57 per cent in 2005 (IEA 2007)) and will account for more than 90 per cent of increased primary energy demand between 2008 and 2030 (IEA *et al.* 2010). Both the IPCC and the consultancy firm McKinsey & Company (henceforth: McKinsey) agree that it is in these rapidly industrialising countries that the greatest potential for mitigating GHG emissions is to be found. Research by McKinsey suggests that all regions and all sectors will have to capture close to the full abatement potential available to them to ensure that the 2°C target is met (McKinsey 2009). Furthermore, McKinsey contends that 70 per cent of this abatement potential is to be found in what it refers to as the 'developing world' (broadly speaking, non-Annex 1 countries).

As called for in the Johannesburg Plan of Implementation (JPOI), which was developed at the World Summit for Sustainable Development in South

Africa in 2002, developed countries must take the lead in supporting emerging and developing economies in their efforts to find more sustainable development paths, for example by means of technology transfer or market-based mechanisms like the clean development mechanism (CDM). Clearly, for fairness[1] and historical reasons, any efforts to reduce emissions in developing and industrialising countries must be supported by developed countries and accompanied by a binding commitment to bring about significant reductions in emissions on their part. To prevent irreversible climate change, however, it is also essential that developing countries identify and implement a number of policies that can reduce GHG emissions while furthering their own (sustainable) development goals. This means finding policies which can generate a number of social, economic and environmental benefits. Without this, mitigating climate change will prove impossible.

If current trends continue, GHG emissions are predicted to increase by between 25 and 90 per cent on 2000 levels by 2030, and considerably more by 2050, if policies are not implemented to reduce emissions significantly (IPCC 2007a:111). Indeed, the International Energy Agency (IEA) predicted in December 2010 that, without significant new climate change commitments (not agreed in Cancun), the concentration of GHGs in the atmosphere is likely to be stabilised at over 650 ppm of CO_2-equivalent, amounting to a likely temperature rise of more than 3.5°C (IEA 2010). In order to prevent irreversible climate change, it is essential that we find ways of reducing emissions in Annex 1 countries while slowing the rate at which emissions are rising elsewhere. It is essential that non-Annex 1 countries do not follow the carbon- and resource-intensive development paths of the West, but 'leapfrog' onto more sustainable, low-carbon development paths, meeting their rapidly increasing primary energy demand not with fossil fuel energy sources, but with renewable sources of energy.

In the light of these trends, the necessity to turn them around, and the failure of climate change negotiations to secure binding commitments to reduce GHG emissions, the question remains: how can measures be agreed to reduce GHG emissions while not compromising sustainable development and poverty reduction measures in non-Annex 1 countries, such as those associated with the Millennium Development Goals (MDGs)? One solution to this problem is the implementation of environmental fiscal reform (EFR). First, because EFR is associated with a number of social, environmental and economic co-benefits which enhance its applicability and palatability to developing and rapidly industrialising economies; and, second, because an essential element in 'greening' our economies is to create prices that are transparent and 'tell the ecological truth'.[2]

1.2. The Co-benefits of Climate Change Mitigation

Measures for climate change mitigation can generate a number of co-benefits. The most direct of these are associated with the improved management of the environment and natural resources, which can contribute directly to poverty reduction, more sustainable livelihoods and pro-poor growth. These linkages are the focus of a joint United Nations Development Programme (UNDP) and United Nations Environment Programme (UNEP) Poverty-Environment Initiative (PEI), which acknowledges the extent to which the poor depend on the environment for their livelihoods and well-being and helps countries to integrate poverty-environment linkages into national and sub-national development planning.[3]

Improvements in the natural environment derived, such as reduced emissions from burning fossil fuels, are also associated with a number of health benefits, such as reduced lung disease. Sustainable ecosystem management can ensure that environmental services contribute to the well-being of many dependent for their livelihoods on natural resources, such as forestry, fisheries, agriculture. Moreover, the impact of climate change will render many poverty reduction measures temporary, as environmental services upon which populations depend are compromised or even destroyed. These linkages are also acknowledged by the United Nations' Committee for Sustainable Development (CSD), which developed a practical plan for how to achieve the MDGs in a 2005 report. In the report, climate change is explicitly mentioned as a factor that could worsen the situation of the poor and make it more difficult to meet the MDGs. For this reason, the CSD suggested adding a number of energy goals to the MDGs to reflect energy security and the role that energy access can play in poverty alleviation (CSD 2005).

Measures that reduce GHG emissions and improve the natural environment also generate a number of related benefits, such as cost savings through enhanced resource and energy efficiency, increased energy security, potential improvements in access to (renewable or low-carbon) energy, reduced local air, water and soil pollution, reduced land degradation and reduced rates of deforestation. EFR complements these co-benefits by raising state revenue, which can be used for poverty alleviation measures, pro-poor investment, pollution control and improved natural resource management.

The Organisation for Economic Co-operation and Development (OECD) has analysed the macroeconomic benefits resulting from climate change mitigation measures (OECD 2003). It suggests that a more resource-efficient society will tend to create new energy and material efficiency-related jobs in a regionally equitable way in manufacturing, the building sector and installation, planning, maintenance, consulting and other services businesses (OECD 2003:19). Green technologies are booming in many parts of the globe, and those countries that develop and manufacture technologies for energy and resource efficiency will have a competitive 'first mover' advantage over other countries within which a market for such goods and services does not (yet) exist. There is also much evidence that the promotion of renewable energy by means of grants and market-based instruments such as feed-in-tariffs can have a considerable impact on employment – in Germany well over 250 000 jobs have been created in the booming wind energy industry (Knigge and Görlach 2005). Similarly, the European Commission's 2006 Renewable Energy Roadmap estimated that 650 000 jobs could be created in the renewable energy sector by 2020 (COM 2006). EFR measures can also reduce market distortions, thus rendering markets more efficient (see below).

It seems likely that placing greater emphasis on these co-benefits might facilitate the implementation of climate change mitigation policies. In the light of this, this chapter will explore the extent to which EFR has the potential to bring about changes in behaviour that will result in GHG emissions reductions while generating additional benefits. First, I will look at the potential sources of GHG emission reductions, particularly those relevant to non-Annex 1 countries. Emissions are often the result of diverse and diffuse emitters – individual consumers, small-scale farmers – and thus, it seems that EFR may be one of the most effective policy measures available to governments to bring about behavioural change. I will go on to explore the most significant barriers to GHG emission reductions – market failures – and suggest that EFR might be the most appropriate instrument to deal with such barriers. I will conclude by analysing ways of progressing towards increased implementation of EFR in the future, which would have the potential to contribute to climate change mitigation and environmentally, socially and economically sustainable development.

2.   POTENTIAL SOURCES OF EMISSIONS REDUCTIONS

2.1.   Introduction to McKinsey's Global Greenhouse Gas Abatement Cost Curve

To be relatively certain that average global temperatures do not increase by more than 2°C relative to pre-industrial era, global GHG emissions should peak before 2020 and reductions of approximately 50 per cent on 2007 levels should be achieved by 2050. In quantitative terms, this means achieving reductions in global GHG emissions of approximately 38 gigatonnes of CO_2-equivalent (Gt CO_2-eq) by 2030. The analysis of mitigation potentials and sources of emissions reductions below is based on these figures.

In 2009, McKinsey published a report, 'Pathways to a low-carbon economy – Version 2 of the Global GHG Abatement Cost Curve', exploring potentials for reducing GHG emissions and stabilising the average increase in global temperature at approximately 2°C. This report identifies a number of measures which can be implemented, at a cost of less than €60 per tonne CO_2-eq, many of which will have a neutral or negative cost during their lifetime, as initial investments will be recouped as a result of significant energy savings during use.

McKinsey developed the global cost curve for GHG abatement to illustrate the results of their research. This identified a number of technological potentials to deliver a reduction in emissions of 38 Gt CO_2-eq relative to business-as-usual emissions of 70 Gt CO_2-eq. They also brought these potentials together under three main headings: energy efficiency (14 Gt CO_2-eq per year in 2030); low-carbon energy supply (12 Gt CO_2-eq per year in 2030); and terrestrial carbon sinks in forestry and agriculture (12 Gt CO_2-eq per year in 2030). They also contended that there is additional abatement potential amounting to as much as 9 Gt CO_2-eq per year in 2030 involving changes in individual consumer behaviour in the buildings, transportation and waste sectors, as well as in other, more expensive technical measures. This latter category is not included in the global cost curve for abatement, as the costs of these changes are subject to a high degree of uncertainty (McKinsey 2009:9). McKinsey also contended that more than 70 per cent of this potential is to be found in developing countries (McKinsey 2009:16). These four categories are discussed below.

2.2.   Category 1: Energy Efficiency

In 2004, *energy-related* CO_2 emissions from fossil fuel combustion, mostly for heat supply, electricity generation and transport, accounted for around 57 per cent of total GHG emissions (IPCC 2007a:103). Energy conservation and energy efficiency measures are amongst the most cost-effective means available to reduce GHG emissions. About one-quarter of all measures identified in the McKinsey global cost curve for GHG abatement are efficiency-enhancing measures *associated with no net cost* (mainly in the buildings, transportation and industry sectors). This means that upfront investments for energy efficiency measures will be outweighed by cost savings in the medium or long term (McKinsey 2009). Particularly in those

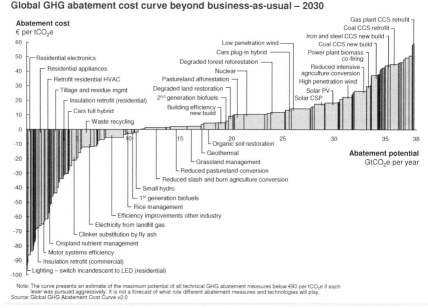

© McKinsey & Company 2009.

Figure 6.1 The McKinsey global GHG abatement cost curve beyond business-as-usual – 2030

countries where ability to pay for energy supply may be limited, such measures have considerable appeal.

Clearly, there are many ways to encourage energy conservation and efficiency measures, not least increasing energy prices by means of an EFR measure, an energy tax, while ensuring that more efficient technologies are available and providing sufficient information for business or private consumers to make an informed choice.

2.3.   Category 2: Low-carbon Energy Supply

Fuel switching from fossil fuels to low-carbon energy sources is fundamental to climate change mitigation and is particularly urgent in the light of upward trends in the carbon intensity of the energy mix in non-OECD countries. McKinsey contends that a shift to renewable or low-carbon energy sources could account for a further 12 Gt CO_2-eq per year in 2030.

One of the most cost-effective and efficient ways of reducing carbon emissions and encouraging fuel shifting would be to increase the price of carbon by means of a carbon tax. While putting a price on carbon alone is unlikely to be sufficient to reduce carbon emissions, with appropriate flanking measures, it could be an extremely effective and efficient instrument for generating incentives for a shift towards a low-carbon economy.

2.4. Category 3: Terrestrial Carbon – Forestry and Agriculture

McKinsey suggest that avoided deforestation, afforestation and carbon sequestration in soils could save as much as 12 Gt CO_2-eq per year in 2030. The IPCC has estimated that at least half of the mitigation potential of the forestry sector can be achieved for < US\$20/t CO_2-eq, the vast majority of this in developing countries, most notably South America and Asia.[4]

Poor and unsustainable forest management is often at least partly attributable to market failures. The environmental services provided by forests, and the goods and services that can be extracted from them, are rarely priced in a way that reflects their actual value. Market-based measures that price forest resources according to their scarcity, such as payment for environmental services (PES)[5] or forest product certification schemes can help create explicit economic advantages in favour of sustainable forest management. This can generate a number of co-benefits, including support for the livelihoods of local populations, creation of new sources of income (agroforestry, forestry management), preservation of watersheds, reduced illegal logging and higher incomes from sale of legally extracted timber resources and from the sustainable extraction of non-wood forest products.

EFR is also highly relevant in relation to reforming environmentally harmful subsidies in the agricultural sector and to changing the farming practices of the diverse and diffuse 22 per cent of the global population that work within the agriculture sector. Price signals have considerable potential to incentivise individuals to change their behaviour. I will return to this argument in relation to category 4, below.

2.5. Category 4: Behavioural Change and Technologies Costing > €60/tCO_2-eq

McKinsey contend that behavioural change across sectors could yield reductions of between 3.5 and 5 Gt CO_2-eq per year in 2030. While behavioural change is difficult to predict and tends to demand the use of comprehensive incentive measures (regulation, economic instruments and information) (UNEP 2009:xvi), there is a large body of evidence that shows that increasing energy prices does bring about changes in behaviour. In Germany, for example, research has shown that increasing energy prices (domestic energy and transport fuels) had a significant impact on individual consumer purchasing decisions in relation to car-sharing, choice of car model, and public transport use (Knigge and Görlach 2005).

McKinsey has also estimated that technologies costing > €60/t CO_2-eq could reduce GHG emissions by a further 3–6 Gt CO_2-eq per year by 2030. Other than to note that EFR measures are one means of raising revenue to fund the application of such technologies, these will not be addressed in more depth here.

3. BARRIERS TO CHANGE – OR WHY EFR CAN CONTRIBUTE TO THE IMPLEMENTATION OF CLIMATE CHANGE MITIGATION POLICIES ALL OVER THE WORLD

3.1. The Single most Significant Barrier to Change – Market Distortions

Perhaps the most crucial argument in favour of implementing EFR is that the single most important barrier to change which could bring about reduced GHG emissions is market distortions. What this means is that prices for goods or services do not reflect the costs associated with producing or consuming them, such as the costs of cleaning up the pollution associated with their production, consumption and disposal. Until these costs are included in the price, they are paid for by somebody else, typically, the taxpayer – and not the polluter. Market distortions can be a result of implicit or explicit subsidy policies like low-interest loans, tax exemptions (see section 3.3. below), but also be distorted for a number of other reasons, such as imperfect information or 'split incentives' that incentivise short-term, unsustainable decision-making.[6]

Market distortions are highlighted by the 2007 IPCC Fourth Assessment Report as being relevant for all sectors – energy supply, industry, residential and commercial buildings, transport and transport infrastructure, agriculture, forestry and waste and waste water. The absence of a price on carbon (at least in most countries) means that the cost of emitting carbon for the polluter does not reflect the potential cost to (global) society of those emissions. Energy prices are too cheap and neither reflect the external costs of energy use nor the scarcity of energy as a limited resource, which results in energy being used less efficiently than it could be in a better regulated market. There are also examples of environmentally harmful subsidies (EHS) in all of these sectors (see section 3.3. below).

3.2.   EFR – A Dynamic Tool for Mitigating Climate Change

Climate change mitigation requires that all economies move onto a green growth paradigm based on low-carbon technologies and lower rates of energy and resource consumption. Finding a means of preventing high rates of growth in rapidly industrialising economies resulting in ever-higher GHG emissions is essential. But reversing this trend by improving energy and resource efficiency at a higher rate than GDP growth is a major challenge. Ernst von Weizsäcker has suggested one possible solution to this problem, namely increasing energy or resource prices in proportion to the efficiency gains of the previous year by means of annual increases in energy and resource taxation (Weizsäcker *et al.* 2009). A resource and energy tax escalator such as this would create a robust and dynamic price signal in favour of constantly improving energy and resource efficiency *and* energy and resource conservation. This could facilitate the 'leapfrogging' discussed in the introduction – i.e., a transition to low-carbon technologies at an earlier stage of development than has been the case in the West. Although such a radical move remains untested, drawing attention to the co-benefits of EFR may enable governments to take such far-reaching steps in the future.

3.3.   The Potential of Subsidy Reform to Reduce GHG Emissions

In many sectors, EHS are a significant cause of market distortions. EHS can be defined as 'all kinds of financial support and regulations that are put in place to enhance the competitiveness of certain products, processes or regions, and that, together with the prevailing taxation jurisdiction, (unintentionally) discriminate against sound environmental practices' (OECD, 1998).

EHS are particularly relevant to fossil fuels and the energy sector. Fossil fuel subsidies encourage wasteful consumption, distort markets, undermine the competitiveness of renewable energies and 'lock in' carbon-intensive electricity generation. In 2007, 81 per cent of total primary energy supply was derived from fossil fuels and only 1 per cent from renewable energy sources (IEA 2009:6). Internationally, however, this imbalance is being addressed. In its 2010 Toronto Summit Declaration, the G-20 countries welcomed the phasing out of fossil fuel subsidies which encourage wasteful consumption. Research conducted by the IEA, OPEC, OECD and World Bank has revealed the scale of fossil fuel consumer subsidies, and the tremendous potential of subsidy phase-out to reduce GHG emissions (IEA *et al.* 2010). Reform is imperative in view of upward trends in the carbon intensity of the energy mix in non-OECD countries, where fossil fuel energy subsidies are 'locking in' high-emitting electricity generation and slowing change. The IEA estimated that fossil fuel consumer subsidies were worth US$312 billion in 2009 (and $557 billion in 2008), and that the removal of all such subsidies would reduce global CO_2 emissions by almost 6.9 per cent or 2.4 Gt by 2020 when compared with a 'business as usual' (BAU) scenario (IEA *et al.* 2010).

Fossil fuel subsidy phase-out is a 'low-hanging fruit' in terms of reducing GHG emissions. The co-benefits of reform are manifold and subject to broad agreement. The IEA, OPEC, OECD and World Bank 2010 joint report on EHS for the G20 emphasised the economic, social and environmental benefits of reform. The OECD has estimated that subsidy removal, particularly in non-OECD countries, would reduce GHG emissions drastically (in some cases by more than 30 per cent relative to BAU by 2050) while raising gross domestic product (GDP) per capita (OECD 2009:100). It has also been suggested that subsidy reform could free up considerable government revenues – estimated to amount to almost 6 per cent of GDP in Russia – which would subsequently be available for compensatory measures, government spending or fiscal consolidation (IEA *et al.* 2010). Other co-benefits might include a more equitable fiscal system, as the poorest 40 per cent of the population is estimated to receive only 15–20 per cent of fuel subsidies, health benefits and an improved natural environment due to reductions in SO2, NOx and particulate emissions; and positive contributions to sustainable development as a result of fuel shifting and increased use of 'clean' energies, to name but a few (IEA *et al.* 2010).

Thus, although subsidy removal tends to be difficult and provokes opposition, there are many arguments in favour of reform. In developing and transition economies, subsidies are often in place with the intention of supporting the access of the poor to basic services like energy and water, yet as a rule, wealthier elements in society benefit most.[7] To avoid any negative consequences and prevent conflict with national poverty alleviation strategies, compensatory and information mechanisms can be implemented alongside gradual and targeted subsidy phase-out.[8] This can help placate opposition and protect populations from the worst impacts of price increases. Public information campaigns can explain policy and inform populations of alternatives to fossil fuels. For example, when coal subsidies were removed in China, poor households received income support to protect them from the impact of increased costs, while cost savings were realised elsewhere in the supply chain to cover these additional expenditures and more efficient stoves were widely introduced to reduce energy demand (World Bank 2005).[9]

4. CONCLUSIONS

4.1. Why has EFR not been Implemented more Widely?

In spite of the strong arguments in favour of the widespread application of EFR to bring about GHG emissions reductions, EFR instruments have thus far been little used, particularly in non-Annex 1 countries. It seems that one major reason for this is a lack of capacity, both in identifying where economic instruments might be applicable to policy objectives, and also in designing and implementing these instruments. Poor financial governance in some countries has in the past undermined the implementation and enforcement of economic instruments: if a fiscal system is not capable of levying, collecting and redistributing revenues, enforcement of economic instruments will be poor and their impact correspondingly minimal. On the other hand, if tax collection systems are well established and functional, environmental taxes, fees and charges can be 'tagged on' to existing tax administration mechanisms and can as a result prove relatively easy to implement. An additional problem faced by many governments is corruption, which also feeds into a lack of political will to implement reform. Political resistance to EFR is often strong and widely felt, and in combination with a lack of communication between ministries of environment and finance, often results in policies not progressing beyond the drawing board. In addition, stakeholders in both industry and society often strongly resist policies that will increase their costs or affect their income, such as energy taxation.[10]

Annex 1 countries have also been far too slow in implementing EFR instruments and in greening their economies, although for different reasons. While all countries in the EU have implemented a number of EFR measures, and all are required to levy a minimum rate of taxation on energy products (the EU Energy Taxation Directive 2003/96/EC[11]), these countries have failed to take sufficiently serious steps to reduce their emissions in line with the achievement of the 2°C target. Without awareness raising and increased political acceptance of both the necessity for climate change mitigation and the application of EFR as a means to achieving that end, it is unlikely that progress will be made in the future.

4.2. Part of the Way Forward – Awareness Raising to Enhance Political Acceptance

There are many subnational, national and international organisations which propose measures to reduce GHG emissions, or campaign on climate change mitigation measures. EFR has typically not been at the forefront of such discussions. However, as shown above, EFR instruments offer an appealing and feasible way of reducing GHG emissions and generating multiple additional benefits.

For this reason, it would be a valuable exercise to communicate and raise awareness about the advantages and co-benefits of EFR measures, and to encourage strongly their implementation in both Annex 1 and non-Annex 1 countries. The work of international organisations such as UNEP/UNDP, IEA, OECD, the World Bank and others on poverty-environment linkages, subsidy reform, green growth and the green new deal has been very welcome, and has driven the debate forward. Placing greater emphasis on the co-benefits of climate change mitigation measures in general and EFR in particular can help to further the willingness of countries to implement measures to reduce GHG emissions and to make firm commitments to bringing about these reductions.

For sufficient implementation to bring about meaningful GHG emissions reductions, worldwide, what is needed is broad promotion of EFR and pervasive dissemination of information on EFR and the principles it can help us to realise in practice (most notably the polluter pays, sustainable development and precautionary principles) – that is, the 'mainstreaming' of EFR as a policy tool. Cross-party acceptance of EFR measures can create the political space governments need to implement long-term measures. This phenomenon has been seen most notably in Scandinavian countries, but also in the UK and Germany, where both left- and right-wing parties have implemented relatively radical EFR measures to reduce GHG emissions and green their economies.

Initiatives such as the European expert platform for EFR Green Budget Europe (GBE) can support this dissemination process and contribute to mainstreaming of EFR policy. GBE brings together representatives of international organisations, such as OECD and UN organisations, with representatives of the European Commission, the EEA, state governments, business, NGOs, policy-makers and members of the research community to compare and contrast their experiences with EFR.[12] Comparable initiatives in other parts of the world can fulfil a similar function – for example, the United Nations Economic and Social Commission for Asia (UN ESCAP) and the Pacific's East Asia low-carbon green growth roadmap.

4.3.   The Financial Crisis – a Window of Opportunity?

The global economic crisis of 2008–10 may in some countries have created a window of opportunity to implement change. How to deal with the economic crisis became the focus of media attention, and, thus, electorates have been thinking much harder about the issue of how to manage our economies in a sustainable way. In addition, many economic recovery packages were targeted towards climate change mitigation and environmental sustainability – most notably those of China, the EU, and Korea, with 38 per cent, 59 per cent and 81 per cent green investments respectively (Robins *et al.* 2009). However, many opportunities have been missed during these crisis years, in spite of many calls for a 'green new deal'. A new window of opportunity has opened up in 2011, as the scale of the deficits in many countries has been revealed. The required change in underlying primary balance to stabilise debt by 2025, in per cent of potential GDP, amounts to more than 4 per cent of GDP in many OECD countries and much more elsewhere (OECD 2010). The need for fiscal consolidation is pressing.

In the light of this shift in mood in approaches to public finance, not least the need to raise revenues to plug budget deficits and to move towards fiscal consolidation, an enabling environment for a shift towards EFR policies has been created. EFR measures appeal to governments in debt, because they can raise revenues to meet budgetary shortfalls, create jobs, increase resource efficiency and have environment benefits as well.[13] The current economic climate offers policy-makers a unique opportunity to green their economies decisively and shift towards low-carbon technologies. Moreover, the potential for such a shift to generate revenues for fiscal consolidation is considerable – for example, research has shown that €5 billion in additional revenues could be raised from EFR measures in Ireland from 2011 to 2014.[14] Moreover, OECD research has revealed that there is a negative correlation between the amount of fiscal consolidation required in OECD countries and the percentage of total tax revenues raised from taxes on energy and pollutants. Thus, there is considerable scope for convergence, as those countries with the highest deficits also have the greatest potential to increase environmental taxation without suffering negative competitiveness effects.[15]

4.4. Final Conclusions

A strong point in favour of mitigation measures worth bringing to the negotiating table in 2011 is the argument made here: many of the measures which bring about reduced GHG emissions also have a number of co-benefits for economy, environment and society. They can make development truly sustainable, by ensuring that poverty alleviation is not undermined by irreversible climate change and an associated deterioration in the natural environment. EFR also has additional appeal, as it can help overcome one of the most significant barriers to mitigation – market distortions.

To ensure that the average global temperature increases by no more than 2°C, a huge shift is essential in the way our economies work and the resources upon which our economies are based. Serious, binding commitments to bring about emissions reductions must be made at the end of 2011 – and not only on the part of Annex 1 countries. This is not to say that Annex 1 countries, for historical and fairness reasons, should not make the greatest commitments to reduce their emissions and does not imply that considerable financial support for technological transfer and for the implementation of mitigation strategies should not be an essential element in any climate agreement. Annex 1 countries must make serious and binding commitments to reduce their emissions significantly, by at least 30 per cent and preferably 40 per cent in 2020.[16] It is simply to say that increased emphasis on the co-benefits of EFR measures, combined with serious commitments to reduce emissions on the part of Annex 1 countries, might help facilitate reduction commitments also on the part of the rest of the world.

Although it has not been published at the time of going to print, expectations are high that the next Chinese Five Year Plan will include a number of measures to implement carbon pricing on a wide scale within the Chinese economy. Already, in the 11th Five Year Plan (2005–2010), targets were set that aimed to reduce energy consumption per unit of GDP by 20 per cent on 2005 levels by 2010.[17] Other countries all over the world would do well to learn from this example. If we do not, the 2°C target will soon be out of reach.

NOTES

1. Fairness here refers to the principle of equity and the notion of 'common but differentiated responsibility' as defined in Article 3 of the UNFCCC – with developing countries taking the lead and special circumstances of developing countries being taken into account in relation to mitigation measures.
2. This phrase was first coined by Professor Ernst Ulrich von Weizsäcker in 1988 in e.g. 'Steuern für die Umwelt', *Der SPIEGEL*, **34**, 86–7.and has since been adopted by many as a rallying cry for environmental taxation, particularly but not only in the German context.
3. See www.unpei.org/index.asp for further information.
4. South America and Asia account for 49 per cent and 21 per cent of mitigation potential from avoided deforestation from 2000 to 2050. Tropical Africa also has considerable potential (IPCC 2007a:552).
5. Forest Trends, the Katoomba Group and UNEP have developed a primer for setting up Payment for Environmental Services, for more information see: www.ecosystemmarketplace.com.
6. The classical example of a split incentive is that of a landlord retrofitting a house. Although the landlord invests, e.g., in installing better insulation to reduce heating

costs by 30 per cent annually, the landlord does not make any direct savings as a result, as it is the tenant who benefits from reduced energy costs.

7. In 1994 in Hyderabad, research showed that 63 per cent of the value of LPG subsidies went to the richest 40 per cent of households, while only 17 per cent went to the poorest 40 per cent of households – despite the subsidy being targeted towards cleaner cooking fuel for low-income households (World Bank 2005).

8. For example, ending subsidised electricity prices can be complemented by setting up 'lifeline' tariffs to ensure that low-income households retain access to electricity, even if prices increase.

9. The 2010 joint report from IEA, OPEC, OECD and the World Bank includes detailed suggestions for policy-makers on how to reform fossil fuel subsidies (see IEA *et al.* 2010: 33–43).

10. For details of barriers to the implementation and enforcement of economic instruments in developing, emerging and transition economies see GTZ (2008), the German Technical Cooperation, which was renamed the GIZ (German Agency for International Cooperation) in 2011.

11. Council Directive 2003/96/EC of 27 October 2003 restructuring the Community framework for the taxation of energy products and electricity.

12. More information on GBE is available at: www.green-budget.eu.

13. To maintain the tax shifting associated with EFR, it may be advisable to implement EFR measures that raise revenues for the general budget at first – to meet urgent budget deficits – but that earmark later revenues for the reduction of labour taxation in the future, e.g. two to three years down the line. This could also enhance the political acceptability of such measures.

14. Information from EEA presentation by Professor Mikael Skou Andersen at the Belgian EU Presidency/GBE international symposium on growth and green tax shifting in an era of fiscal consolidation, see: www.foes.de/internationales/green-budget-europe/.

15. For more information, see the presentation made by Jens Lundsgaard, OECD, link as note 13 above.

16. A unilateral move to increase the EU's GHG emission reduction target to 30 per cent has been proposed by Climate Commissioner Connie Hedegaard and called for by the French, British and German governments. Impact assessments carried out in 2010 estimated that such an increase in the EU reduction target would have cost no more than 0.2 per cent of GDP in 2020 (statistics taken from a leaked impact assessment from the European Commission on increasing the EU GHG reduction target to 30 per cent by 2020).

17. Unfortunately, however, GDP growth rates of more than 50 per cent over the same time period offset improvements in energy efficiency.

REFERENCES AND FURTHER READING

Cottrell, J., Milne, J.E., Ashiabor, H., *et al.* (eds) (2009), *Critical Issues in Environmental Taxation: International and Comparative Perspectives, Vol. VI*, Oxford, Oxford University Press.

COM (2006) 848 final, *Communication from the Commission to the Council and the European Parliament – Renewable Energy Roadmap – Renewable Energies in the 21st century: building a more sustainable future*, Brussels, European Commission.

CSD (2005), *Investing in Development: A Practical Plan to achieve the Millennium Development Goals*, New York, United Nations Commission on Sustainable Development.

IEA (2010), *Energy Subsidies: Getting the Prices Right*, Paris, IEA.

IEA (2009), *Key World Energy Statistics*, Paris, IEA.

IEA (2008), *Worldwide Trends in Energy Use and Efficiency*, Paris, IEA.

IEA (2007), *World Energy Outlook 2007*, Paris, IEA.

IEA, OPEC, OECD and World Bank (2010), *Analysis of the Scope of Energy Subsidies and Suggestions for the G20 Initiative: IEA, OPEC, OECD and World Bank Joint Report*, Paris, IEA.

GTZ (2008), *Environmental Fiscal Reform in Developing, Emerging and Transition Economies: Progress and Prospects*, Bonn, GTZ.

GTZ (2006), *Policy Instruments for Resource Efficiency*, Bonn, GTZ.

IPCC (2007a), *Fourth Assessment Report: Working Group III: Mitigation of Climate Change*, Cambridge, Cambridge University Press.

IPCC (2007b), *Fourth Assessment Report: Working Group III: Executive Summary for Policy Makers*, Cambridge, Cambridge University Press.

IPCC (2007c), *Fourth Assessment Report: Working Group III: Technical Summary*, Cambridge, Cambridge University Press.

Knigge, M. and Görlach, B. (2005), *Effects of Germany's Ecological Tax Reforms on the Environment, Employment and Technological Innovation*, Berlin, Ecologic.

McKinsey & Company (2009), *Pathways to a Low-Carbon Economy: Version 2 of the Global Greenhouse Gas Abatement Cost Curve*, Stockholm, McKinsey & Company.

OECD (2010), *OECD Economic Outlook 88*, Paris, OECD.

OECD (2009), *The Economics of Climate Change Mitigation: Policies and Options for Global Action beyond 2012*, Paris, OECD.

OECD (2008), *Instrument Mixes for Environmental Policy*, Paris, OECD.

OECD (2003), *The Forgotten Benefits of Climate Change Mitigation: Innovation, Technological Leapfrogging, Employment and Sustainable Development*, Paris, OECD.

OECD (1998), *Improving the Environment through Reducing Subsidies*, Paris, OECD.

Robins, N., Clover, R., Singh, C. (25 Feb 2009), *A Climate for Recovery: The Colour of Stimulus Goes Green*, London, GTZ HSBC Bank plc.

Schmidt, S., Prange, F., Schlegelmilch, *et al.* (2009), *Sind die Deutsche Konjunkturpakete Nachhaltig?*, Berlin, WWF/Green Budget Germany.

Stern, N., (2007), *The Economics of Climate Change: The Stern Review*, Cambridge, Cambridge University Press.

UNEP (2009), *Reducing Emissions from Private Cars: Incentive Measures for Behavioural Change*, Geneva, UNEP.

von Weizsäcker, E., Hargroves, K., Smith, M., *et al.* (2009), *Factor 5: Transforming the Global Economy through 80 per cent Increase in Resource Productivity*, London, Earthscan, UK.

World Bank (2005), *Environmental Fiscal Reform – What Should be Done and How to Achieve It?*, Washington, World Bank.

7. Carbon tax policy progress in north-east Asia

Xianbing Liu, Kazunori Ogisu, Sunhee Suk and Tomohiro Shishime

1. INTRODUCTION

Both carbon tax policy and cap and trade schemes aim to discourage the use of fossil fuels by making carbon emissions more costly. Many economists support a carbon tax due to its advantages over an emissions trading scheme (ETS). Carbon tax can be levied upon carbon emissions from all sectors while an ETS requires accurate monitoring of emissions, and thus is only applicable to large emitters. Fair allocation of carbon credits is almost impossible in an ETS. Uncertain carbon prices in an ETS cause companies to become myopic and thereby discourage their reduction efforts. Conversely, a fixed carbon tax rate is more straightforward for companies and allows them to make decisions for the medium and long term. Additionally, it is easier to minimize the number of losers by using carbon tax revenues, either to reduce other taxes or to lower the burden on energy-intensive sectors. Recently, several famous economists have even argued that an international carbon tax is systematically better and could be agreed upon more easily as a post-Kyoto scheme than a global cap and trade scheme (e.g. Mankiw, 2007).

Carbon tax was first introduced in Finland in 1990 and then levied in some other European countries, such as Sweden, Norway, the Netherlands and Denmark. Although obvious differences were found between the carbon tax policies implemented in Europe (Cansier and Krumm, 1997), they have shown broadly positive effects in reducing the use of fossil fuels and CO_2 emissions and in increasing employment, while bringing about only very slightly negative impacts on economic growth (Anderson and Ekins, 2009).

The progress of policy on appropriate pricing of carbon emissions in Asian countries, either by taxation or ETS, has been much slower. The three large economies of north-east Asia, Japan, China and the Republic of Korea, all make the list of the top ten CO_2 emitters in the world. However,

103

their policy countermeasures on climate change remain sparse, particularly in relation to the adoption of market-based instruments. Aiming to close the policy gap, this chapter provides an overview of emerging discussions on carbon tax in the region. The remainder of this chapter is arranged as follows. Section 2 provides a glimpse of the latest climate policies in the target countries; section 3 summarizes related analyses of carbon tax at the country macro-level; section 4 overviews the actual progress of carbon tax policy using available information; section 5 identifies opportunities for and barriers to introduction of carbon tax policy from multiple viewpoints; and section 6 concludes the findings and suggests a way forward for development of this policy.

2. CURRENT CLIMATE POLICIES IN THE THREE TARGET COUNTRIES

2.1 State of Carbon Emissions in the Three Target Countries

China has surpassed the US to become the largest carbon emitter in the world. CO_2 emissions increased by 152.8 per cent in 2006 compared with 1990 figures, with an annual growth rate of 5.1 per cent during this period. The CO_2 emissions of the Republic of Korea also increased rapidly with a total change of 96.7 per cent and an annual average growth of 4.2 per cent between 1990 and 2006. The CO_2 emissions of Japan were stable over the same period but showed a slight increasing trend, with the average growth rate being 0.6 per cent. From the viewpoint of averages, per capita CO_2 emissions in China were much lower in 2006, around half that of Japan and Korea and one-quarter that of the US. Nevertheless, CO_2 emission intensity by gross domestic product (GDP) in China was over three times that of Japan and twice that of the US (sourced from World Development Indicators, World Bank).

According to estimations of the International Energy Agency (IEA), about 68 per cent of China's 2005 greenhouse gas (GHG) emissions arose from fuel combustion; 5 per cent evaporated as methane from energy-related systems; 10 per cent arose from industrial processes; 14 per cent was from agriculture; and waste and miscellaneous sources shared the remaining 4 per cent. The energy use of the industrial sector is the largest source of CO_2 emissions in Japan, despite a decreasing share from 42.2 per cent in 1990 to 34.5 per cent in 2008. CO_2 emissions from the transport sector, as well as commercial and residential sources, increased during this period. In 2008, the residential sector accounted for 14.1 per cent of the total, and the transport and commercial sectors each equally shared 18.9 per cent (sourced from Ministry of the Environment, Japan). Likewise, industries contributed to 66 per cent of CO_2 emissions in Korea in 2007. The residential sector accounted for 10 per cent, a decrease of 16 per cent compared with 1990 levels, due to energy substitution from coal to clean energies such as natural gas and electricity in the 1990s (sourced from the website of Green Growth Committee, Korea, www.greengrowth.go.kr/english/en_main/index.do).

2.2 The Latest Climate Policies in the Three Target Countries

Under the Kyoto Protocol, Japan has committed to reduce its 1990 GHG emissions by 6 per cent between 2008 and 2012. As a mid-term target, Japan has pledged to reduce GHG emissions by 25 per cent from 1990 levels by 2020. However, this commitment is premised upon an agreement on aggressive reduction targets being achieved by all major emitting countries. Japan also announced its long-term target to reduce GHG emissions by 80 per cent from 1990 levels by 2050. The main climate countermeasures of Japanese industries include energy efficiency-related policies, the shift to low carbon energy and carbon capture and storage (CCS) for large sources of GHG emissions to be introduced after 2020 (MOE, 2010). The Keidanren's (nationwide business association of Japan) Voluntary Action Plan, a trial domestic ETS, a carbon offset scheme and carbon financing have been implemented. A calculation, reporting and disclosure system for GHG emissions has been running since 2006. Regarding legal measures, 'The Basic Act on Global Warming Countermeasures' is under discussion. Various measures are listed in the draft act toward achieving medium- and long-term reduction targets.

China's climate policy was outlined in its National Climate Change Programme of 2007 and Climate Change White Paper of 2008. While China has traditionally avoided policies that explicitly target CO_2 emissions, its energy and forestry programmes have provided the basic framework for its National Climate Change Programme. The central government set two key policy targets in 2006. One is to reduce national energy intensity by 20 per cent by the end of 2010. The other is to increase renewable energy in the energy mix to 15 per cent by 2020. Both are ambitious for China as a developing country. The Chinese government further pledged in November 2009 to cut CO_2 emissions per unit of GDP by 40 to 45 per cent by 2020 compared with 2005 levels. These targets represent voluntary actions to tackle climate change problems based on China's own conditions. China's climate policy is diverse and includes targets and quotas, industrial processes and equipment standards and financial incentives and penalties. China has gained some experience in the carbon market through clean development mechanism (CDM) projects. On the energy supply side, improving the energy efficiency of the power sector has been a major task. The IEA (2009) estimates that by 2011, 80 per cent of China's coal-fired power plants will be modernised with capacities above 300 MW, and that this number will rise to over 90 per cent by 2020. On the energy demand side, the Top 1,000 Enterprises Programme is part of key efforts to reduce industrial energy intensity. Started in 2006, this programme accounts for a large portion of the 20 per cent energy intensity reduction target by directly targeting around 1000 of the largest state-owned enterprises, the majority in heavy industries. The programme goal was satisfied in the first year (Price *et al.*, 2008).

On 15 August 2008, the Republic of Korea proclaimed 'Low Carbon, Green Growth' as its new national vision to shift the current quantity-oriented and fossil fuel-dependent economy to quality-oriented growth. On 17 November 2009, the Green Growth Committee announced a decision to adopt a 30 per cent reduction target of GHG emissions by 2020, compared with 'business as usual' (BAU) levels. Along with the mid-term mitigation goal, countermeasures include the adoption of a legal and regulatory framework, carbon emissions trading and the creation of a national GHG inventory reporting system by 2010, in addition to raising public awareness. Other measures include: adoption of new auto emissions standards; a waste-to-energy programme; promotion of low-carbon transportation; introduction of light-emitting diodes (LEDs); stricter heat insulation standards for buildings; and development of CCS technologies.

3. ACADEMIC DISCUSSIONS ON CARBON TAX POLICY RELATED TO THE THREE TARGET COUNTRIES

The literature contains several analyses of carbon tax policy related to Japan, China and the Republic of Korea at the national level. This literature provides meaningful discussions on policy impacts.

Nakata and Lamont (2001) examine the impacts of using carbon and energy taxes to reduce CO_2 emissions in Japan. A partial equilibrium model of the energy sector was constructed to evaluate energy system changes up to 2040. Their results confirm that a carbon tax would suppress CO_2 emissions. At a tax rate of US\$160/t-C (US\$43.6/t-CO_2), total emissions would be 391 Mt-C, corresponding to a reduction of 100 Mt-C. Using a multi-sector dynamic computable general equilibrium (CGE) model allowing for 27 sectors over 100 years, Takeda (2007) examines the double dividend of a carbon tax in Japan. His model assumes that government revenues remain constant and that carbon tax is utilised to alleviate distorted taxes. A strong double dividend does not arise when labour and consumption taxes are reduced, but arises when the capital tax is reduced. Although Japanese industries strongly oppose carbon tax policy, a carbon tax could possibly be introduced if it could be combined with reductions in capital tax (Takeda, 2007).

Liang *et al.* (2007) established a CGE model simulating carbon tax policy in China. By referring to existing policy schemes in Europe, the authors define different tax scenarios based on whether adoption of tax relief is assumed or not for the production sectors. Their results confirm that the negative impacts of carbon tax could be alleviated if relief or subsidies are provided to the production sectors. The carbon tax rate for different reduction targets was estimated under a preferable scheme with tax completely exempted for iron and steel, building materials, chemicals, non-ferrous metals and the paper industries, while being identical for all other sectors. The tax rate is 163 CNY/t-C (5.4 US$/t-$CO_2$ at the 2002 constant price) when the reduction target is set at 5 per cent compared with the baseline. The rate is 348 CNY/t-C (about 11.5 US$/t-$CO_2$) in the case of a 10 per cent reduction target.

Kwon and Heo (2010) first showed the impacts of carbon tax on commodity prices in the Republic of Korea using an input-output model and a simple CGE model. Their results suggest that an upstream carbon tax equivalent to 36,545 KRW/t-CO_2 (about 31 US$/t-$CO_2$) must be imposed to achieve the government's mid-term target. A carbon tax system with revenue recycling enhances income redistribution, and a lump-sum transfer of the revenue would make this policy progressive. Their findings re-emphasise the relative advantages of a tax system over an ETS in that the latter is less likely to collect a substantial amount of government revenue to be recycled.

4. ACTUAL PROGRESS OF CARBON TAX POLICY IN THE THREE TARGET COUNTRIES

4.1 Progress of Carbon Tax Policy in Japan

4.1.1 Existing energy-related taxes in Japan

The existing energy-related taxes in Japan include: automobile fuel-related taxes (gasoline tax, regional gasoline tax, diesel tax and liquefied petroleum gas tax); aviation fuel tax; petroleum and coal tax; and a promotion of power resources development tax. Table 7.1 summarises the tax rates and revenues. Energy taxes in Japan may help mitigate energy use and corresponding CO_2 emissions. The tax rates vary considerably if converted by the carbon contents of the fuels. The highest rate is 24 052 JPY/t-CO_2 for gasoline and the lowest is 291 JPY/t-CO_2 for coal. Energy-related taxes are estimated to contribute to 0.9 per cent of CO_2 emissions reductions (Kawase *et al.*, 2003).

Table 7.1 *Existing energy-related tax rates and revenues in Japan*

Fuel	Unit	Energy tax							Total: JPY	
		Gasoline tax	Regional gasoline tax	Petroleum and coal tax	Diesel tax	Promotion of power-resources development tax	LPG tax	Aviation fuel tax	Per unit	Per t-CO_2
Tax collector		National	National	National	Prefectural & municipal	National	National	National		
Taxation position		Upstream[2]	Upstream	Mainly upstream[1]	Downstream[3]	Downstream	Downstream	Downstream		
Gasoline	JPY/l	48.6	5.2	2.04					55.8	24 052
Diesel	JPY/l			2.04	32.1				34.1	13 034
Heavy oil	JPY/l			2.04					2.0	753
Jet fuel	JPY/l			2.04				26	28.0	11 386
Coal	JPY/kg			0.7					0.7	291
LNG	JPY/kg			1.08					1.1	400
LPG	JPY/kg			1.08			17.5		18.6	6,193
Electricity	JPY/kWh					0.375			0.4	675
Tax revenue (2010)	100 million JPY	25 760	2756	4800	8432	3300	240	910		

Notes: [1] Mainly upstream: taxation at import or extraction stage; [2] Upstream: taxation at shipment stage out of manufacturing site; [3] Downstream: taxation at supply stage to the consumer.

4.1.2   Carbon tax proposals of the MOE of Japan

Carbon tax policy has been discussed since the early 1990s within the Ministry of the Environment (MOE), Japan. Options have been narrowed down into two streams: a high tax rate or a low tax rate in combination with subsidies for climate change mitigation activities. The Central Environmental Council (CEC) (2003) suggests that CO_2 reduction through levying of a carbon tax with a low rate (e.g. 3400 JPY/t-C) where all revenue (approximately 950 billion JPY) is directed to a specific budget for climate change mitigation efforts might equal a reduction by levying a high rate carbon tax (e.g. 45 000 JPY/t-C). From 2004 to 2006, the MOE presented carbon tax proposals on three occasions, as listed in Table 7.2. Considering a lack of civic support, strong resistance from business lobbyists and the indifference of the Ministry of Finance (MOF), these proposals outlined a low-rate tax earmarked for global warming countermeasures.

Table 7.2 Carbon tax proposals of the MOE of Japan from 2004–06

	Proposal 2004	**Proposal 2005**	**Proposal 2006**
Tax rate	2400 JPY/t-C (655 JPY/t-CO2, 5.45 US$/t-CO2)		
Revenue	490 billion JPY	370 billion JPY	360 billion JPY
(Industry: Service: Household)	(150:200:140)	(160:110:100)	
Use of revenues	Subsidy for climate change and forestry (340); reduction of social security (150)	General budget; subsidy for climate change and forestry	General budget; subsidy for climate change and forestry
Special treatment	Exemption for steel, agriculture, forestry and fishery; reduction for heavy industry, diesel, small firms and household	Exemption for steel; 50% reduction for large emitters that perform reduction activities; 50% reduction for kerosene; put-off motor fuel	Exemption for steel and fishery; 80% reduction for large emitters that undertake reduction activities; 50% reduction for kerosene; put-off motor fuel

The MOE's FY2010 proposal considered imposing tax on importers and companies that exploit fossil fuels. Carbon tax on gasoline levied on refinery companies has been considered, but a tax on diesel is pending. As shown in Table 7.3, the sum of this newly added carbon tax and existing energy taxes of Japan is much lower than the average of European countries. The MOE estimates that a total of 2.0 trillion JPY in revenues could be raised through the introduction of this proposed carbon tax. The carbon tax proposal of FY2010 also considers tax exemptions for the following items: (a) fossil fuels such as raw materials like naphtha; (b) coal and cokes for iron and steel manufacturing; (c) coal for cement manufacturing; and (d) bunker A fuel oil for agriculture, forestry and fisheries. The companies subject to a domestic ETS would receive relief once the domestic ETS was introduced. The FY2010 proposal suggests that carbon tax revenues should be assigned to the general budget, preferentially to use for expenditures to counter global warming.

Table 7.3 The FY2010 carbon tax proposal of Japan and existing taxes of EU countries (unit: JPY/t-CO$_2$)

Country		Gasoline	Diesel	Heavy oil	Coal	Natural gas
Japan	Energy tax	24 052 (12 831*)	13 034	753	291	400
	Carbon tax	8531*	1064**	1064	1174	1064
	Total	21 362*	14 098	1817	1465	1464
UK		45 543	40 368	7200	1083	1820
Germany		45 388	28 915	1458	587	1930
France		42 087	26 333	989	588	1044
Netherlands		47 780	25 632	24 777	865	12 002
Finland		43 481	22 374	3583	3375	1622
Denmark		38 651	25 506	17 429	15 256	23 692
EU average		*43 822*	*28 188*	*9239*	*3626*	*7018*

Notes: * The carbon tax rate for gasoline is set with a precondition that the existing temporary energy tax on gasoline will be changed to the number in parentheses. ** Additional tax on diesel is under consideration.

Source: Ministry of the Environment website (www.env.go.jp/), as of 6 September 2010.

The latest 'Package of Tax Revision of FY2011', concluded by the Japanese cabinet on 16 December 2010, outlines a roadmap for specific taxes aimed at climate change mitigation. The updated rates for these taxes are 760 JPY per kl of petroleum and oil products; 780 JPY per ton of gaseous hydrocarbon; and 670 JPY per ton of coal. These rates are the equivalent of

289 JPY/t-CO_2 and are much lower than the earlier proposals of the MOE. Taxes are scheduled to be phased in in three stages. From 1 October 2011, taxes with rates one-third of those listed above will be introduced. Another one-third will be added on from 1 April 2013. Finally, the taxes will be fully implemented from 1 April 2015. Besides maintaining relief measures for existing energy-related taxes, the tax revision package of FY2011 lists some other newly added exemptions and refunds of the special anti-climate change tax.

4.2 Progress of Carbon Tax Policy in China

4.2.1 Existing energy-related taxes in China

In China, taxes related to the environment and resources include resource taxes, consumption taxes, vehicle and vessel usage taxes and a vehicle purchase tax. Some are related to energy use and are therefore summarised in Table 7.4.

Table 7.4 Taxes related to energy use and carbon emissions in China

Tax	Item	Tax rate	Note
Resource tax	Crude oil	8–30 CNY/t	Except oil refined from bituminous shale
	Natural gas	2–15 CNY/1000 m³	Except natural gas from coal mines
	Coal	0.3–5 CNY/t	Referring to raw coal, excluding. washed and separated coal
Consumption tax	Gasoline	0.2 CNY/l	
	Diesel	0.1 CNY/t	
	Motorcycle	10%	
	Automobile	3–8%	
Vehicle and vessel usage tax	Vessel	1.2–5.0	Unit: CNY per ton per year; classified by the tonnage of vessel
	Vehicle	16–320	Unit: CNY per year; different by the purpose of use and type
Vehicle purchase tax	Vehicle	10%	

4.2.2   Carbon Tax Policy Proposals in China

In recent years, experts at research institutes under the Ministry of Environmental Protection (MOEP), the Ministry of Finance (MOF) and the State Administration of Taxation (SAT) have actively discussed how to develop carbon tax policy in China.

Carbon tax in China would be limited to fossil fuels including coal, oil and natural gas. Li (2010) suggests that carbon tax should not be levied on electricity because coal-fired power plants are major electricity suppliers in China. Double taxation may occur if both coal and electricity are taxed. Li (2010), Wang *et al.* (2009) and Su *et al.* (2009) further suggest that two options exist for carbon taxation. One is to impose a carbon tax on the producers of fossil fuels. The other would target the wholesalers, retailers and users of fossil fuels. Under the first option, the producers would pass costs downstream to customers. In this case, the price pressure from the carbon tax would decrease along the supply chain of fossil fuels and lead to a relatively weak effect on CO_2 emissions reduction (Li, 2010). Nevertheless, considering the cost of tax collection, Cao (2009) suggests that carbon tax should be imposed at the source of energy exploitation or the energy distribution hub. Particularly for coal, petroleum and natural gas, taxes should be paid by the exploitation companies; for refined oils such as gasoline and diesel, taxes should be paid by the refinery companies. Li (2010) proposed another option: to impose taxes on secondary energy products, such as oil, kerosene and gas, on the wholesalers and retailers in the middle.

Considering the cost of CO_2 emission reductions in the long run as well as resulting impacts on the economy, tax rate setting should be a gradual process and differential tax rates should be adopted. Rates should be low at the early stages and then rise gradually. Su *et al.* (2009) conducted a simulation study of carbon tax using a CGE model. Suggested tax rates are shown in Table 7.5.

Table 7.5 Proposal for carbon tax rates in China

Tax	Tax rate	
	From 2012	From 2020
Carbon tax (CNY/t-CO_2)	10	40
Carbon tax on coal (CNY/ton)	19.4	77.6
Carbon tax on oil (CNY/ton)	30.3	121.2
Carbon tax on gasoline (CNY/ton)	29.5	118
Carbon tax on kerosene (CNY/ton)	31.3	125.2
Carbon tax on natural gas (CNY/1000 m^3)	2.2	8.8

Li (2010) suggests several carbon tax relief measures referring to international experiences with China's actual conditions. First, energy-intensive industries should enjoy preferential measures only under certain conditions, such as signing agreements with the government to reduce CO_2 emissions and engage in efforts toward energy saving. Secondly, tax refunds could be provided as incentives to companies with significant reductions, increased investment in energy saving or improved energy efficiency via use of advanced technologies. For low-income groups, tax returns should be offered to guarantee a basic standard of living and to maintain social stability.

Any imposition of a carbon tax must overcome obstacles from taxpayers and take domestic and international conditions into consideration. Su *et al.* (2009) point out that according to the Bali Roadmap, not only are developed countries required to commit to extensive emissions reductions, but developing countries as well must take action to reduce GHG emissions. China will face increasing pressure to control its GHG emissions after 2012. Imposition of a carbon tax around 2012 is consistent with the Chinese strategy of adding policies to control CO_2 emissions.

4.3 Progress of Carbon Tax Policy in the Republic of Korea

4.3.1 Energy-related taxes in the Republic of Korea

Transportation, energy and environmental taxes are in place in the Republic of Korea. According to Lee (2005), refinery prices of gasoline and diesel were 0.21 and 0.20 US$/l respectively in 1999. After-tax prices were 0.94 and 0.40 US$/l, making energy taxes for gasoline and diesel 0.73 and 0.20 US$/l respectively at that time. Korea had a higher energy tax rate (74.8 per cent) for gasoline than Japan (56.2 per cent) and the US (31.0 per cent), but a lower tax rate (39.9 per cent) for diesel than Japan (52.4 per cent) and the UK (72.1 per cent). This implies that the Korean government has generally supported industrial rather than household fuel use. The Korean government has taken steps towards reforming its energy taxes (Kim *et al.*, 2001). One of its key targets is to narrow the price differences of different transportation fuels by increasing the price of diesel and LPG up to 80 per cent and 65 per cent of gasoline respectively. For industrial fuels, one proposal was to increase the price of bunker C fuel oil by 28 per cent and keep the price of LNG unchanged.

4.3.2 Discussions on carbon tax proposals in the Republic of Korea

Debate is ongoing in the Republic of Korea regarding the introduction of carbon tax policy. A simple method would be to levy tax on fuels containing carbon, which would satisfy the polluter pays principle (PPP) (Kim,

2008). Kim (1997) argues for an indirect tax rather than a direct method. As the production structure of Korea has a lower substitutability for other energy inputs, carbon tax would stimulate the substitution effect, which could transform the economic structure through energy-saving technologies (Park, 2003). Choi *et al.* (2000) assert that large fluctuations in prices by industry would occur with a high carbon tax rate and suggest application of relief measures for industries with large price changes. Cho (2005) explains potential negative and positive aspects of carbon tax in the Republic of Korea. A negative aspect is the possibility of transference of the carbon tax burden from producers to consumers. A decrease in demand due to a price increase may lead to shrinking production, which in turn may contribute to lower wages and unemployment. A positive aspect is the possibility of enhancement of the competitiveness of industries through investment in research and development. In the long run, the initial impacts on energy price increases due to carbon tax can turn into economic benefits. Kim and Shin (2007) rationalise that Korea depends on petroleum and coal products more than China, Japan and the US. If a carbon tax is introduced, the Republic of Korea will suffer more heavily than its main trading partners. Nevertheless, the general attitude toward a carbon tax is rather positive among environmental scholars.

The Korea Institute of Public Finance (KIPF) initially proposed detailed carbon tax rates for fossil fuels in 2008, as listed in Table 7.6 (Kim *et al.*, 2008). These rates were calculated according to the carbon price of the EU-ETS (€25/t-CO$_2$, equivalent to 31 328 KRW/t-CO$_2$). The total expected annual revenue from the proposed carbon tax was to be 8.5–9.1 trillion KRW (UD$7.38–7.91 billion) based on 2007 emissions in Korea. KIPF suggests that a carbon tax be implemented from 2010, replacing the existing transportation tax, which was originally scheduled to end in 2009. A later option for introducing a carbon tax would be 2012, as the maximum rates of income tax and corporate tax are planned to be abated by then. According to a later report of Kim *et al.* (2009), considering that income tax and corporation tax has been cut off after the launch of new government in 2008, carbon tax should be introduced separately at much lower rates than those listed in Table 7.6 without cutting the existing taxes at early stages. In the medium and long term, it is preferable to increase the rates of carbon tax or energy tax simultaneously with the reduction of the existing income taxes, such as personal income tax, corporation tax and social security contributions, to keep the national tax reform to be revenue-neutral. The revenue of carbon tax should be recycled in the form of investment for renewable energy and R&D for clean technologies, and various incentives for the export sectors to absorb a possible shock due to the phase-in of carbon tax. In addition, tax exemption and direct support for low-income people was proposed in parallel when introducing this new tax.

Table 7.6 Proposal for carbon tax rates in the Republic of Korea

Tax	Tax rate
Carbon tax on gasoline (KRW/l)	67.5
Carbon tax on diesel (KRW/l)	82.4
Carbon tax on kerosene (jet fuel) (KRW/l)	77.7
Carbon tax on B-C oil (KRW/l)	95.5
Carbon tax on butane (KRW/l)	53.2
Carbon tax on propane (KRW/kg)	92.0
Carbon tax on LNG (KRW/m³)	71.0
Carbon tax on coal (anthracitic) (KRW/kg)	58.9
Carbon tax on coal (bituminous) (KRW/kg)	33.7

5. A COMPARATIVE ANALYSIS OF THE CARBON TAX PROPOSALS OF THE THREE TARGET COUNTRIES

Considering the cost and difficulty of tax collection, each of the carbon tax proposals in the three target countries opts to levy taxes on fuels containing carbon. The importers, producers, wholesalers and retailers of fossil fuels at the furthest point upstream or along the upstream spectrum would be the targets of the carbon tax. Concerning the negative impacts of carbon tax on economies and industrial competency, especially for energy and carbon-intensive sectors, proposed carbon tax rates are low. The latest carbon tax proposal of the MOE of Japan suggests a rate of 289 JPY/t-CO_2 (around US\$3.40/t-CO_2) for the fuels under consideration. This rate is much lower than the rate recommended by Nakata and Lamont (2001) (US\$43.6/t-CO_2). Similarly, the carbon tax proposed by experts in China is even lower (about US\$1.5/t-CO_2 from 2012), a large gap with the rate suggested by Liang et al. (2007) (US\$5.4–11.5/t-CO_2). The proposed carbon tax in the Republic of Korea is also set at quite a low rate (Kim et al., 2009). As described earlier, all discussions on carbon tax policy in the three target countries consider relief measures. The proposed carbon tax policy in Japan excludes fuels for some specific purposes. Appropriate tax exemption and a return mechanism are suggested for the energy-intensive industries in China (Li, 2010). Principally, a carbon tax refund is preferred to act as an incentive for the energy-saving efforts of companies. Experts in the Republic of Korea suggest applying measures for industries with large cost changes due to the introduction of carbon tax (Choi *et al.*, 2000).

Nevertheless, various barriers exist and hinder the actual introduction of policy in the region. In Japan, strong resistance from industrial lobby groups such as the Keidanren has been the most crucial factor blocking introduction in the past. Multifaceted political issues like environmental tax reform require cooperation between competent ministries such as the MOF, Ministry of Economy, Trade and Industry (METI, responsible for energy policy), Ministry of Land, Infrastructure and Transportation (MLIT, responsible for spending of gasoline tax revenue), Ministry of Agriculture, Forestry and Fisheries (MAFF) and MOE. Although a roadmap for introducing a climate change mitigation tax has been determined by the cabinet, difficulties have arisen in coordination of the interests of related ministries. An encouraging sign in Japan is the growing support of the public for this policy. Proponents of carbon tax have increased to 40.1 per cent in 2007, while 32.0 per cent of the population is opposed. More than 70 per cent of the proponents prefer that the total of tax revenue be earmarked for climate change countermeasures (Cabinet Office of Japan, 2007). In 2005, only 24.8 per cent of respondents in a similar survey were in favour, and 32.4 per cent were against a carbon tax. Chinese experts are optimistic about the introduction of carbon tax in China. The 2009 research report of the Energy Research Institute (ERI) on a carbon tax scheme points out that the loss of GDP would be less than 0.5 per cent by 2025 due to introduction of such policy (Jiang, 2010). The attitudes of related ministries, such as the MOEP, National Development and Reform Commission (NDRC), MOF and SAT, are positive regarding environmental tax reform. However, as carbon tax is a new type of tax in China, companies may be reluctant at the beginning, and it will take time for the public to fully understand this new tax. Korean policy-makers must overcome various obstacles in the creation of a carbon tax (*The Korea Times*, 2010). It is vital to advance structural reform of the nation's economy and industries so that companies can adjust themselves to the low-carbon strategy. It is necessary to push ahead with overall tax reform, and the government must make efforts to build public consensus on carbon tax in particular.

6. CONCLUSION

This chapter provides a preliminary overview of emerging discussions on carbon tax policy in three target countries in north-east Asia. A comparative analysis identified opportunities for and barriers to introduction of carbon tax in this region. It is indicated that the design of a carbon tax scheme, including the scope, tax rate, collection and utilisation of the tax, is very important and must be adapted to the actual situations of each country. Further discussion is required to convince decision-makers. A short comparison identified problems in target countries in implementing carbon tax policy. As carbon taxation may cause a shift from coal to other low-carbon energies, existing energy tax with a supplementary carbon tax would be a stable and acceptable way for Japan and the Republic of Korea, which rely heavily on energy imports. As a way forward, discussions on acceptance by individual companies of carbon tax are definitely necessary to overcome industrial resistance to this policy. Industry's reactions to optional tax schedules and corresponding behavioural changes, especially technological inventions, innovations and the choice of cleaner technologies, require in-depth observation.

REFERENCES

Andersen, M.S. and Ekins, P. (eds) (2009), *Carbon Taxation: Lessons from Europe*, Oxford and New York, Oxford University Press.

Cabinet Office of Japan (2007), 'Public opinion on anti-global warming', available at: www8.cao.go.jp/survey/h19/h19-globalwarming/index.html [in Japanese].

Cansier, D. and Krumm, R. (1997), 'Air pollution taxation: an empirical survey', *Ecological Economics*, **23**(1), 59–70.

Cao, J. (2009), 'Low carbon development: China's carbon policy design and CGE model analysis', *Journal of Financial Research* [in Chinese], **12**, 19–29.

CEC (Central Environmental Council) (2003), 'Concrete plan for anti-global warming taxes (in Japanese)', Report of Central Environmental Council of Japan.

Cho, Y. (2005), 'Environmental strategy of OECD members', *Journal of Economics and Management*, **5**(1), 153–91.

Choi Y.H., Lim W.Y. and Kim S.H. (2000), 'The price variable effect of carbon tax per industry', *Quarterly Review of Economics and Business*, **28**(1), 1–17.

IEA (International Energy Agency) (2009), *Cleaner coal in China*, pp.104–117.

Jiang, K.J. (2010), 'The loss of GDP due to carbon tax is less than 0.5%', available at: http://finance.jrj.com.cn/people/2010/05/2709097536091.shtml [in Chinese].

Kawase, A., Kitamura, Y. and Hashimoto, K. (2003), 'CO2 emission reduction effect by energy tax and reform of green taxation plan – simulation analysis by applied general equilibrium model', *Japan Economy Research* [in Japanese], **48**, 76–8.

Kim, H.G. (2008), 'On the views of carbon tax in Korea', *American Journal of Applied Sciences*, **5**(11), 1558–61.

Kim, H.G. and Shin, H.J. (2007), 'An analysis of changes in production and trade of US, Japan, China and Korea affected by levy of carbon tax', *International and Area Study Review*, **11**(1), 273–91.

Kim, S.H. (1997), 'A study on the effect of carbon taxes on the industrial sector in Korea', *Journal of Regional Development*, **3**, 263–84.

Kim, S.H., Kim, T.H., Kim, Y.D., *et al.* (2001), 'Korean energy demand in the new millennium: outlook and policy implications, 2000–2005', *Energy Policy*, **29**(2001), 899–910.

Kim, S.R., Park, S.W. and Kim, H.J. (2008), *A Study on Green Tax and Budget Reform in Korea*, Seoul, KIPF (Korea Institute of Public Finance) [in Korean].

Kim, S.R., Song, H. and Kim, J.Y. (2009), *Fiscal Policy Directions for Low-carbon Green Growth Industries in Korea*, Seoul, KIPF (Korea Institute of Public Finance) [in Korean].

Korea Times, The (2010), 'Carbon tax: time to put green growth strategy into action', 2010, available at: www.koreatimes.co.kr/www/news/opinon/2010/02/137_60889.html.

Kwon, O.S. and Heo, D.Y. (2010), 'The incidence of green tax in Korea', paper presented at the 1st Congress of East Asian Association of Environmental and Natural Resource Economics, Hokkaido University, Sapporo, Japan, 18–19 August 2010.

Lee, M.K. (2005), 'Reviewing tax system and its reform plan for the fuel market in South Korea', *Energy Policy*, **33**(2005), 475–82.

Li, C.X. (2010), 'Study of carbon tax policy framework for addressing climate change', *Law Science Magazine* [in Chinese], **6**, 20–22.

Liang, Q.M., Fan, Y. and Wei, Y.M. (2007), 'Carbon taxation policy in China: How to protect energy and trade-intensive sectors', *Journal of Policy Modeling*, **29**(2007), 311–33.

Mankiw, G. (2007), 'One answer to a global warming: a new tax', *New York Times*, 16 September 2007.

MOE (Ministry of Environment, Japan) (2010), 'Medium and long term roadmap related to global warming countermeasures', sourced from: www.env.go.jp/earth/ondanka/domestic.html.

Nakata, T. and Lamont, A. (2001), 'Analysis of the impacts of carbon taxes on energy systems in Japan', *Energy Policy*, **29**(2001), 159–66.

Park, J.S. (2003), 'An economic approach to climate change policy', *Journal of Social Science*, **20**(2), 233–59.

Price, L., Wang, X.J. and Yun, J. (2008), 'China's top-1000 energy-consuming enterprises program: reducing energy consumption of the 1000 largest industrial enterprises in China, LBNL-519E', available at: http://ies.lbl.gov/iespubs/LBNL-519E.pdf.

Su, M., Fu, Z.H., Xu, W., *et al.* (2009), 'Research on levying carbon tax in China', *Review of Economic Research* [in Chinese], **72**, 2–16.

Takeda, S. (2007), 'The double dividend from carbon regulations in Japan', *Journal of the Japanese and International Economies*, **21**(2007), 336–64.

Wang, J.N., Yan, G., Jiang, K.J., *et al.* (2009), 'The study of China's carbon tax policy to mitigate climate change', *China Environmental Science* [in Chinese], **29**(1), 29–32.

8. Approaching environmental fee to plastic bag waste management in Ho Chi Minh City supermarkets

**Le Nguyen Thuy Trang and
Nguyen Thi Hai Yen**

INTRODUCTION

Since the 1960s, plastics have permeated virtually every aspect of daily life, paving the way for new inventions, and replacing materials in existing products. The success of these materials has been based on their properties of resilience, resistance to moisture, chemicals and biodegradation, their stability, and the fact that they can be moulded into any desired form (Lardinois and van de Klundert 1995). In Germany, plastics account for 5% of the 30 million tons of domestic waste collected each year, and about 75% of this waste consists of packaging materials (Halbekath 1989). At Metro Manila in the Philippines, in 1982, plastics accounted for 7.5% of the weight of solid waste generated (film plastics 5.9%, hard plastics 1.6%). By 1990, this proportion had increased to 12.4% (film plastics 11.5%, hard plastics 0.9%) (CAPS 1992).

Being a non-biodegradable product, plastic waste can stay in the environment for a considerable length of time, causing all sorts of problems (Halbekath, 1989). A plastic bag measuring 30×20 cm, after a single use, would litter an area of 0.06 m² in a year, increasing to 0.12 m² in two years, and litter marine biodiversity of 3.5 g/year (ExcelPlas *et al.* 2004). The management of plastic waste through combustion is not environmentally friendly and sustainable as this releases carbon dioxide, a major contributor to global warming. Landfilling with plastic waste causes land and water pollution that impacts on wildlife, human health, livelihood, and so on (Ellis *et al.* 2005). Plastic recycling, an advanced technology applied in plastic waste management, has been in use since the 1980s (Lardinois and Klundert 1995). The plastic 'life cycle' analyses showed that the use of recycled pellets in the production of plastic bags saves around 70% in energy use and 90% in water use compared with the use of pellets made of virgin material. This recycling can reduce from 60% up to 80% of greenhouse gas emissions (Henstock 1993, Tinney *et al.* 2002). However, only around 3% of these bags are recycled each year (Planet Ark 2005).

Application of environmental taxation has focused primarily on producer-generated pollution. Typical policies aimed at consumers attempt to reduce the volume of materials in the waste stream through deposit–refund systems, or user charges for waste collection (Bohm 1981, Callan and Thomas 1999). In 1994, Denmark introduced a tax on plastic bags for retailers and promoted using alternatives to shoppers, resulting in a 66% drop in plastic bag use, though has leveled out (Dikgang *et al.* 2010). The Republic of Ireland was consuming 1.2 billion plastic shopping bags per year before introducing the PlasTax – a charge to customers of €0.15 per bag introduced in 2002. This level of PlasTax is six times higher than the average maximum willingness to pay (WTP), around €0.024 (Convery *et al.* 2007). The first year saw a dramatic reduction in use by over 90% – just fewer than 90 million bags were bought by the public and this fell to less than 85 million in 2003. Since 2007, the levy has been increased to €0.22 (Randal *et al.* 2008). The measurement of PlasTax implementation showed that between January 2002 and April 2003 the number of 'clear' areas had increased by 21%, while of the number of areas without 'traces'16 had increased by 56% (Convery *et al.* 2007).

Ho Chi Minh City (HCMC), located near the Mekong Delta, is the largest city in Vietnam. The total area of HCMC is about 2095 km^2 with 18 inner urban districts occupying an area of 140 km^2. The population grew from roughly 5 million people in 1997 to more than 6.2 million in 2005, or a 2.8% annual rate of growth, with migration contributing roughly 63% of the total growth (Sherbinin and Martine 2007). It is the most important economic centre in Vietnam with 300 000 businesses and the economy growth is at an astounding 11% per annum (Sherbinin and Martine 2007). According to the Recycling Fund Program, HCMC consumes about 5–9 million plastic bags daily (Le 2008). At present, about 6000 tons of solid waste is generated daily from activities in HCMC (Nguyen and Nguyen 2009).

The plastic bags are given free of charge to customers by shopkeepers and cashiers at the supermarkets, and generally the bags are only used once, so about 30–50 tons of plastic bags is transported to the landfill daily (Le 2008, and Pham and Huynh 2009). There are 61 supermarkets in HCMC, which are classified into three groups based on their area and the number of products on sale. Supermarkets with an area larger than 5000 m^2 and offering more than 20 000 products are classified as Group I (large); those with an area of between 2000 m^2 and 5000 m^2 and stocking more than

10 000 products are classified as Group II (medium); and supermarkets with an area of between 500 and 2000 m² and stocking more than 4000 products are classified as Group III (small). Following this classification, there are 20 (33%) supermarkets in Group I, 16 (26%) in Group II, and 25 (41%) in Group III. The great number of plastic bags released to the environment is from these 61 supermarkets. Management of plastic bag waste in HCMC should be given more attention. Therefore, the aim of this study was to examine the quantity of plastic bags given out by the supermarkets and the total cost of their recycling to propose an environment fee on plastic bags to support plastic bag waste management.

METHODOLOGY

Six supermarkets in HCMC were randomly selected for study, drawing two from each of the three groups mentioned above.

- Group III: Family supermarket (978 m², three cashiers) and Co-op Mart An Dong supermarket (1326 m², eight cashiers).
- Group II: Co-op Mart Nguyen Dinh Chieu (2600 m², 28 cashiers) and Co-op Mart Cong Quynh (3200 m², 29 cashiers).
- Group I: BigC Mien Dong (10 000 m², 29 cashiers) and Co-op Mart Ly Thuong Kiet (11 266 m², 35 cashiers).

The number of plastic bags given out by each supermarket was surveyed over 98 hours, 14 hours per day from 8 a.m. to 10 p.m. for seven consecutive days, Monday to Sunday, of a particular survey week. During the 14 survey hours of a given day, the counting was carried out for both central and marginal cashiers. The number of plastic bags in a given size given to customers at a surveyed cashier was recorded by the Handy Tally Counter during the survey time. The estimation of number of plastic bags of a given size released from a survey supermarket for a year is based on Equation 1:

$$TPB_{ai} = \Sigma^n N_j H_{ob}^{-1} \times mC_{op} \times H_{op} \times D_{op}^{-year} \qquad \text{(Equation 1)}$$

TPB_{ai} is a total number of plastic bags in size ai given out per year at a selected supermarket; n is the number of customers passing the surveyed cashier during a unit of survey time H_{ob}; N_j is the number of plastic bags that the customer j^{th} got from the cashier; mC_{op} is the number of operation cashiers during the survey time; H_{op} is the number of opening hours; and D_{op}^{-year} is the total number of opening days in a year.

Three managers/owners of three recycling and purifying plastic bag production enterprises were interviewed to provide an understanding of the life cycle of plastic bags and to estimate the total recycling and/or purifying cost (*Cryc*) of one kilogram of plastic bags. The life cycle of a plastic bag includes several stages: in order, film blowing (plastic bag), used by customer, waste, collection, washing and drying, sorting, cutting, shredding, agglomeration, palletizing to produce the granular form, extrusion, injection moulding, and film blowing. The total cost of the plastic bag life cycle including labor payment and materials for each stage was estimated by the enterprises' owners. The cost for each plastic bag is calculated in Equation 2:

$$Pryc_{ai} = Cryc_{ai} / X_{ai}$$ (Equation 2)

$Pryc_{ai}$ is the recycling cost of a plastic bag of size *ai*; $Cryc_{ai}$ is the total cost needed to recycle or purify 1 kg of plastic bags having size *ai*; and X_{ai} is the number of bags in 1 kg of bags having size *ai*. The $Pryc_{ai}$ value is the environmental fee proposed to apply for a plastic bag having size *ai*.

The Pearson correlation and ANOVA statistical tests were employed to examine the relationships between the scope of supermarkets and the number of plastic bags released. The significant indication of statistical tests was important information that would support the decision-maker in the estimate the number of plastic bags given out by any supermarket, and further to apply the same environmental fee to any supermarkets within a group.

RESULTS

The survey results showed that there were seven sizes of plastic bags used in six selected supermarkets, as follows.

- Type 1: 20 × 26 cm.
- Type 2: 20 × 30 cm.
- Type 3: 20 × 38 cm.
- Type 4: 26 × 40 cm.
- Type 5: 30 × 50 cm.
- Type 6: 34 × 62 cm.
- Type 7: 50 × 70 cm.

The surveys of the plastic bag production manufacturers showed that total number of bags per kg of each type of bag is as follows:

- Type 1: 271 bags/kg.
- Type 2: 260 bags/kg.
- Type 3: 186 bags/kg.
- Type 4: 136 bags/kg.
- Type 5: 94 bags/kg.
- Type 6: 67 bags/kg.
- Type 7: 45 bags/kg.

Of these types of plastic bag, Types 2, 4 and 7 were commonly used in the Co-op Mart system supermarkets, Types 3 and 6 were found in supermarkets of the BigC system, and Type 1, the smallest bag was only found in Family supermarkets (see Table 8.1). In general, data analysis showed that the average number of bags given out per observed hour at a given cashier increased at the weekend (Saturday and Sunday) compared with weekdays (Monday to Friday) (Type 1: 10–17 bags; Type 3: 5–9 bags; Type 4: 6–9 bags; Type 5: 15–19 bags; Type 6: 19–25 bags; Type 7: 10–13 bags, while the number of bags of Type 2 was 5–6 bags every day). Data analysis also showed that the number of bags given varied across the 14 opening/ observed hours. The number of bags given out was generally higher at lunchtime (11–12 a.m.), dinner (4–6 p.m.) and early evening (7–8 p.m.) times (Figure 8.1).

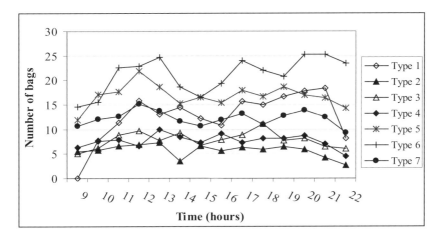

Figure 8.1 Number of bags given out by hour

The average number and standard deviation of plastic bags given out per observed hour and cashier of each selected supermarket is presented in Table 8.1. The number of small-sized bags (Types 2 and 4) was higher in the smaller supermarkets than in the larger supermarkets. In contrast, the number of bigger bags (Types 5 and 7) was higher in the larger supermarkets than in the smaller supermarkets. ANOVA statistical tests showed that there was a significant ($P < 0.05$) correlation between the number of plastic bags of Type 2, 4, 5 or 7 given out and the area (m^2) of the supermarket.

Table 8.1 Average number of bags released in one observation hour by one cashier

Supermarket	Group	Type of bag (dimensions cm^2)						
		Type 1 (20x26)	Type 2 (20x30)	Type 3 (20x38)	Type 4 (26x40)	Type 5 (30x50)	Type 6 (34x62)	Type 7 (40x70)
Family	III	13.6 ± 6.3	NA	NA	3.6 ± 3.3	NA	NA	4.9 ± 5.2
Co-op Mart An Dong	III	NA	7.6 ± 3.3	NA	14.5 ± 4.3	14.4 ± 3.9	NA	8.6 ± 3.5
Co-op Mart Cong Quynh	II	NA	5.5 ± 2.9	NA	6.1 ± 3.1	12.5 ± 3.6	NA	14.0 ± 3.6
Co-op Mart Nguyen Dinh Chieu	II	NA	5.1 ± 3.3	NA	7.3 ± 3.9	15.5 ± 5.0	NA	16.1 ± 4.8
Co-op Mart Ly Thuong Kiet	I	NA	4.3 ± 2.6	NA	6.4 ± 2.7	14.2 ± 5.0	NA	17.0 ± 4.3
BigC Mien Dong	I	NA	NA	7.8 ± 3.6	NA	27.4 ± 8.0	21.1 ± 5.5	NA

(NA: not applicable)

Based on the Equation 1 in the previous section, the estimation of total number of bags of each type of bag given out per year from each of the surveyed supermarket is shown in Figure 8.2. The total weights of each type of bag given out per year were:

- Family supermarket: 1585.95 kg.
- Co-op Mart An Dong: 10 439.36 kg.
- Co-op Mart Nguyen Dinh Chieu: 41 780.36 kg.
- Co-op Mart Cong Quynh: 36 450.48 kg.
- Co-op Mart Ly Thuong Kiet: 52 562.67 kg.
- BigC Mien Dong: 64 756.61 kg.

The life cycle of the plastic bag has many stages, as summarised in Figure 8.3. In Figure 8.3, A is the market price of 1 kg of plastic bags that are made

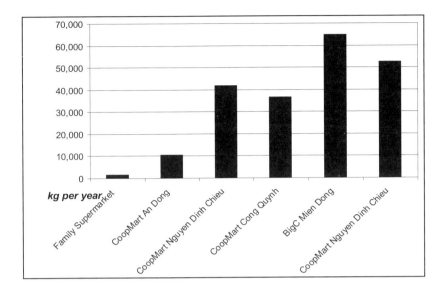

Figure 8.2 Estimation of total number of bags given out per year

from purified or recycled granular plastic; *B* is the cost to pay the labor for collecting, washing, drying and separating plastic bags that are collected from waste; *C* is the cost for extruding granular plastic from the materials made from collected plastic bags; and *D* is the cost of the film-blowing process to produce 1 kg of plastic bags from granular plastic. This cost is included in market price of 1 kg of plastic bags. The estimated cost of *B* varied by manufacturer and time. The survey and interviews showed that the film-blowing process (*D*) costs about VND 2750/kg; the extrusion (*C*) costs VND 3850/kg; while the cost of collecting, washing, drying and separating the waste plastic bags varied from VND 2200/kg to VND 22 000/kg. The environmental fee ($Cryc_{ai}$) applied for 1 kg of waste plastic bags in size a_i is derived from the market price (*A*) and the required recycling cost (*B* + *C*): $Cryc_{ai} = A + B + C$. The market price (*A*) of 1 kg of plastic bags made from purified and recycled granular plastic was around VND 29 590–53,900 and VND 8800–28 600 respectively. The environmental fee estimated for each plastic bag is shown in Table 8.2. The environmental fee was higher when applied to the plastic bags made from purified granular plastic than the plastic bags made from recycled granular plastic, because the price of purified granular plastic is higher than that of recycled granular plastic.

From these prices of purified and recycled granular plastic bags, it can be seen that consumers who use plastic bags have to spend an amount

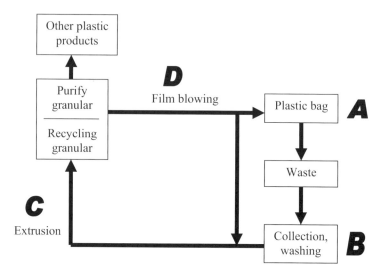

Figure 8.3 Life cycle analysis of plastic bags

corresponding to VND 132–1772 and VND 55–1210 per bag respectively (Table 8.2). This amount also corresponds to the cost of a plastic bag (€0.05–0.10) in countries such as Germany and Ireland.

Table 8.2 Environmental fee estimated for each type of plastic bag

		Environmental fee (VND per bag)						
		Type 1	Type 2	Type 3	Type 4	Type 5	Type 6	Type 7
Bag made from purified granulars	Minimum	132	137	192	262	379	532	792
	Maximum	294	307	429	586	848	1190	1772
Bag made from recycled granulars	Minimum	55	57	80	109	158	222	330
	Maximum	201	209	293	400	579	813	1210

(Exchange rate: US$1 = VND 19 500)

The environmental fees shown in Table 8.2 would be charged to each customer on any bag which he or she requests from the cashier at the supermarket. However, the environmental fee would also be applied to each supermarket based on the number of bags that supermarket released into the environment by unit of time. Table 8.3 indicates the environmental fee that each of the surveyed supermarkets would pay per year. These environmental fees would be also applied to any supermarket in the same group as defined in the Methodology section.

Table 8.3 Deserve-to-pay sum as an environmental fee per year for each supermarket

Supermarket	Group	Number of plastic bags released (kg/year)	Environmental fee (VND per year)	
			Maximum	Minimum
Family	III	1723	44 535 212	10 423 135
Co-op Mart An Dong	III	11 340	293 142 872	68 607 906
Co-op Mart Nguyen Dinh Chieu	II	45 386	1 173 238 400	274 587 711
Co-op Mart Cong Quynh	II	39 597	1 023 569 588	239 558 840
BigC Mien Dong	I	70 346	1 818 436 987	425 591 635
Co-op Mart Ly Thuong Kiet	I	57 099	1 476 017 590	345 450 925
Total		225 491	5 828 940 650	1 364 220 152

DISCUSSION

The plastic bag is a special product since it is only used once (single-use bag). Thus, an environmental fee for plastic bags is necessary. Based on the plastic bag's life cycle, the environmental fee can be applied to a certain size of plastic bag.

Therefore, if someone requests a plastic bag, he or she will pay an amount of money to include both the cost of the bag and the environmental fee ($Cryc_{ai} = A + B + C$. Accordingly, the formula is similar to ones used in other countries, such as Ireland (Akullian *et al.* 2006) and New Zealand (Mallon 2010).

A scenario of the environmental fee for the plastic bags set up from the lowest to the highest cost as in Table 8.2 can be applied to any supermarket in the same group. In addition, this amount also corresponds to the cost of a plastic bag (€0.05–€0.10) in countries as Germany and Ireland. Besides, Equation 1 and 2 can be applied totally to supermarkets of different sizes, together with the total number of plastic bags in 1 kg to calculate the environmental levy for plastic bags in particular sizes.

Scientists these days try to calculate environmental costs based on the environmental economy. In particular, the environmental fee includes the cost of CO_2 emissions from the production and transportation process and treatment process or disposal. However, it is quite difficult to estimate costs for the transportation of plastic bags from a factory to retailers and shops. In Vietnam, there is still no research on CO_2 emissions during the production and transportation process. Hence, it is further research on CO_2 emissions is needed to provide s more accurate environmental costs.

REFERENCES

Akullian, A., Karp, C., Austin, K., *et al.* (2006), 'Plastic Bag Externalities and Policy in Rhode Island'.

Bohm P. (1981), *Deposit Refund Systems: Theory and Applications to Environmental, Conservation, and Consumer Policy. Resources for the Future*, Baltimore, John Hopkins University Press.

Callan S.J. and Thomas J.M. (1999), Adopting a unit pricing system for municipal solid waste: policy and socio-economic determinants, *J Environ. Resour. Econ.*, **14**(4): 503–18.

CAPS (1992), *Recycling Activities in Metro Manila*, The Netherlands, WAREN-project, WASTE Consultants.

Convery, F., McDonnell, S. and Ferreira, S. (2007), The most popular tax in Europe. Lessons from the Irish plastic bags levy, *J Environ. Resourc. Econ.*, **38**: 1–11.

Dikgang, Johane, Leiman, Anthony and Visser, Martine (2010), 'Analysis of the plastic-bag levy in South Africa', Policy Paper 18, Economic Research Southern Africa, July.

Ellis, Sara, Kantner, Sarah, Saab, Ada, *et al.* (2005), *Plastic Grocery Bags: The Ecological Footprint*, Vancouver Island Public Interest Research Group, University of Victoria, Canada.

ExcelPlas Australia, Centre for Design (RMIT), and Nolan ITU (2004), *The Impacts of Degradable Plastic Bags in Australia, 2004. Final Report to Department of the Environment and Heritage*, Canberra, Department of the Environment and Heritage, Commonwealth Government of Australia.

Halbekath, J. (1989), 'The hazards of recycling plastics', *GATE*, No. 3.

Henstock, Michael E. (1993), 'Plastics recycling vindicated', *Warmer Bulletin*, **36**, 12.

Lardinois, I. and van de Klundert, A. (1995), *Plastic Waste: Options for Small Scale Recovery*, Gouda, The Netherlands, Waste Consultants.

Le, V.K. (2008), Policy Measures to Reduce the Use of Plastic Bags in Ho Chi Minh City aiming at a Sustainable Consumption Society, Ho Chi Minh City, Vietnam, Ho Chi Minh City Recycling Fund.

Mallon, Sean (2010), *Report of Council Refuse Bag Price Increase*, AS-10–813, 25 February, New Zealand, Corporate Business Committee.

Nguyen, P.D. and Nguyen, T.V. (2009), 'Status and strategies on solid waste management in Ho Chi Minh City', *International Journal of Environment and Waste Management*, **4**(3–4), 412–21.

Pham, H.N. and Huynh, T.H. (2009), *Studying the Building Regulations for Waste Plastic and Paper Cards in HCMC*, Ho Chi Minh City, Vietnam, Institute of Tropical Technology and Environmental Protection.

Planet Ark (2005), 'Plastic bag reduction', Plastic Bag Fact Sheet, Plastic Bags Just Say 'No', Sydney, Australia, Planet Ark Campaigns.

Rucker, Randal R., Nickerson, Peter H. and Haugen Melissa P. (2008), 'Analysis of the Seattle bag tax and foam ban proposal', Northwest Economic Policy Seminar, Seattle, US, 25 July.

Sherbinin, A. and Martine, G. (2007), Urban Population, Development and Environment Dynamics, Paris, Committee for International Cooperation in National Research in Demography (CICRED).

Tinney, Anthea, Barnes, Sally, Esler, Nancy, *et al.* (2002). Plastic Shopping Bags in Australia, Sydney, National Plastic Bags Working Group, National Packaging Covenant Council.

PART III

Environmental Taxes to Reduce Vehicle
Emissions in Asia-Pacific

9. Mandating emission targets can significantly reduce road transport emissions in Australia

Anna Mortimore

In 2003, the Australian government and the Federal Chamber of Automotive Industry (FCAI) reached a third agreement to improve fuel efficiency of all new passenger vehicles powered by petrol, by setting a voluntary target of 6.8 l per 100 km by 2010, which is equivalent to an emission target of 159 g CO_2 per kilometre. Australia failed to meet its third voluntary fuel efficiency target, illustrating that voluntary fuel efficiency targets do not work. The FCAI introduced an emission target of 222 g CO_2/km by 2010, which was not agreed to by the Australian government.

In 2009, the Final Report by the Vehicle Fuel Efficiency Working Group recommended mandating emission targets. However, the May 2010 Final Report of Australia's Future Tax System stated that such targets are not required if a cap and trade system, known as a carbon pollution reduction scheme (CPRS), is introduced, as supplementary policies such as regulations will not achieve more abatement than the CPRS alone. In September 2010, the Australian government expressed commitment to introduce mandatory emission targets, but not until 2015.

This chapter examines whether a CPRS would have significantly reduced road transport emissions when fuel price increases can be inelastic and consumer behavioural anomalies may lead to market failure or whether a command and control regulation emission standards need to be mandated, to compel car manufacturers to increase technological advancement and the supply of low emission vehicles.

A comparative study with the EU will indicate whether the proposed Australian mandatory emission standards are harmonized with international standards, and whether Australia has considered the lessons learned from other countries in the design of their emission standards.

TECHNOLOGICAL DEVELOPMENT OF LOW EMISSION VEHICLES

According to the International Energy Agency (IEA) current policies are insufficient to stop road vehicle energy use rising above current levels and with projected car ownership worldwide set to triple to over 2 billion by 2050, global transport emissions will double without strong government action. (IEA 2009)

Julia King reported in the 2008 UK *Review of Low-carbon Cars* (*King Review*) that considerable CO_2 emission savings of up to 30–50 per cent can be achieved through enhancing the conventional vehicle systems and using technology, that is 'close to the market', through advances in hybrid and battery technology. (King 2008:6) An almost decarbonisation' of road transport could achieve an 80–90 per cent reduction in road emissions. (King 2007:4)

Therefore to limit the growth of road emissions, and the accumulation of high polluting vehicles, new cars sold each year need to be low emission vehicles. This will be dependent upon governments introducing 'strong' fiscal instruments to increase the demand and supply of low emission vehicles.

AUSTRALIA PREFERS MARKET MECHANISMS

In response, the Australian government released a White Paper in 2008 outlining Australia's preference for market mechanism, a 'cap and trade' permit system, known as a 'carbon pollution reduction scheme' (CPRS). (Aust. Govt 2008)

The CPRS was scheduled to commence in 2010, but failed to receive bipartisan support. Consequently on 27 April 2010, the former Prime Minister announced that the government would delay the implementation of the CPRS.

It is outside the scope of this chapter to discuss the proposed CPRS in detail. Principally, the CPRS employs a 'cap and trade' emission trading mechanism to limit greenhouse gas emissions, where the right to emit greenhouse gas emissions becomes scarce and scarcity entails a price. (Aust. Govt 2008:5–7) The CPRS assumes consumers follow the rational economic model. That is, according to the Pigou theory (1932), the permit price per tonne of CO_2, or the carbon price would increase fuel prices by the cost of emitting carbon and, over time, this would provide the necessary price signal for consumers to reduce their demand for fuel and encourage a shift to fuel-efficient vehicles. (Aust. Govt 2008:6–5) However, consumers may not necessarily respond to the increase in fuel prices, nor consider fuel efficiency in making their final choice of vehicle.

FUEL PRICES CHANGES MAY BE INELASTIC

It is argued that the CPRS will have minimal to no effect in encouraging demand for fuel-efficient low emission vehicles, if the 'carbon price' is not the 'correct price'. But what 'price' will encourage a behavioural change to low emission vehicles? For example, even EU fuel prices, which are more than double Australian fuel prices because of high fuel taxes,[1] did not abate the growth of carbon emissions in the EU. (Aust. Govt 2005:para. 8.4)

The UK Energy Research Centre (ERC) explains that demand response to fuel price changes is relatively inelastic, particularly when people become so dependent on their vehicles that they have little choice but to adapt to higher fuel prices. (UK ERC 2009:98) However, the fuel price elasticity of fuel demand is higher when fuel prices are higher, but this depends on the absolute level of price. (OECD/ITF 2010c:8). For example, reducing fuel demand in the passenger transport sector by 25 per cent may require a price rise of 41.7 per cent. (UK ERC 2009:100) This means that a high carbon price may be required to increase fuel prices to that level. But a high carbon price may not be acceptable by other sectors of the economy. It is also regressive, as it impacts on consumers who do not have the financial capacity to change to low emission vehicles.

CONSUMER BEHAVIOURAL ANOMALIES

The CPRS assumes a rational consumer will respond to the higher fuel prices by considering future fuel savings and respond by choosing a fuel-efficient vehicle. Observations by economists Turrentine and Kurani consider consumers' fuel economy decision-making is more complex than any single economic model and 'almost certainly do not make their decisions according to the strict model of rational economic behaviour.' (US EPA 2010:5) On the contrary, consumer behavioural anomalies, or certain patterns of behaviour such as loss aversion and hyperbolic discounting, can impact on consumer's final choice of vehicle. (OECD/ITF 2010b:24)

Loss aversion can influence decision-making when consumers give potential losses greater weight than potential gains. That is, consumers are reluctant to pay up front for uncertain reduction in fuel expenditure. (Reeson and Dunstall 2009:5), and require large financial benefits before switching to a smaller car or a car with a smaller engine. (King 2008:para 4.9)

According to economic theory, such 'behavioural anomalies' are described as irrational (Reeson and Dunstall 2009:3) and can lead to market failure, thus creating uncertainty for manufacturers in deciding whether to increase the supply of low emission vehicles, and may explain their underinvestment in energy efficiency when consumers are risk averse. (OECD/ITF 2010b:10)

Since it takes a long time for low emission vehicles to become dominant in the vehicle fleet, and rather than waiting for consumers to change their preference to low emission vehicles, it is argued that emission standards need to be mandated so that all vehicle manufacturers can invest with certainty in the technological development of low emission vehicles and the future decarbonisation of the road transport sector.

REGULATING EMISSION STANDARDS

Mandatory and voluntary emission targets adopted by the EU, Australia and Japan are shown in the Table 9.1

Table 9.1 Projected national average carbon emissions (NACE) for all new light or passenger vehicles

	NACE (current, 2007) (g CO_2/km)	Target (g CO_2/km)	Coverage	Code
Australia	226.1	222.0 (2010)	New light vehicles < 3.5 tonnes gross mass	Voluntary
EU	160.0	140.0 (2008)	Newly registered vehicles, including SUVs	Voluntary
EU	160.0	120.0 (2012)	Newly registered vehicles, including SUVs	Mandatory
Japan	165.6	125.0 (2015)	Cars and light trucks	Mandatory

Source: Australian Government, Department of Innovation Industry, Science and Research (2008), *A New Car Plan for a Greener Future*, p. 63: 'A precise comparison between the European Union and other regulatory regimes is difficult because of differences in fleets and test methods.'

VOLUNTARY EMISSION STANDARDS IN AUSTRALIA

Australia has a 'complete voluntary' agreement between the Australian government and the motor vehicle industry, known as the Federal Chamber of Automotive Industries (FCAI), where participation in agreements is solely at the discretion of the participating entity, and there is no serious pressure from government to compel the entity to join. (IPCC 2007:7.9.2.1) The FCAI developed a code of practice for reducing the fuel consumption of new passenger cars (IEA 2008:23), which is voluntary and not enforceable. The IEA reported that Australian automotive industries introduced two sets of voluntary targets in 1978 and 1987, which contributed to fuel efficiency improvements, and both targets failed because of consumers' preference for bigger cars. (IEA 2008:26) Obviously the Australian government's fiscal measures are 'strong' to shift consumers to low emission vehicles.

In 2003, the Australian government reached a third agreement with the FCAI to improve fuel efficiencies of all new passenger vehicles fuelled by petrol, by setting a 'voluntary target' of 6.8 l/100 km by 2010. (Aust. Govt 2007:38) The national average fuel consumption (NAFC) target applied to all new passenger vehicles sold by a manufacturer or importer in a given year. (ACIL 1999) The target represented the majority of passenger vehicles as 85.2 per cent of all passenger vehicles used petrol as at 31 March 2008. (ABS 2009)

In 2004, the FCAI and the Australian government commenced negotiations to change the above voluntary NAFC target to reflect the international challenge to reduce carbon emissions from motor vehicles and established a 'national average carbon emissions' (NACE) target. However, according to the Australian Transport Council, the parties were unable to agree on a revised target. (ATC and EPHC 2009:16) Even though there has been no agreement, the emission target shown in Table 9.1 is the target referred to by the FCAI in assessing the performance of Australia's fleet vehicles.

The NACE target proposed by the FCAI of 222 g CO_2/km by 2010 applies to all new vehicles under 3.5 tonnes. (FCAI 2008a) Vehicles include not only new passenger vehicles, but all new light vehicles such as SUVs and light commercial vehicles, and all types of fuel (petrol, diesel, LPG, etc.). (ABS 2009) FCAI claims that this enlarged list of vehicles and all types of fuels makes the target for reducing CO_2 more challenging. (FCAI 2008b) Consequently the FCAI argues that a comparison with other countries (see

Table 9.1) is difficult when international targets only apply to new passenger vehicles and SUVs. It is argued that failure to adopt a uniform target that is internationally uncompetitive fails to harmonise emission targets internationally and avoids scrutiny by masking the true performance of locally manufactured new vehicles. In addition the European Commission is proposing to adopt separate emission targets for light commercial vehicles that are more tailored to specific vehicle segments (IEA 2010a:25) such as longer model life; differences in CO_2 emission may vary because of vehicle size, shape, the load carried, the number of start-stops, and so forth. (European Automobile Manufacturers Association (ACEA) 2010b:5).

INTERNATIONAL TARGETS

In 1998, the Association of European Car Manufacturers (ACEA), which represents 80 per cent of new registrations in the EU, entered into 'Memorandum of Common Understanding' with the European Commission, a voluntary agreement to 'limit average emissions from newly registered passenger cars to 140g/km by 2008' (see Table 9.1). (EC 1998) An intermediate target was set at 165–170 g CO_2/km by 2003. In 1999, voluntary agreements with the same targets were entered into with the Japan Automobile Manufacturers Association (JAMA), which represents over 10 per cent of annual registrations in the EU, and with the Korean Automobile Manufacturers Association (KAMA), which represents less than 5 per cent of annual registrations. (Europa 2000) The EC agreed that if JAMA and KAMA were selling vehicles in the EU, they would also be required to achieve the EU target of 140 g CO_2/km by 2008.

The European Commission would report to the European Parliament and to the Council on the progress of the emission performance standards for new passenger cars. (Europa 2000) The above three manufacturers' associations would be required to confirm their progress regarding CO_2 emissions. In 2009, JAMA achieved an average CO_2 emission of 142.6 g CO_2/km and KAMA, 141.8 g CO_2/km for. In spite of achieving significant reduction in emissions since their 2003 interim targets of 165–170 g CO_2/km, both associations were unable to reach to reach the 140 g CO_2/km target by 2008–09.

The voluntary agreements requiring fuel efficiency improvements accounted for high levels of dieselization of the passenger car market in the EU, but further reductions in emissions would need to be met through technological developments. However, this required new strategies and technological approaches, but manufacturers did not adopt these 'quickly enough and trends towards larger, heavier vehicles continued to offset much of the technology uptake.'(IEA 2010b:21) Therefore the Commission reported to the Council and the European Parliament on 7 February that the target of 120 g CO_2/km set by the EU would not be met by 2012, unless additional measures were taken. (EC 2007)

The proposal was met with heavy lobbying from the car industry. The point of contention was that the manufacturers of large and heavy cars could be in a disadvantageous position compared with manufacturers of smaller, lighter and lower emitting cars if a similar target was applied to all types of cars. (EC 2008).

The European Council and European Parliament adopted the Commission's proposal and set the most ambitious emission performance standards of 130 g CO_2/km by 2012 for all new passenger vehicles registered in the EU, mandated by the European Parliament and Council on 23 April 2009 (Regulation 443/2009/EC).[2] A further reduction of 10 g CO_2/km will be delivered by other technological improvements such as tyre pressure monitoring systems, more effective air conditioning systems and by an increased use of sustainable biofuels. The Commission recommended improving vehicle labelling and encouraging sales of vehicles with low fuel consumption taxation measures. (EC 2010b) The emission performance standards will be enforceable through charging penalties for manufacturers whose fleet's average CO_2 emissions exceed the limit in any year after 2012 (Regulation 443/2009/EC, Article 9). The penalties will be based on the number of g CO_2/km that an average vehicle sold by the manufacturer is above the target, multiplied by the number of vehicles sold by the manufacturer. From 2012 to 2015, the penalties will be: a premium of €5 per vehicle for the first g CO_2/km; €15 for the second; €25 for the third gram; €95 for the fourth, and onwards. From 2019, manufacturers will pay €95 for each g CO_2/km exceeding the target (Regulation 443/2009/EC, Article 9). Manufacturers expect to meet the target to avoid the significant penalties. The regulation applies to all manufacturers that sell new cars in Europe, which includes the US Japanese and Korean manufacturers.

The EU mandatory targets have provided certainty to the EU motor vehicle industry by providing long-term targets of 95 g CO_2/km for 2020, and encouragement through providing manufacturers incentives by granting them super credits for vehicles with CO_2 emission below 50 g/km, where each vehicle is counted as 3.5 cars in 2012 and 2013, as 2.5 cars in 2014, 1.5 cars in 2015, and one car from 2016 (Regulation 443/2009/EC, Article 5). It is projected that this measure will contribute to more than one-third of the emission reduction from non-emission trading scheme sectors by 2020. (EC 2010a)

COMPARISON OF AUSTRALIAN AND EUROPEAN TARGETS

A comparison of the Australian and EU emission targets is possible as test methods used in measuring vehicle emissions are directly comparable in both countries. (Aust. Govt NTC 2009:25)

In 2009, the FCAI reported that Australia achieved a NACE of 218.5 g CO_2/km, an improvement of 1.8 per cent compared with the 2008 NACE of 222.4 g CO_2/km. In response the FCAI stated: 'Australia's new vehicle market had reached a new environmental milestone with average carbon dioxide the lowest on record, helped by improvements in engine technology.' (FCAI 2010) However, the 2009 Final Report of Australia's Vehicle Fuel Efficiency noted that it was 'not aware of any data or information that demonstrates that voluntary NAFC target has had any influence on the modest reductions in fuel consumption achieved to date.' (ATC and EPHC 2009:22)

The above 2009 NACE of 218.5 g CO_2/km for new light vehicles less than 3.5 tonnes gross mass represents the following vehicles: passenger cars CO_2 average of 195.5 g/km (down from 201.7 g/km in 2008); SUVs at 246.3 g CO_2/km and light commercial vehicles (LCVs) at 253.6 g CO_2/km. (Martin 2010) These ratings may have met the FCAI target, but not the Australian government's fuel efficiency target for new passenger vehicles of 6.8 l/100 km, fuelled by petrol, which is equivalent to an emissions target of 159 g CO_2/km. (Green Vehicle Guide 2010) None of the Australian manufactured vehicles reached these targets. The National Transport Commission reported that in the period January–August 2009, GM Holden (Australia) had the highest average emissions of 279/km, and 'showed virtually no improvement (–0.1 per cent) in the average vehicles emissions from 2005 to Jan-Aug 2009.' (Aust. Govt NTC 2009:21), demonstrating that voluntary targets are ineffective when they are not mandated.

The EU-27 achieved a NACE of 145.7 g CO_2/km in 2009 (EU 2009), 33 per cent less than Australia's NACE of 218.5 g CO_2/km. Australia's voluntary targets are less ambitious, less environmentally effective and more economically inefficient than other fiscal measures.

Consequently Australia's new passenger fleets are one of the world's most polluting. The FCAI explained that the differences in the reported NACE targets for each jurisdiction are principally due to differences in consumer preferences for factors such as fuel type and vehicle size. (FCAI 2008b) However, it is argued that Australia's voluntary targets and lack of fiscal measures penalizing the acquisition of high polluting vehicles has allowed the importation of high emitting vehicles such SUVs, which are increasing in popularity. For example, in 2010 Toyota (Australia) sold more HiLux utilities, with a CO_2 rating of 217 g/km, than Corolla's, with a rating of 173 g CO_2/km (Dowling 2010), and the lowest emitting vehicle in Australia, the Prius (89 g CO_2km), sold one for every ten LandCruiser 4WDs sold. Thus the voluntary targets have failed to encourage the acquisition of low emission vehicles such as the hybrids, and have failed to encourage the acquisition of fuel-efficient vehicles that use diesel, as 84 per cent of Australia's fleet in 2009 was registered with petrol type. (ABS 2009) In the EU, mandatory targets and fiscal incentives have encouraged the use of diesel, which has the advantage of producing less CO_2/km than equivalent petrol vehicles. For example, in 2009, the highest diesel usage recorded was in Belgium at 72 per cent, and France at 70 per cent. (OECD ITF 2010a:25)

AUSTRALIA CONSIDERS MANDATORY EMISSION STANDARDS

In 2008, the Council of Australian Governments requested the Australian Transport Council (ATC) and the Environment Protection and Heritage Council (EPHC) to form a Vehicle Fuel Efficiency Working Group, representing the federal and state/territory transport, environment and industry representatives, to evaluate potential vehicle fuel efficiency measures. (ATC and EPHC 2009:9) The working group report provided the framework for Australia's National Transport Policy, within which to incorporate and report progress towards potential vehicle fuel efficiency measures. (ATC and EPHC 2009:17)

The working party identified that a CPRS would not adequately address potential market failures caused by 'non-price barriers' such as consumers' choice of vehicle.(ATC and EPHC 2009:20) Therefore the working party report was made on the understanding that additional 'complementary' measures would work in parallel with the CPRS, to assist in the transition to a 'low carbon economy.' (ATC and EPHC 2009:18)

In response the working party recommended there was a case for mandating fuel consumption/CO_2 standards for new light vehicles sold in Australia, and advised that before appropriate legislation could be introduced, a 'regulatory impact statement' (RIS) would be required to assess the costs and benefits of such an approach. (ATC and EPHC 2009:26) This analysis would: consider the design of the standard; assess the technological options to achieve the various CO_2 emission targets; address the timing of the standard, providing initial and longer-term targets; consider how the target would support programmes such as the Australian government's

Green Car Innovation Fund and Green Car Challenge; and how the standard can account for emerging technologies such as plug-n electric hybrid vehicles, fully electric vehicles and vehicles designed to operate on emerging low carbon fuels. (ATC and EPHC 2009:25)

Despite the good results achieved by the EU mandatory targets, the working party declined to harmonize their targets with international targets with proposed emission target scenario's for all light vehicles up to 350 tonnes as follows:

- NACE target between 160 and 180 g CO_2/km in 2015; and
- NACE target of 150 g CO_2/km in 2020; or
- NACE target of 115 g CO_2/km in 2025 (ATC and EPHC 2009:50).

However, these regulatory standards are not as stringent as the EU targets. The targets combine both passenger vehicles and light vehicles, which have varying sales-weighted, average CO_2 emissions, making it difficult to make international comparisons. For example, the proposed NACE for 2020 of 150 g CO_2/km does not even meet the target achieved by the EU-27 of 145.7 g CO_2/km in 2009. But the level of emissions achieved by the EU only refers to passenger vehicles. Separate targets for passenger vehicles and LCVs would need to be set to make a proper assessment of the target's performance. Also the delay of introducing and adopting the above proposed targets will fail to 'allow industry time to adapt product development.' (IEA 2010a:19)

Additionally, the above standards fail to adopt the recommendations made the IEA for existing standards to be more stringent and harmonized in 'as many aspects of fuel efficiency standards' to enable comparison of targets between countries. The IEA states that such measures will reduce industry costs and remove barriers to trade. (IEA 2010a:19)

In response to the public discussion on the vehicle fuel efficiency enquiry, the motor vehicle manufacturers opposed mandating emission targets. GM Holden (Australia) made submissions to the working party in November 2008, that 'mandating emission targets should only be considered as a last resort, because they are an 'extremely blunt instrument, costly, require significant government resources to effectively enforce, and generally will constrain innovation and disrupt normal market forces.' (GMH 2008a:25) The fact is that if the NACE targets were enforceable, Australia may end up not having a car manufacturing industry.

Naturally Australia's motor vehicle industry would be supportive of voluntary targets, as it is party to the negotiations and may have some influence over the targets. (Thalmann and Baranzini 2008). It would also be supportive of agreeing to a CPRS market mechanism, which may have less impact to the industry and may defer the introduction of more challenging measures such as taxes or command and control regulation.

The Australian FCAI also criticized the use of regulation in its submission to the Public Discussion Paper on Vehicle Fuel Efficiency, claiming 'Japan, the United States and the EU have introduced second best measures to address fuel efficiency and emissions such as mandatory emissions targets, because they do not have a more efficient market based measure such as a CPRS.' (FCAI 2008b:11)

The Australian Treasury's Final Report on Australia's Future Tax System, published on 2 May 2010, stated that once a CPRS was operational 'additional measures that seek to reduce emissions (in sectors not covered by CPRS) and which are not justified on other grounds should be phased out.' (Aust. Govt 2010a:360) The Final Report concurred with the above submissions made by GM Holden and the FCAI, that implementing non-market approaches through regulations was inefficient in achieving environmental outcomes and was likely to impose significant costs on business and households. (Aust. Govt 2010a:347)

It is argued that the additional costs of command and control regulation are outweighed by the certainty that manufacturers wish to bring forward to the market the technological development and supply of fuel-efficient vehicles, which requires a long lead-time of up to five years to design and produce such vehicles and a further seven years for automotive manufacturers to recover their investment.

At the time of writing this chapter, the Australian government announced in September 2010 that it was committed to introduce mandatory emissions standards for light vehicles in 2015, but made no announcement on the emission targets.

GOVERNMENT'S ROLE IN SUPPORTING MANDATORY FUEL EMISSION TARGETS

It is argued that Australia has no independent government body, such as the European Commission to monitor and regulate the performance of the new passenger cars and SUVs in achieving emission targets. The Australian government did not have detailed information on average emission from new passenger cars and LCVs until 2010. The National Transport Commission (NTC) identified this shortcoming and the information has now been compiled. (Aust. Govt NTC 2009:1) However the NTC findings showed there are no comprehensive reports available for CO_2 emissions by vehicle segment, buyer type or manufacturer for Australia. (Aust. Govt NTC 2009:2)

It was the FCAI that prepared reports on Australia's NACE performance. The FCAI was responsible for introducing all three voluntary fuel efficiency targets and the 2004 NACE target. All fuel efficiency targets failed, and the Australian government did not agree to the 2004 NACE target.

Reviews of the motor vehicle industry performance in reducing emissions by automotive associations such as the Australian FCAI are likely to be biased to meet the needs of the industry rather than the environment, and the targets are less likely to be stringent. All submissions made by GM Holden to Australia's future tax system were supported by the FCAI, both opposing all taxes and mandatory regulations on carbon emissions.

The ATC, established in June 1993, is not a regulatory body, but provides advice to governments on the 'co-ordination and integration of all surface transport and road policy issues at a national level.' (ATC 2010) It was only at the request of the Council of Australian Governments in 2008 that the ATC prepared a report in 2009, identifying Australia's poor vehicle fuel efficiency and carbon emission standards record, when compared with international standards. Even then the proposed mandatory emission targets discussed earlier are not internationally compatible.

It is the role of the Australian government to recognize the shortcomings of the proposals – they are not in accord with the IEA's 2008 recommendations for harmonized fuel efficiency standards across countries.

Yet it appears that the Australian government will not adhere to the IEA's 2008 recommendations, considering the announcement made by the Prime Minister[3] in July 2010 outlining future mandatory emission targets (Stanford 2010):

- NACE target of 190 g CO_2/km in 2015; and
- NACE target of 155 g CO_2/km in 2024.

These targets are even less stringent than the targets proposed by the working party, discussed earlier. In response, the Australian government has been criticized for 'dragging the chain on the issue of vehicle emissions in an attempt to protect the local car industry, which builds large six-cylinder sedans, utility vehicles and four-wheel-drives.'(Blackburn 2010)

Like the EU, the Australian local car industry will be able to meet the above targets and reduce emissions by converting their new passenger fleet from petrol to diesel. However, experience from the EU indicates that such targets will not 'push' the local car industry to reduce road transport emissions significantly without innovation and technological advances of low emission vehicles that will reduce the consumption of fossil fuels. Local Australian car manufacturers will not be competitive if stringent emission targets such as the EU's mandatory target of 120g g CO_2/km by 2012 for new passenger vehicles is not adopted.

INTERNATIONAL HARMONIZATION OF AUTOMOBILE EMISSION STANDARDS

The IEA strongly recommends harmonizing as many aspects of fuel efficiency standards as possible across countries. (IEA 2010a:19) Europe has been at the forefront of international harmonization efforts with the 1958 Agreement of the United Nations Economic Commission for Europe (UNECE) on technical standards. (European Automobile Manufacturer's Association (ACEA) 2010) China and Japan have also adopted internationally harmonized regulations for emissions established for Europe by the UNECE. They have adopted target values in each class, divided by vehicle mass. (IEC, 2008:31)

Hence it is argued that international harmonization is important as the automotive sector is of a global nature, and is engaged in international trade. Harmonizing global standards and regulations will encourage more stringent targets and bring certainty to manufacturers by increasing the competiveness of the industry and reducing industry costs and barriers of trade. (IEA 2010a:19)

For example, the automobile manufacturers associations active in the EU, namely the ACEA, the JAMA and the KAMA, are engaged in 'international harmonization' in meeting the mandatory standards of the European Parliament and Council, in order to be able to register their cars for sale in the EU. These automobile manufacturers account for 60 per cent of the world's new passenger vehicles; with the EU 27 producing 33 per cent of the world passenger car production; JAMA producing 20 per cent and KAMA producing 7 per cent. (Worldometers 2010)

Australia will not be engaging in the international harmonization of regulatory standards if the federal government adopts the proposed mandatory regulatory standards. Not only will the Australian vehicle manufacturers continue be uncompetitive, but the proposed mandatory emission targets will benefit the 81 per cent of vehicles imported into the country, as the targets are not stringent and will fail to restrict high emitting vehicles from being imported into the country.[4]

CONCLUSION

It was argued that a cap and trade market mechanism such as a CPRS will not bring certainty to manufacturers in increasing the supply of low emission vehicles, because behavioural anomalies may create market failure and the possibility of price inelasticities of demand if fuel prices are not high enough. Rather than waiting for consumers to make a behavioural shift to low emission vehicles, it was more effective to introduce command and control regulatory emission standards, to create certainty for manufacturers to increase supply and invest in the technological advancement of low emission vehicles.

In 2010 the Australian government announced its commitment to introduce mandatory emission targets in 2015. However, Australia's proposed mandatory target will not be harmonized with other countries, nor will it be as effective or stringent as that of the EU – the EU achieved Australia's proposed target for 2020 in 2009. In effect Australia's proposed targets will not push local car manufacturers to use technological advancement to produce low emission vehicles, nor restrict the importation of high emitting vehicles, consequently failing to cut the country's road transport emissions significantly.

NOTES

[1.] Australia's excise duty on unleaded petrol is AUS$0.38143 per litre, which is the fourth lowest tax rate of the OECD-30 countries.
[2.] Article 4, phasing in requirements where in 2012 65 per cent of each manufacturer's newly registered cars must comply on average with the limit value set by the legislation. This will rise to 75 per cent in 2013, 80 per cent in 2014 and 100 per cent from 2015 onwards.
[3.] Prime Minister Julia Gillard.

REFERENCES

ACIL Consulting (1999), *Study on Factors Impacting on Australia's National Average Fuel Consumption Levels to 2010*, This is a report made to the Australian Greenhouse Office by economic advisors ACIL Consulting, who were retained by the Australian government.

Australian Bureau of Statistics (ABS) (2009), '9309.0 Motor Vehicle Census, Australia, 31 Mar 2009', available at: www.abs.gov.au/AUSSTATS/abs@.nsf/Lookup/9309.0Main+Features131%20Mar%202009 (accessed 10 December 2010).

Australian Government (2008), *Carbon Pollution Reduction Scheme: Australia's Low Pollution Future*, White Paper.

Australian Government, National Transport Commission (NTC) (2009), 'Carbon emissions from new Australian vehicles', available at: www.ntc.gov.au/filemedia/general/carbonemissionsfromnewausvehicle.pdf (accessed 10 December 2010).

Australian Government, Treasury (2005), 'International comparison of Australia's taxes', available at: http://comparativetaxation.treasury.gov.au/content/report/html/10_Chapter_8–03.asp (accessed 16 November 2010).

Australian Government, Treasury (2010a), *Final Report Australia's Future Tax System*.

Australian Government, Department of Climate Change (2010b), 'Australian national greenhouse accounts greenhouse gas inventory', available at: www.climatechange.gov.au/climate-change/.../media/publications/greenhouse-acctg/national-greenhouse-gas-inventory-2008.as (accessed 24 October 2010).

Australian Transport Council (ATC) (2010), available at: www.atcouncil.gov.au/ (accessed 11 December 2010).

Australian Transport Council (ATC) and Environment Protection and Heritage Council (EPHC) (2009), *Vehicle Fuel Efficiency Working Group Final Report*, available at: www.atcouncil.gov.au/ (accessed 13 November 2010).

Blackburn, R. (2010), 'Australia lags behind on emission control', criticism by Senator Christine Milne, *The Age*, 19 June, available at: http://theage.drive.com.au/motor-news/australia-lags-behind-on-emission-control-20100618-ym1w.html (accessed 13 November 2010).

Dowling, J. (2010), 'Cash for clunkers', available at: www.carsales.com.au/news/2010/cash-for-clunkers-hides-new-co2-target-20188 (accessed 31 October 2010).

Energy Research Centre, UK (2009), 'What policies are effective at reducing carbon emission from surface passenger transport', available at: www.ukerc.ac.uk/support/TransportReport (accessed 11 November 2010).

Environment Protection Agency (EPA), US (2010), 'How consumers value fuel economy: a literature review', available at: www.epa.gov/oms/climate/regulations/420r10008.pdf (accessed 12 November 2010).

Europa (2000), 'Summaries of EU legislation', available at: http://europa.eu/legislation_summaries/internal_market/single_market_for_goods/motor_vehicles/interactions_industry_policies/l28055_en.htm (accessed 19 November 2010).

European Automobile Manufacturers' Association (ACEA) (2010a), 'European commercial vehicle manufacturers jointly develop evaluation tool to help further reduce CO2 emissions', available at: www.acea.be/index.php/news/news_detail/european_commercial_vehicle_manufacturers_jointly_develop_evaluation_tool_t (accessed 20 November 2010).

European Automobile Manufacturers' Association (ACEA) (2010b), 'The importance of streamlining regulation and technical standards in boosting automobile industry competitiveness', available at: www.acea.be/index.php/news/news (accessed 20 November 2010).

European Commission (1998), 'Communication from the Commission to the Council and the European Parliament – Implementing the Community strategy to reduce CO2 emissions from cars: an environmental agreement with the European automobile industry', Brussels, 29 July1998, available at: http://eur-lex.europa.eu/smartapi/cgi/sga_doc?smartapi!celexplus!prod!DocNumber&lg=en&type_doc=COMfinal&an_doc=1998&nu_doc=495 (accessed 19 November 2010).

European Commission (2007), 'Communication from the Commission to the Council and the European Parliament of 7 February 2007', COM(2007) 19, Official Journal C172 of 12 July 2005.

European Commission (2008), 'European roads to reduce cars' CO2 2missions', available at: http://ec.europa.eu/environment/etap/inaction/pdfs/jan08_cars_co2.pdf (accessed 19 November 2010).

European Commission (2009), Council Regulation (EC) No. 443/2009 of the European Parliament and of the Council of 23 April 2009.

European Commission (2010a), 'Reducing CO2 emissions from light-duty vehicles', available at: http://ec.europa.eu/environment/air/transport/co2/co2_home.htm (accessed 30 November 2010), p. 9.

European Commission (2010b), 'Report from the Commission to the European Parliament, the Council, and the European Economic and Social Committee', available at: Http://ec.europa.eu/clima/policies/transport/vehicles/docs/strategy_report_post_isc_e-greffe_en.pdf (accessed 16 November 2010).

European Union (2009), 'Cars: greenhouse gas emissions – ACEA agreements', available at: www.dieselnet.com/standards/eu/ghg_acea.php (accessed 3 December 2010).

Federal Chamber of Automotive Industry (FCAI), Australia (2008a), 'National Average Carbon Emissions', media release 31 March, available at: www.fcai.com.au (accessed 16 November 2010).

Federal Chamber of Automotive Industry (FCAI), Australia (2008b), 'Response to the public discussion paper on vehicle fuel efficiency', available at: www.fcai.com.au/library/publication/1264747485_document_fuel_efficiency_response_to_public_discussion_paper.pdf (accessed 2 December 2010).

Federal Chamber of Automotive Industry (FCAI), Australia (2010), 'Presidents report 2010', available at: www.www.fcai.com.au/about/president's-report-2010 (accessed 30 October 2010).

GM Holden (2008), 'GM Holden submission to the public discussion paper on vehicle fuel efficiency "Potential measures to encourage the uptake of more fuel efficient, low carbon emission vehicles"', available at: www.environment.gov.au/archive/settlements/transport/publications/vfe-paper/submissions/63gmhol (accessed 10 December 2010).

International Energy Agency (IEA) (2008), 'Review of International Policies for Vehicle Fuel Efficiency' Paris, France. OECD/IEA

International Energy Agency (IEA) (2009), 'Transport, energy and CO2: moving toward sustainability – how the world can achieve deep CO2 reductions in transport by 2050', press release 27 October, available at: www.iea.org/press/pressdetail.asp?PRESS_REL_ID=293 (accessed 28 October 2010).

International Energy Agency (IEA) (2010a), *Transport Energy Efficiency Implementation of IEA Recommendations since 2009 and Next Steps*, Paris, OECD/IEA.

International Energy Agency (IEA) (2010b), 'Transforming Global Markets for Clean Energy Products', Paris, OECD/IEA.

International Energy Agency (IEA) (2010c), 'Transforming Global Markets for Clean Energy Products', Paris, OECD/IEA.

Green Vehicle Guide (2010), available at: www.greenvehicleguide.gov.au.

Intergovernmental Panel on Climate Change (IPCC) (2007), 'Climate Change 2007: Working Group III: Mitigation of climate change', available at: www.ipcc.ch/publications_and_data/ar4/wg3/en/ch7s7-9-2.html (accessed 18 November 2010), para. 7.9.2.1.

King, J., Department of Transport, UK (2007) *The King Review of Low-carbon Cars*, Part I: 'The potential for CO2 reduction', available at: http://webarchive.nationalarchives.gov.uk/+/dft.gov.uk/pgr/sustainable/climatechange/king/ access 20 November 2010

King, J., Department of Transport, UK (2008), *The King Review of Low-carbon Cars*, Part II: Recommendations for action', available at: www.physics.harvard.edu/~wilson/energypmp/2008_King_II.pdf (accessed at 20 November 2010).

Martin, T. (2010), 'New-Car CO2 emissions under review', available at: www.goauto.com.au/mellor/mellor.nsf/story2/7BFED44A028545B9CA2576D 90006F3C1 (accessed 31 October 2010).

Organisation for Economic Co-operation and Development (OECD) and International Transport Forum (ITF) (2010a), L. Bastard, 'The Impact of economic instruments on the auto industry and the consequences of a fragmenting markets', discussion paper no. 2010–8, 18–19 February, Paris, OECD.

Organisation for Economic Co-operation and Development (OECD) and International Transport Forum (ITF) (2010b), D. Green, 'Why the market for new passenger cars generally undervalues fuel economy', discussion paper no. 2010–6, 18–19 February, Paris, OECD.

Organisation for Economic Co-operation and Development (OECD) and International Transport Forum (ITF) (2010c), 'Stimulating Low-Carbon Vehicle Technologies', discussion paper no. 2010–13, 18–19 February, Paris, OECD.

Reeson, A. and Dunstall, S. (2009), *Behavioural Economics and Complex Decision-Making' Implications for the Australian Tax and Transfer System*, The Commonwealth Scientific Industrial Research Office (CSIRO).

Stanford, J. (2010), 'Australia to follow US and Europe with Co2 emissions standards under Gillard policy', available at: www.goauto.com.au/mellor/mellor.nsf/story2/FD7221E399E9CD11CA25776D00123BF7 (accessed 31 October 2010).

Thalmann, P. and Baranzini, A. (2008), 'Gradual introduction of coercive instruments in climate policy', *Critical Issues in Environmental taxation*, **V**, 53–74.

Worldometers (2010), 'Cars produced in the world', available at: www.worldometers.info/cars/ (accessed 20 November 2010).

10. Enhancing green tax measures concerning energy use in Hong Kong

Yuzhu Lu

I. INTRODUCTION

Hong Kong, a compact city with a population of seven million and with few natural resources, has undergone remarkable economic growth over the past few decades. Hong Kong is a regional centre for international business, and its economy consists almost entirely of trade and services.

At the same time, however, the city has developed severe environmental problems, especially referring to its air pollution and climate change problems. The high average temperature and continuous rising sea level in Hong Kong are convincing evidence of its climate change problem: according to the Hong Kong Observatory, the average temperature in Hong Kong is rising at rate of 1.2°C per 100 years; the rate has accelerated to 0.28°C per decade between 1980 and 2009; and the records of Hong Kong's tide gauge station show that the mean sea level in the Victoria Harbour has risen at an average rate of 2.4 mm per year during the period 1954 to 2008.[1] Referring to air pollution in Hong Kong, the air quality monitoring data show that the ambient air quality has worsened on average by 13–47% (by comparing monitoring data between 1990 and 2008) for some pollutants. 'Reduced visibility' days, defined as those with a visibility of less than 8 km and relative humidity not exceeding 80%, increased by 207% between 1997 and 2006.[2] Transport emissions and emissions from heating and energy generation are the main sources of the air pollution and greenhouse gases in Hong Kong, except for pollutants from neighbouring Guangdong Province. In 1997, local power generation was the source of 33% of particulates, 84% of SO_2 and 51% of NO_x emissions, and in 2007 it contributed to 89% of the total emissions.[3] Consequently, there is an urgent need for strong and immediate action to address the climate change and air pollution problems in Hong Kong.

In today's world, green taxes have been accepted and applied by more and more countries, especially those in the Organisation for Economic Co-operation and Development (OECD), among which the Scandinavian nations are the forerunners. Green tax is known for many of its advantages over traditional command-and-control instruments. For example, static cost minimisation, dynamic efficiency, lower compliance and administrative costs, important revenue source and so on. However, Hong Kong has still rarely used the tax tool as an integral part of the government's anti-pollution strategy.

Besides my concern over the environment, following my studies in Hong Kong taxation, comparatively speaking, the taxation system in Hong Kong is a simple and old system. Hong Kong's taxation system has the following main characteristics: first, taxes are imposed at low rates – the standard tax rate of 15% (for the year of assessment 2009/10) and corporation profits tax rate of 16.5% (for the year of assessment 2009/10) are relatively low, compared with other developed countries. Second, the system is mainly territorially driven. That means, income taxes (i.e. salaries tax, profits tax and property tax) are charged on income which has a Hong Kong source. Stamp duty is charged on instruments which relate to Hong Kong assets. The residence status of a taxpayer does not normally affect his tax liability. Third, it has a small tax base (the Hong Kong Inland Revenue Department only collects the following taxes and fees: salaries tax, property tax, profits tax, stamp duty, business registration fee and betting duty. There is no tax on capital gains or dividend income, and there is no goods and services tax). The total tax revenue in the sum of HK$200 696.5 million was 12.15% of GDP for 2007/08 and had been maintained at around 10% for the previous 20 years.[4] This ratio is very low when compared with that of other developed countries, many of which range from 28.3% (United States) to 43.6% (France).[5] As a result, it may affect the role of government with respect to macroeconomic control. There is a need for more stable sources of revenue that will be less affected by the cycles in the economy and by any sudden jolts that it may encounter. In conclusion, at present, the tax base is too narrow and needs to be broadened. The Hong Kong government has been considering options for new broad-based taxes for a very long time. It concluded that a goods and services tax (GST) is the best choice for Hong Kong and intended to introduce it in 2006,[6] but this proposal was generally and strongly opposed by the public and as a result was dropped by the government. Inferring from a survey about tax reform conducted by the *South China Morning Post* in Hong Kong in 2006, the introduction of green tax is supported by 73% of those surveyed, ranking it second among 15 tax options (the first is tax on luxury goods – 82%).[7] It can be concluded that, overall, the introduction of green taxes could be an option that is more suitable for Hong Kong and relatively more acceptable by the public.

As a result, the major objective of this chapter is to make proposals for improving the use of green taxes related to energy use and transportation in Hong Kong, by learning from more advanced overseas experiences. This chapter provides a good opportunity to make a contribution to the improvement of both the air quality and taxation system in Hong Kong, help address the wider climate change problem and contribute to the literature.

The chapter proceeds as follows. The next section elaborates on the green tax measures currently existing in Hong Kong concerning the energy use and transportation situation. Proposals are made on improving existing green tax measures, introducing new green taxes, using the revenue from these taxes and dealing with implementation issues in Section 3. A summary and a discussion of future research are provided in the final section.

2. CURRENT GREEN TAX MEASURES CONCERNING ENERGY USE IN HONG KONG

As mentioned in the introduction, Hong Kong is mainly faced by two air pollution issues, namely local street-level pollution and the power station emission problem. However, currently there are only a limited number of green tax measures existing in Hong Kong to address these problems. Especially, to date, Hong Kong still has no tax or charge levied on energy use for power generation, and only a few depreciation allowance measures exist.

2.1 Green Tax Measures Concerning Transport Sector

2.1.1 First registration tax (FRT) and vehicle licence fee (VLF)

The Transport Department in Hong Kong regulates that during the first registration of a vehicle, it is necessary to pay the FRT for the registration and to pay the VLF for licensing of the vehicle. The FRT is calculated basing on the taxable value of the vehicle, and the Motor Vehicles Valuation Group of the Customs and Excise Department is responsible for the assessment of the taxable value of each motor vehicle which is to be used in Hong Kong. Since 1982, the level of FRT was increased to discourage private car ownership and also as an incentive to buy smaller, more efficient cars; smaller cars have less tax levied on them. The VLF is set on a gradated scale with the fee rising with the engine size, and different tax levels are applied to different types of vehicles (including private car, goods vehicle, bus, taxi, motor cycle and motor tricycle and electrically powered passenger vehicle) with the highest level on private cars and the lowest level on buses.[8]

2.1.2   Excise duties on motor fuels

There is no tariff on goods entering Hong Kong, but excise duties are payable on hydrocarbon oil (other than ultra low sulphur diesel and Euro V diesel) at the following rates:[9]

- aircraft spirit: HK$6.51/l;
- light diesel oil: HK$2.89/l;
- leaded petrol: HK$6.82/l;
- unleaded petrol: HK$6.06/l.

Additionally, since July 2008 Euro V diesel has been zero-rated, and there is no tax on liquefied petroleum gas (LPG) to encourage taxis and light buses to switch from diesel to LPG-burning engines.

Hong Kong sits alongside one of the world's busiest shipping lanes, but there is no fee levied on the use of fuel by ships (Cheung, 2008). One reason might be that Pearl River Delta ports, including the Kwai Chung container terminal in Hong Kong, comprise one of the busiest port facilities in the world, handling about 12% of global container traffic, and the government is concerned that levying fees on bunker fuel would impose financial burdens on business operators and hamper the port's competitiveness. However, the harmful aspect of burning bunker fuel provokes serious concern. Bunker fuel is a viscous and highly polluting substance left over from refining oil. It has high nitrogen oxide contents and contains as much as 4.5% sulphur, making its exhausts especially noxious for those who inhale them. (Derwent *et al.*, 2005). 'At least 3.8 million people living around Kwai Chung Container Port had been exposed to health risks because of port-related air pollution.'[10]

2.1.3   Tax incentives for environment-friendly petrol private cars

Starting from 1 April 2007, a 30% reduction in FRT was offered to buyers of newly registered environment-friendly petrol private cars, subject to a cap of HK$50 000 per car.[11] There are also qualifying standards for environment-friendly petrol private cars, including Emission Requirements and Fuel Efficiency Requirements, which are set out by the Environmental Protection Department (EPD). The EPD will review the qualifying standards annually in the light of technological advancement to restrict the tax incentive to vehicles of truly outstanding emission and fuel efficiency performance.[12]

2.1.4 Tax incentives for environment-friendly commercial vehicles

Starting from 1 April 2008, buyers of newly registered environment-friendly commercial vehicles, including taxis, light/medium/heavy goods vehicles, public/private light buses, public/ private non-franchised buses and special purposes vehicles, could receive a reduction on the FRT. The rates of reduction of the first registration taxes for different vehicle classes qualified under the scheme are as follows:

- 100% for taxis, light buses, non-franchised buses and special purpose vehicles;
- 50% for goods vehicles (except van-type goods vehicles up to 1.9 tonnes permitted gross vehicle weight); and
- 30% for van-type goods vehicles up to 1.9 tonnes permitted gross vehicle weight.

As a start, the qualifying standard for environment-friendly commercial vehicles is set at Euro V level, and the qualifying standards for environment-friendly commercial vehicles also will be reviewed annually by the EPD.[13]

2.1.5 Tax incentives for electric cars

To encourage the use of electric cars in Hong Kong, the government offered exemption from FRT for electric vehicles. This exemption was first granted in the financial year 1994/95 and has been extended several times since. Moreover, the annual licence fee costs only HK$440, compared with the minimum annual charge of HK$3929 for conventional private cars.[14]

2.1.6 Tax deduction for capital expenditure on environment-friendly vehicles

With the aim to encourage the business sector to purchase more electric vehicles, hybrid vehicles and other environment-friendly commercial vehicles instead of other types of vehicles, in the HKSAR government's 2010/11 budget, enterprises will be able to enjoy a 100% profits tax deduction in the first year of purchasing environment-friendly vehicles.

2.2 Green Tax Measures Concerning Energy Use

At present, there is a tax concession scheme on environment-friendly facilities. Starting from the year of assessment, 2008/09, there will be a tax concession if capital expenditure was incurred on any environment-protection machinery or installation (collectively 'environmental protection facilities'). Eligible environmental protection machinery will receive a

100% deduction of the cost from the year of assessment instead of 60% of the cost as was previously the case. Eligible environmental protection installations will now receive an accelerated rate of 20% deduction of cost for five consecutive years.[15]

In conclusion, it will be seen from the discussion in Section 3 that, considering the poor air quality in Hong Kong, the government's action is not sufficient to control the major causes of air pollution and climate change problems. Additionally, given the need to broaden the tax base in Hong Kong, there is a large scope and an urgent need for the government to enhance its use of green tax measures.

3. RECOMMENDATIONS TO ENHANCE GREEN TAX MEASURES RELATED TO ENERGY USE AND THE TRANSPORT SECTOR IN HONG KONG

The experience of Scandinavian countries shows that they all have several kinds of taxes levied on fossil fuels used for energy purposes, mostly including energy tax, CO_2 tax and sulphur tax (Sweden also has an NO_x tax). But in Hong Kong the energy used for heating and power generation has not been subject to any kind of tax or charge. Furthermore, according to European experiences, green taxes on transportation can be divided into taxes/fees levied on motor vehicles and energy-related taxes levied on transport fuels. As a result, this section discusses recommendations for gradually revising existing green tax measures and introducing new ones in Hong Kong. Additionally, recommended ways of using revenue generated by green taxes and ways to build the political and public acceptance of green tax are also discussed.

3.1 Recommendations to Enhance Green Tax Measures Concerning Energy Use

3.1.1 Extending excise duties to fossil fuels

Regarding the energy structure in Hong Kong, the predominant energy sources are coal, fuel oil, naphtha and natural gas. However, excise duties are not levied on any of these fossil fuels, but only on transport fuels. By contrast, all the Scandinavian countries have excise duties on fossil fuels in order to regulate and restrict the use of energy. Therefore, it is recommended that excise duties are extended to these fossil fuels in Hong Kong. According to the Nordic experience, the tax could adopt differentiated tax rates according to the energy content or the pollution intensity of each specific fuel type to provide consumers with financial incentives to save energy.

3.1.2 CO_2 tax

Before describing the CO_2 tax proposal for Hong Kong, it is better to explain the two crucial arguments involved in the design of a CO_2 tax – the choice between an upstream and downstream tax base and the choice between a specific and *ad valorem* tax rate.

First, an upstream CO_2 tax would be one that is levied early in the chain of production and processing, i.e. on raw energy sources at the point where they are mined or extracted (coal mines, oil wells, etc.), and if a country/region does not have its own raw energy sources and all the energy used by the country/region is imported, then the upstream carbon tax would be one levied at the time of importation. A downstream CO_2 tax, on the other hand, would not be levied until much later in the chain of energy production and processing, i.e. at the point where energy sources had been converted into final fuel products sold to business and domestic energy consumers (Pearson and Smith, 1992). According to Vollebergn (2008), an upstream CO_2 tax is better than the downstream tax, because the upstream CO_2 tax establishes the best linkage to (potential) emissions – it implicitly accounts for emissions in the production stage of the final fuel products by taxing the carbon content of the raw materials.

Second, with regard to CO_2 tax, specific rate is expressed as a fixed amount per ton of carbon and *ad valorem* rate is expressed as a percentage of the price of energy products (Pearson and Smith, 1992). Specific tax rates are superior to *ad valorem* rates if the aim is to use taxes as regulatory devices, because a specific tax on the carbon content of a fuel is the best-targeted (indirect) instrument in the case of climate change, whereas an *ad valorem* tax would also penalise characteristics that are responsible for the heating potential of energy products but not for climate change (Vollebergn, 2008).

In all the four Scandinavian countries, CO_2 tax is upstream-charged, and at the same time, almost all the fossil fuels used in Hong Kong are imported, so the CO_2 tax in Hong Kong would better be designed as an upstream tax; in other words, the CO_2 tax would be levied on the importer. Because of the lack of taxes or charges regulating energy use in Hong Kong and, as can be seen, the proposed CO_2 tax is easily to collect, it is recommended that a CO_2 tax is introduced in the near future. The tax could be levied on the primary fossil fuels used in Hong Kong: coal, fuel oil, naphtha and natural gas and could be charged based on the carbon emission from their combustion and a fixed rate per tonne of CO_2 adopted regardless of the fuel type – in other words, the less CO_2 emitted by the fuel during combustion, the lower the tax to be paid. As a result, economic incentives for using less CO_2-intensive energy are available to energy users. According to the Nordic nations' experiences, the tax rate could be set at a low level at first and increased gradually in the future – to increase the feasibility. Currently, coal is the major source of heating and power generation in Hong Kong, and in order to encourage the three main suppliers[16] of electricity and gas to use more natural gas, which is less carbon intensive, the natural gas could be exempted from the CO_2 tax at first, and at an appropriate time in the future this exemption provision of CO_2 tax on natural gas should be removed.

3.2 Recommendations to Enhance Green Tax Measures Concerning the Transport Sector

3.2.1 Green taxes levied on motor vehicles

Hong Kong has the FRT and VLF to charge for the purchase and use of motor vehicles. But the imposition of these two charges does not seem to have had much effect on restricting the number of motor vehicles in Hong Kong, and the higher level of tax on private cars also appears not to have decreased the number of private cars in HKSAR – there are 385 675 licensed private cars, accounting for 67% of all vehicles as at the end of June 2009. Furthermore, there are about 283 licensed vehicles for every kilometre of road, amongst the highest in the world, and the topography makes it increasingly difficult to provide additional road capacity in the heavily built-up areas.[17] It can be inferred from this that, in economic terms, the likely reason why the FRT and VLF have not had much effect in reducing the vehicle population is that the FRT and VLF are currently not set enough to reflect the real externalities produced by road travel. As a result, there is still opportunity for the rate of FRT and VLF to be increased.

3.2.2 Taxes levied on motor fuels

First, excise duties on motor fuels are suggested to be revised and improved in Hong Kong. Currently the tax rates on petrol are set according to its lead content, and the rates on diesel oil are set according to its sulphur content. The variable tax rates have had a positive effect in changing people's motor fuel-using behaviour and encouraging people to choose more environmentally sound fuel types, but following Finland's experience, where tax rates on petrol are differentiated not only according to the lead content but also according to the sulphur content with the aim of controlling air pollution caused by vehicle emissions more effectively, it is suggested that Hong Kong should set the differentiated tax rates on petrol as Finland does. Additionally, the scope of excise duties should be extended to the fuels used by ships, which are much dirtier than the fuels used by trucks.

Second, although the motor fuels used in Hong Kong generate less air pollution and greenhouse gases than power plants, as mentioned in the introduction, the combustion of motor fuels is still a major source of air pollution and climate change problems in Hong Kong. As a result, when the CO_2 tax is introduced, it would be advisable also to levy it on the combustion of motor fuels, in order to reduce the CO_2 emissions generated by motor vehicles effectively.

3.3   Recommendations for Revenue Use

Generating revenue is one important advantage of green taxation. Concerning the current situation in Hong Kong, besides the role of stable sources of revenue for the government, if part of the revenue was specifically spent on environmental protection-related activities or facilities, as several countries do, the newly revised or introduced green tax measures would not only give a greater contribution to environmental protection, but would also be more acceptable to the public. In light of this, some recommended ways for the Hong Kong government to spend revenues generated from the proposed green taxes are as follows.

3.3.1   Provide incentives for development of renewable energy sources

For example, the government could grant funds to wind energy projects,[18] solar energy projects and energy-saving projects. Additionally, nuclear power is a comparatively clean energy source. As a near zero emission fuel source, it has significantly reduced emissions of sulphur dioxide, NO_x and particulates in Hong Kong. It has also saved more than 130 million tonnes of CO_2, which is equal to about three times Hong Kong's annual CO_2 emissions.[19] CLP Power Hong Kong Limited has had a nuclear electricity supply contract since 1994, through which CLP receives 70% of the nuclear electricity supply generated from the Daya Bay nuclear power station. In September 2009, the Hong Kong government approved an extension of this contract for another 20 years from 2014. As a result, the government should continue the tax exemption on nuclear-generated electricity importation. It is also suggested that green tax revenue be used to grant funds for CLP to buy more nuclear electricity, thereby to increase the proportion of nuclear-generated electricity in Hong Kong's total electricity demand (the current proportion is 25%),[20] so that emissions from burning environmentally harmful fuel (e.g., coal) could be further reduced.

3.3.2   Enhance the efficiency of the public transport system

The government could provide funds to, for example, the subway system and the light railway, especially; the government could give subsidies to promote franchised bus companies to use the smaller, lighter and high-technology buses, so that ticket fees could be kept at a relatively stable level or even a lower level, encouraging citizens to choose public transport rather than private cars and insuring that low-income households can afford the fees for their daily trip.

3.3.3   Promote the use of electric vehicles

There is a scheme to promote electric cars in Hong Kong. But the current set-up is not developed sufficiently to encourage the use of electric cars. For example, their operation depends heavily on the infrastructure of recharging stations, but at present there are only 21 recharging stations in Hong Kong (Lam, 2009). The green tax revenue could be used to make electric cars more convenient to use – building more recharging stations and maintenance stations, so improving the feasibility of the electric car scheme.

3.4   Political and Public Acceptance

Considering the theoretical advantages of green taxes mentioned in the introduction and their at least partial success to date in Hong Kong, it is surprising that green tax measures have not been more widely applied. However, it can be seen that the above recommendations on green tax measures would be difficult for the Hong Kong government to put into practice. Possible reasons for this are discussed below, and then some approaches to encourage acceptance of green tax in Hong Kong are suggested.

3.4.1   Obstacles for imposing green tax measures in Hong Kong

In Hong Kong, there are mainly two possible obstacles that hinder green taxes being widely used. First is the increasing gap between rich and poor. Because of the income regressive characteristic of some green taxes, poorer households pay a disproportionate share of their income in these taxes relative to the richer households. The wide income disparities in Hong Kong mean that any broadening of the tax base is open to the criticism that it redistributes the tax burden onto those least able to afford it. Second, Hong Kong's political structure can make it difficult for the government to pursue policies in the face of vested interests. In particular, functional constituencies give various groups influence in the legislature and thus over government. Thus it would be very difficult for the government to take any action that may impact on these groups' interests. As a result, approaches are necessary to be worked out to enhance the political and public acceptance of green tax in Hong Kong.

3.4.2 Building acceptance of green tax measures

It should be noted that there is already a supportive foundation, to some extent, for green tax in Hong Kong. First, public support for green taxes was proved by a public opinion survey conducted by Cullen and Simmons (2007). The survey's finding suggests that with a 7-point scale from 1 (strongly disagree) through 4 (neutral) to 7 (strongly agree), there was fairly strong support (4.75) for the proposition that the government is not doing enough to address Hong Kong's serious environmental concerns through the use of green taxes. Second, when officials from the EPD were interviewed,[21] they said that, 'Green tax measures will play a more and more important role in tackling environmental problems in the government's future environmental policies', confirming the government's support for green taxes.

In addition to the above supportive foundation, it is recommended that the following approach is taken to build acceptance further.

First, the application of green tax measures could start with tax incentives. Current tax incentives on environment-friendly vehicles and facilities should be continued, and new tax incentives could be provided to promote the use of renewable energy in Hong Kong, for example, wind power and solar energy.

Second, when introducing a new green tax, the tax could start with a low rate and with exemptions to specific types of energy. For example, as discussed in Section 3.1.2, we can exempt natural gas from CO_2 tax when the tax is first introduced, as Scandinavian countries did – they all offered some exemption provisions to the energy-intensive industries to reduce the negative impacts on international competitiveness. The tax rates then could be increased step by step, and other new green taxes could be introduced gradually over the years.

Third, relief should be provided to low-income households when introducing or increasing the tax. For example, as electricity and heating costs might increase due to the extension of excise duties and the introduction of CO_2 tax, low-income households should be provided with relief. Additionally, the recommendations on revenue use put forward in Section 3.3 could help to build acceptance.

Fourth, although not discussed in detail in this chapter, it is worth noting that the Scandinavian nations have all adopted 'environmental tax reform' (ETR) while implementing green tax measures – in simple terms, using revenue from green taxes to lower taxes on valuable economic activities such as employment or investment. Moreover, when the revenues of environmental taxes are used to reduce other distorting taxes, the economic outcome is better than if those revenues are not so distributed (Hoerner and Bosquet, 2001). Thus, the ETR might be a very good way to encourage acceptance of green taxes, and the Hong Kong government should consider adopting the reform or some elements of the reform in the future.

Finally, the government should enhance its communication with public and make the 'green' purpose of the introduction of green taxes clearer to the public. 'Public acceptance of noticeable increases in the cost of electricity, gas, public transportation and petrol would depend in large part on the government's ability to communicate that Hong Kong's continuing prosperity requires both that the revenue base be broadened and that more be done to improve the environment' (VanderWolk, 2010).

4.   CONCLUSIONS AND FURTHER STUDY

Hong Kong has developed severe air pollution problems. Additionally, the taxation system in Hong Kong is relatively old and limited, and there is a strong need to broaden the tax base. However, Hong Kong still has not adequately used the tax tool as an integral part of the government's anti-pollution strategy, and what the government has done so far does not seem to be enough. Thus after learning from more advanced experience overseas, recommendations for green tax measures concerning energy use and the transport sector in Hong Kong are finally made. Moreover, recommendations for using the revenue generated by green taxes are also provided. Finally, this chapter recommends some ways for the Hong Kong government to make green tax measures more acceptable to its citizens.

One characteristic of environmental problems is that they do not only result from the polluting activities of a single city or region and, according to the interview with officials in EPD,[22] most of air pollutants in Hong Kong come from the neighbouring Guangdong province of China. Since this chapter does not consider trans-boundary environmental issues, future study could concentrate on this issue and investigate the coordination of green tax measures between the two regions.

NOTES

[1.]   Hong Kong Observatory (2010), *Observed Climate Change in Hong Kong*, Hong Kong Special Administrative Region (HKSAR), HKSAR Government.
[2.]   EPD (2009), *A Report on the Results from the Air Quality Monitoring Network (AQMN) – 2008*, HKSAR, HKSAR Government.

3. *ibid.*
4. Census and Statistics Department (2009), *Statistical Table 030 and 193*, HKSAR, HKSAR Government.
5. OECD (2008), *Country Statistical Profiles 2008*, available from the OECD StatExtracts database, http://stats.oecd.org/Index.aspx.
6. For details see 'Final Report to the Financial Secretary by the Advisory Committee on New Broad-Based Taxes', available at: www.fstb.Gov.hk/tb/acnbt/English/finalrpt/btfinal-report.htm.
7. *South China Morning Post*, 'Tax reform, fiscal health and the proposed goods and services tax', 3 January 2007.
8. Transport Department (2010), 'Fees & Charges: Vehicle License', available at: www.td.gov.hk/en/ public_services/fees_and_charges/index.html.
9. Customs and Excise Department (2009), *Dutiable Commodities in HKSAR*, HKSAR, HKSAR Government.
10. Cheung, C.F. (2008), 'Use policies on fuel tax to lower port pollution', *South China Morning Post*, 18 June 2008. p. 2.
11. Environment-friendly petrol private cars emit about 50% less hydrocarbons (HCs) and nitrogen oxides (NO_x) and consume about 40% less fuel than conventional petrol Euro IV private cars. Owing to their higher fuel efficiency, they also emit about 40% less carbon dioxide (CO_2), a key greenhouse gas contributing to global warming.
12. EPD (2010), *Tax Incentives for Environment-friendly Petrol Private Cars*, HKSAR, HKSAR Government.
13. EPD (2010), *Tax Incentives for Environment-friendly Commercial Vehicles*, HKSAR, HKSAR Government.
14. EPD (2010), *Air – Problems and Solutions*, HKSAR: HKSAR Government.
15. EPD (2009), *Tax Concession Scheme on Environmental-Friendly Facilities*, HKSAR, HKSAR Government.
16. Currently, there are three main suppliers in Hong Kong: China Light and Power (CLP), Hong Kong Electric (HKE) and Hong Kong and China Gas (Towngas).
17. Transport Department (2009), *Hong Kong: The Facts – Transport*. HKSAR, HKSAR Government.
18. Lamma Winds on Lamma Island, Hong Kong's first commercial-scale wind power station, started operation in 2006.
19. CLP Holdings Limited (2009), 'CLP Welcomes Hong Kong SAR government's approval for an extension of nuclear electricity supply contract', 22 September, available at: www.clpgroup.com/ourcompany/news/Pages/22092009.aspx.
20. *ibid.*
21. Mr David Wong, Principal Environmental Protection Officer, EPD, was interviewed on April 21, 2010.
22. Mr David Wong, Principal Environmental Protection Officer, EPD, was interviewed on April 21, 2010.

REFERENCES

Cheung, D. (2008), 'Hong Kong: green taxes and their debate, enforcement and future', in Bronwyn Spicer, *Environmental Taxes: A Global Perspective*. US: BNA International Inc., pp. 64–9.

Cullen, R. and Simmons, R.S. (2008), 'Tax Reform and democratic reform in Hong Kong: what do the people think?', *The British Tax Review*, **6**, 667–90.

Derwent, R.G., Stevenson, D.S., Doherty, R.M., *et al.* (2005). 'The contribution from shipping emissions to air quality and acid deposition in Europe', *Ambio.*, **34**(1), 54–9.

Hoerner, J.A. and Bosquet, B. (2001), *Environmental Tax Reform: The European Experience*, Washington, DC, Centre for a Sustainable Economy.

Lam, T. (2009), Hong Kong sets up free charging stations for electric cars, *CNN-HK*, 10 November, available at: www.cnngo.com/hong-kong/none/hong-kong-sets-free-charging-stations- electric-cars-153750#ixzz0Zm4TP6QS.

Pearson, M. and Smith, S. (1992), *The European Carbon Tax: An Assessment of the European Commission's Proposals*, London, Institute for Fiscal Studies.

VanderWolk, J. (2010), 'Green tax measures for Hong Kong: a policy proposal', presented at the 2nd International Conference of The Taxation Law Research Programme, Hong Kong University, Hong Kong. January 2010.

Vollebergn, R.J. (2008), 'Lessons from the Polder: energy tax design in the Netherlands from a climate change perspective', *Ecological Economics*, **64**(3), 660–72.

FURTHER READING

Cheung, D. (2010), 'New tax measures in the 2010–11 budget – their analysis and implications', *News Update – ACCA Hong Kong's Magazine for Students*, Summer, pp. 12–18.

Hong Kong Institute of Certified Public Accountants (HKICPA) (2007), *Broadening Hong Kong's Tax Base*, Hong Kong, HKICPA.

Hong Kong Observatory (2003), 'Global warming – the Hong Kong connection', available at: www.hko.gov.hk/wxinfo/news/2003/pre0801e.htm.

Leverett, B., Hopkinson, L., Loh, C., *et al.* (2007), *Hong Kong's Environmental Policy in a Ten Year Stall 1997–2007*, Hong Kong, Civic Exchange.

OECD (1989), *Economic Instruments for Environmental Protection*, Paris, OECD.

OECD (2001), *Environmentally Related Taxes in OECD Countries: Issues and Strategies*, Paris, OECD.

Sin, D. (2009), 'Tax-break plan fails to put more green cars on the road – few take up cost-saving scheme to dump polluting vehicles', *South China Morning Post*, 2 February, p. 2.

Speck, S. (2007), 'Overview of environmental tax reforms in EU member states, in *Competitiveness Effects of Environmental Tax Reforms*, Final Report to European Commission, DG Research and DG Taxation and Customs Union.

Speck, S. and Andersen, M.S. (2006), 'Environmental tax reform and competitiveness', in Alberto Cavaliere, Janet Milne, Kurt Deketelaere, *et al.*, *Critical Issues in Environmental Taxation – International and Comparative Perspectives, Volume III*, Oxford University Press, USA, pp. 285–97.

Speck, S., Andersen, M.S., Nielsen, H., *et al.* (2006), *The Use of Economic Instruments in Nordic and Baltic Environmental Policy 2001–2005*, Denmark, Aarhus, National Environmental Research Institute.

Speck, S., Mcnicholas, J. and Markovic, M. (2004), 'National experiences with pollution taxes: what have we learned?, in Janet Milne, Kurt Deketelaere, Larry Kreiser*, et al.*, *Critical Issues in Environmental Taxation – International and Comparative Perspectives, Volume I*, Oxford University Press, USA, pp. 269–88.

11. Prospects of South African vehicle emissions tax reducing CO_2 emissions

Rudie Nel and Gerhard Nienaber

INTRODUCTION

The global community is facing immense challenges in dealing with the environmental issues brought about by pollution and the concomitant ecological degradation which is not confined within geographical boundaries – actions on climate change are therefore required across all countries (Anjum 2008:1).

Climate change is a major cause of global warming, and is one of the negative results of pollution and greenhouse gas emissions. Based on the figures released by the World Resources Institute (2000), CO_2 emissions represent 77 per cent of greenhouse gases and the transport sector contributes 13.5 per cent to the total CO_2 emissions. In a bid to address the transport sector's increasing CO_2 emissions, vehicle green taxes have been introduced by the governments of various countries. The purpose of these vehicle green taxes is to serve as a deterrent to people who do not act in the best interest of the environment. This is done by attempting to influence either consumers' driving habits (for example, fuel taxes) and/or their purchasing decisions (encouraging the acquisition of lower CO_2-emitting or better fuel-economy vehicles).

The concept of vehicle green taxes is also not entirely new in South Africa as transport levies have existed for years. As one aspect of fiscal reform the South African government introduced a vehicle emissions tax with effect from 1 September 2010 (SARS 2010). The purpose of the vehicle emissions tax is to attempt to reduce CO_2 emissions by influencing consumer purchasing decisions (encouraging the purchase of lower CO_2-emitting vehicles).

However, the prospects for the vehicle emissions tax achieving its purpose in South Africa could be affected by the following factors (Nel 2009:4).

- **The design of the vehicle emissions tax.** This refers to the stage at which the vehicle green tax is levied (purchase, ownership or usage taxes). According to Hayashi *et al.* (2001:124), it is important to have a spread of taxes across all three stages. Their study also suggests that levying taxes in certain stages might be more effective in reducing CO_2 emissions than in other stages.
- **Legislation.** According to Nieuwoudt (2001:45), legislation would influence fiscal policy and planning as well as the effectiveness of the tax base or the instruments used. Legislation is therefore important in that it could be used as a means of enforcement and of providing possible incentives.
- **Consumer attitudes.** Consumers do not always fully appreciate the impact of their actions on the environment (Kunert and Hartmut 2007:315). However, this is a limitation in the market that could be avoided if the fiscal reform policy did not target only consumers in an attempt to address environmental concerns.

The international perspective conveyed in literature reviewed shows that more comprehensive studies on fiscal reform involving vehicle green taxes have been conducted in developed countries. However, the principle of environmental fiscal reform is considered to be the same in developed and developing countries and the implementation thereof is not limited to developed countries alone (Speck 2008:1). Due to the lack of available literature on vehicle green taxes in developing countries literature from three developed countries (Japan, the USA and EU countries) were considered to identify possible weaknesses in, and alternatives to, the South African vehicle emissions tax.

1 NEED FOR AND OBJECTIVE OF THE STUDY

The purpose of the vehicle emissions tax in South Africa is to reduce CO_2 emissions. The objectives of this chapter are to evaluate:

- the prospects of the vehicle emissions tax achieving its purpose; and
- the deductibility of the vehicle emissions tax in terms of the South African Income Tax Act 58 of 1962 ['the Act'].

The prospects will be evaluated according to possible weaknesses in the design of, and alternatives for, the vehicle emissions tax. The design will be evaluated based on a study performed by Hayashi *et al.* (2001) that concluded on the impact purchase, ownership and usage taxes had on reducing CO_2 emissions. Alternatives and weaknesses will be identified by considering the current purchase, ownership and usage taxes levied on vehicles in South Africa. A comparative study between similar taxes levied in EU countries and the USA is undertaken to evaluate whether the current taxes levied in South Africa can be expanded or possible new taxes/levies introduced to address CO_2 emissions.

Deductibility in terms of the Act will be evaluated, as legislation would influence fiscal policy and planning as well as the effectiveness of the tax base or instruments used (Nieuwoudt 2001:45). Provision of the Act will be considered to evaluate whether a deduction will be allowed if the vehicle emissions tax is incurred.

2   VALUE OF THE RESEARCH

The initial proposal to incorporate CO_2 emissions as an assessment base for levying taxes on certain vehicles in 2009 was met with a mixture of outrage and relief by consumers and the local motor industry in South Africa (Philander 2007). Some people might recognise the need for reform as result of their carbon footprint. The local motor industry has, however, heavily criticised the proposal having regards for the impact such tax could have on consumers as well as the motor industry in the current economic situation in South Africa.

This chapter wishes proactively to identify certain weaknesses in, and alternatives for, the vehicle emissions tax. The provisions of the Act will be considered in order to identify sections which might have to be amended as it could possibly affect the prospects of the vehicle emissions tax achieving its purpose of reducing CO_2 emissions. The chapter could therefore facilitate further discussions regarding the vehicle emissions tax and could serve as a basis for further studies regarding other possible vehicle green taxes in South Africa in the future.

3 COMPARATIVE STUDY

3.1 Purchase Taxes

Purchase taxes in South Africa include non-recurrent value added tax [VAT], registration fees and *ad valorem* excise duties. The vehicle emissions tax will be classified under this category as it would be a tax incurred on initial purchase of the vehicle and will not be recurrent in nature (which might be the case with ownership or usage taxes).

Hayashi *et al.* (2001:135–8) suggest that purchase taxes are not particularly effective in reducing CO$_2$ by influencing either consumers' decisions on purchasing vehicles or their driving patterns.

The different purchase taxes currently levied in South Africa (VAT, registration fees, *ad valorem* customs and excise duties and the vehicle emissions tax) were considered and compared to similar taxes levied in EU countries and the USA in order to identify whether these taxes could be expanded and possible alternatives for the vehicle emissions tax (the results of this comparison are summarised in Table 11.3).

3.1.1 VAT
In South Africa, VAT is an indirect tax which is currently levied at 14 per cent on the value of taxable supplies. For VAT purposes, the value of a vehicle would normally refer to its selling price (excluding VAT) and does not incorporate any environmental criteria such as CO$_2$ emissions.

The VAT levied in South Africa is also lower than that levied in 26 of the 27 EU countries (Kunert and Hartmut 2007:307). Sales tax levied in the USA, which is also an indirect tax, is levied differently in the different states, the highest being 9.36 per cent in Tennessee (Tax Foundation 2008).

The VAT currently levied in South Africa is comparatively lower than that levied in the majority of the EU countries and higher than the sales taxes levied in the USA. Keeping in mind that other taxes are levied in the USA (for example, 'gas-guzzler taxes' – see section 3.1.4) which might justify lower sales taxes.

3.1.2 Registration fees
In addition to VAT, non-recurrent registration fees are levied in all nine South African provinces (Nel 2009:42). In all the provinces, the current registration and licensing fees are levied according to the tare weight (which represents the unloaded weight of the vehicle), without taking into account any environmental considerations such as CO$_2$ emissions.

Registration fees are levied in 18 of the EU countries, representing a non-recurrent administrative fee of up to €170 for a standard-sized vehicle

(Kunert and Hartmut 2007:307). Based on an exchange rate of R10.96 for €1 as at 30 June 2009 (South African Reserve Bank 2009), this could amount to R1863 payable on a standard-sized vehicle at registration (Kunert and Hartmut 2007:307).

Registration fees levied in the USA differ from state to state. They may be a flat fee or one based on the weight, age or value of the car and are recurrent in nature. The average annual registration fee for the USA is $185.38 (Idaho Transportation Department 2008:2). Based on an exchange rate of R7.77 for US$1 as at 30 June 2009 (South African Reserve Bank 2009), this could amount to a registration fee of R1441.

The registration fee levied in Gauteng is the highest of those in all nine South African provinces, amounting to R82 (Gauteng (South Africa) 2009). However, it is comparatively lower than the fees levied in the EU countries and the average fee in the USA.

3.1.3   *Ad valorem* customs and excise duties

Ad valorem excise duties currently levied in South Africa are based solely on price and do not incorporate any environmental criteria (SARS 2009:11). Currently *ad valorem* excise duties levied on vehicles in South Africa are solely based on the retail price and do not incorporate any environmental assessment base (see Table 11.1)

Table 11.1 Ad valorem *excise duty tax rates on motor vehicles*

Retail price (ZAR)	Current rate (%)	Retail price (ZAR)	Current rate (%)
100 000	1.7	500 000	11.3
150 000	2.9	600 000	13.7
200 000	4.1	800 000	18.5
300 000	6.5	864 500 or more	20.0
400 000	8.9	–	–

Source: SARS Budget Tax Proposals (2009:11).

The registration tax levied in 19 of the EU countries (Kunert and Hartmut 2007:307) is similar to the *ad valorem* taxes levied in South Africa. However, the former is recurrent and could be equivalent of R164 412 non-recurrent for a standard-sized vehicle (Nel 2009:26). In South Africa a retail price of R500 000 would result in *ad valorem* (Table 11.1) of R56 500 (R500 000 ×

11.3 per cent) which is comparatively lower than the registration fees levied in EU countries.

3.1.4 Vehicle emissions tax
Vehicle emissions tax will be levied at R75 per gram per kilometre (g/km) of CO_2 emissions which exceed 120g/km (SARS 2010:192) as indicated in Table 11.2.

Table 11.2 Vehicle emissions tax example of tax per vehicle and tax incidence

Average CO_2 emissions (g/km)	CO_2 emissions above 120 g/km	Vehicle emissions tax (ZAR)	Average price (ZAR)	Average tax rate (%)
120 or less	–	–	170 000	–
170	50	3750	166 000	2.3
200	80	6000	293 000	2.0
320	200	15 000	551 000	2.7
370	250	18 750	947 000	2.0
410	290	21 750	606 000	3.6

Source: SARS (2010:192).

In principle the vehicle emissions tax in South Africa is similar to the 'gas-guzzler taxes' in the USA. Both are aimed at increasing the cost of vehicles with higher fuel consumption (or higher CO_2 emissions), with a view to curbing the demand for such vehicles. The study by Greene *et al.* (2005:762) showed that USA 'gas-guzzler' taxes were effective in increasing more efficient fuel consumption, thereby lowering CO_2 emission, which suggests that the vehicle emissions tax might achieve its purpose of reducing carbon emission in South Africa. In the USA, the 'gas-guzzler taxes' range between $1000 and $7700 (Internal Revenue Services 2005). Based on an exchange rate of R7.77 for US$1 as at 30 June 2009 (South African Reserve Bank 2009), this could amount to an equivalent of up to R59 872.

According to the South African Revenue Service (SARS 2010:192), the average vehicle emissions tax in South Africa would be R4350 (SARS 2010:192), which is lower than the theoretical maximum 'gas-guzzler' tax of R59 872 in the USA. Both these taxes, however, result in adherence to the principle of the 'polluter pays', as vehicles with higher CO_2 emissions would be taxed at higher rates than vehicles with lower CO_2 emissions.

Table 11.3 Comparative table – vehicle purchase taxes

Stage	Vehicle purchase taxes
Effect on CO_2 emissions	Not particularly effective in reducing CO_2 emissions by influencing the decisions of consumers regarding their vehicle purchases and/or driving patterns (Hayashi *et al.* 2001:135–8).
EU countries	VAT levied at rates between 7.6% and 25% in 27 countries, with Sweden being the only country where only VAT is levied on initial purchase (Kunert and Hartmut 2007:307).
	Registration taxes levied in 19 countries (of which only 8 countries include ecological factors when assessing their taxes).
USA	No VAT levied, but in some states non-refundable sales tax is levied at rates ranging between 9.36% and 4.38% (TaxFoundation 2008).
	'Gas-guzzler' taxes levied which range between $1000 and $7700, depending on the fuel economy of the vehicle (Internal Revenue Services 2005).
South Africa	VAT levied at 14%.
	Ad valorem duty levied based solely on selling price of vehicle. (SARS 2009:12).
	Vehicle emissions tax, which is to similar 'gas-guzzler' tax levied in the USA and registration fees levied in EU countries. Currently the only purchase tax in South Africa which incorporates CO_2 emissions as environmental concern.

Source: Compiled based on the literature review performed in the preparation of this chapter.

3.2 Ownership Taxes

Ownership taxes in South Africa include annual licensing fees. These taxes are recurrent in nature but not levied in proportion to usage. In South Africa, annual licensing fees are levied in all nine provinces (Nel 2009:46). In each province, the levy is based on the tare weight (which represents the unloaded weight of the vehicle) without taking into account any environmental considerations such as CO_2 emissions. For a standard-sized passenger vehicle, with a tare weight between 1251 kg and 1500 kg, the highest annual licensing fees of R411 are payable in the Western Cape (2009:7).

The results of the study performed by Hayashi *et al.* (2001:135–8) suggest that increases in ownership taxes showed a minimal effect on the reduction of CO_2 emissions unless the ownership tax rate is set in proportion to fuel efficiency or CO_2 emissions. Furthermore increasing ownership taxes for specific classes of vehicles could also result in a shift to another class of vehicle. This approach could be effective in reducing CO_2 emissions if the ownership taxes on fuel-efficient vehicles or lower CO_2-emitting vehicles were reduced to encourage their acquisition.

The vehicle taxes levied in EU countries are recurrent (Kunert and Hartmut 2007:307) and similar to the annual licensing fees levied in South Africa. For a standard-sized vehicle, the annual vehicle tax amounts to up to €600 (Kunert and Hartmut 2007:308). Based on an exchange rate of R10.96 for €1 as at 30 June 2009 (South African Reserve Bank 2009), this could amount to R6576 per annum.

Registration fees levied in the USA vary from state to state. They may be in the form of a flat fee or may be based on a car's weight, age or value and are recurrent. In certain states, annual safety inspections are also compulsory, and according to the New York Department of Motor Vehicles (2009) such inspections can cost up to $10.

Table 11.4 Comparative table – vehicle ownership taxes

Stage	Vehicle ownership taxes
Effect on CO$_2$ emissions	Would have a minimal effect on the reduction of CO_2 emissions unless the ownership tax rate was set in proportion to fuel efficiency/CO_2 emissions.
	Technology aimed at reducing CO_2 emissions is important (Hayashi *et al.* 2001:138)

Stage	Vehicle ownership taxes
EU countries	Recurrent annual vehicle tax levied in 24 countries which could amount to €600.
	In addition insurance taxes and para-fiscal charges on insurance premiums levied in certain countries.
	Lower fuel consumption and modern exhaust systems honoured by the ownership tax schemes of 11 countries.
USA	Registration fees are levied in all states and the average annual registration fee is $185.38. Highest annual registration fees are $941.78 (Idaho Transportation Department 2008:2).
	Annual safety inspection fees and emissions ('smog') fees also levied in some states.
South Africa	Registration fees levied in all nine provinces.
	Annual licensing fees levied in all nine provinces based solely on the tare weight (see section 3.2).
	None of the ownership taxes considered incorporates CO_2 emissions as environmental concern.

Source: Compiled based on the literature review performed in the preparation of this chapter.

Usage taxes are directly linked to the use of a vehicle and will affect the day-to-day decisions of consumers with regard to the vehicles. Transport levies represent the most significant usage tax levied in South Africa and consists of different components, as indicated in Table 11.5.

According to Hayashi *et al.* (2001:138), usage taxes (which include fuel levies) are the most effective fiscal instrument that could be used in reducing CO_2 emissions.

Table 11.5 Transport fuel levies in South Africa

Tax year	2008/09		2009/10		2010/11	
Description	Petrol	Diesel	Petrol	Diesel	Petrol	Diesel
General fuel levy (ZAR)	127.00	111.00	150.00	135.00	167.50	152.50
Road Accident Fund levy (ZAR)	46.50	46.50	64.00	64.00	72.00	72.00
Customs and excise levy (ZAR)	4.00	4.00	4.00	4.00	4.00	4.00
Illuminating paraffin marker (ZAR)	–	0.01	–	0.01	–	0.01
Total (ZAR)	177.50	161.51	218.00	203.01	243.50	228.51
Pump price: Gauteng (ZAR)	750.00	732.30	43.00	649.35	785.00	701.85
Taxes % of pump price	23.7%	22.1%	33.9%	31.3%	31.6%	32.8%

Source: 2010 Budget Review (SARS 2010:81).

It is clear that, based on the budget, increases are budgeted for all the components of transport levies except for the customs and excise levy, up to the end of the 2010/11 tax year. According to SARS (2009:15), because of the increasing use of diesel in passenger vehicles in South Africa, the aim is to equalise, over time, the general fuel levy on diesel and petrol.

Petroleum taxes are levied in all of the 27 EU countries. As a percentage of the consumer prices, these taxes on petrol range between 31 per cent and 52 per cent and on diesel between 26 per cent and 45 per cent (Kunert and Hartmut 2007:308). Compared with the percentage fuel taxes levied in the EU countries in 2007 (Kunert and Hartmut 2007), transport levies on petrol and diesel in South Africa for 2007/08 are lower than in all 27 EU countries (Nel 2009:49).

Fuel taxes have also been implemented in the USA. Compared with the percentage fuel taxes levied in the USA in 2008 (Energy Information Administration 2009), transport levies in South Africa for 2007/2008 are slightly higher for both petrol and diesel (Nel 2009:49). Although it is slightly higher in South Africa the fact that a mixture of vehicle green taxes, including the 'gas-guzzler' taxes, have been introduced in the USA might justify lower fuel taxes in the USA.

Table 11.6 Comparative table – vehicle usage taxes

Stage	Usages taxes
Effect on CO_2 emissions	Could result in highest possible reduction in CO_2 emissions – because usage taxes are directly linked to vehicle usage and will therefore affect the day-to-day decisions. Most of the reduction in CO_2 emissions as result of the decrease in driving distance (Hayashi *et al.* 2001:135).
EU countries	Petroleum taxes are levied in all 27 countries. As percentage of the consumer prices these taxes range on petrol between 31% and 52% and diesel between 26% and 45%.
	In addition to the petroleum taxes, VAT is also levied on both petrol and diesel in all of the 27 countries and ranges (Kunert and Hartmut 2007:308).
USA	Fuel taxes are levied in 50 states. The average fuel taxes, as a percentage of the retail price, are 20% on gasoline and 21% on diesel (Nel 2009:37).
	In addition, sales taxes on both gasoline and diesel are levied in 11 states (Williams 2002:7).
South Africa	Fuel taxes for the 2008/09 tax year, as a percentage of the retail price, are 23.7% on petrol and 22.1% on diesel (see section 3.3).
	No VAT is levied on petrol and diesel in South Africa.

Source: Compiled based on the literature review performed in the preparation of this chapter.

4 POSSIBLE WEAKNESSES IN THE VEHICLE EMISSIONS TAX

Although the vehicle emissions tax incorporates CO_2 emissions as environmental criteria, which is a step in the right direction, a few weaknesses were identified. These might affect the prospects for the vehicle emissions tax achieving its goal of reducing CO_2 emissions. The weaknesses relate, in principle, to the overall design of the vehicle emissions tax and are as follows.

4.1 Focus on Consumers

The vehicle emissions tax is aimed at consumers in the transport sector. The additional cost to consumers could have a negative effect on their attitude towards these taxes. Consumers might perceive these taxes simply as an income-generating exercise by government and may consequently not fully value the benefit of reducing CO_2 emissions (Kunert and Hartmut 2007:315).

Even if consumers did value the benefit of reducing CO_2 emissions, it would still have to be considered whether or not this would influence consumers' choices and behaviours in reducing CO_2 emissions. Studies performed in other countries have concluded that consumers' choices between higher or lower fuel economy vehicles were not noted as a significant contributing factor in improving fuel economy (Greene *et al.* 2005:759; Kunert and Hartmut 2007:315). These findings support the fact that focusing only on consumers might not be the most effective way to attempt to reduce CO_2 emissions.

The focus should rather be shifted from targeting consumers to providing incentives for vehicle manufacturers to invest in fuel economy technology (i.e. fuel standards that would result in the best possible fuel consumption and the lowest possible CO_2 emissions). Implementing a 'feebate' policy (see section 5.1) is a possible alternative which could facilitate shifting the focus away from consumers

4.2 Focus on New Vehicles

The focus of the vehicle emissions tax is on new vehicles only, and no policies on existing used vehicles have yet been proposed. There is an argument favouring the view that older vehicles, in most cases, emit more gases than newer vehicles as a result of advances in fuel technologies (Atson and Smith 2007). Therefore, environmental fiscal reform with regard to older vehicles should also be considered, as focusing only on new vehicles could result in an increase in sales of older (second-hand) vehicles on which vehicle emissions tax is not levied.

4.3 Current Status of Motor Industry

There could be a risk that the vehicle emissions tax results in decreased revenue for the motor industry and an increase in the informal market for second-hand vehicles. If the motor industry loses revenue it would add to the existing pressure of maintaining sales in the current economic climate. This, in turn, could affect international competitiveness and could also result in job losses if sales volumes decreased significantly. The concern is therefore that the implementation of the vehicle emissions tax would increase the pressure on the motor industry and should have been postponed, possibly until the motor industry is in a healthier position (Donnelly 2009).

Implementing a 'feebate' policy (see section 5.1) could possibly provide some financial relief to vehicle manufacturers in the motor industry if incentives are introduced.

4.4 No Distinction between Petrol- and Diesel-driven Vehicles

During the past few years up until 2009/10, as in the EU countries, the total fuel taxes on diesel were lower than those on petrol (see Table 11.5). It therefore appears that, although diesel is already taxed at a lower rate, the improved fuel consumption of diesel-driven vehicles is of inherent benefit in levying fuel taxes.

Kunert and Hartmut (2007:314) commented in their European study that, as diesel-driven vehicles have inherently lower fuel consumption, this could imply that, in levying fuel tax, the CO_2 emissions resulting from diesel consumption might in effect already be taxed at a lower rate than petrol. While there is an argument in favour of taxing diesel at a lower rate in the public sector (in order to promote the use of public transport by reducing costs) this preferential treatment in the private sector might not be justified. However, if the proposed fuel taxes during 2010/11 (see Table 11.5) are implemented diesel vehicles will be taxed at a higher rate than petrol which will start in addressing this weakness in South Africa.

5   POSSIBLE ALTERNATIVES TO THE VEHICLE EMISSIONS TAX

Based on the literature review carried out in preparing this chapter, the following are considered alternatives for expanding on the vehicle emissions tax and improving the prospects for it achieving its purpose:

- implementing a 'feebate' policy and investing in fuel technology; and/or
- increasing transport levies (for example, fuel levies).

5.1 A 'Feebate' Policy and Investing in Fuel Technologies

The introduction of the vehicle emissions tax (purchase taxes) in South Africa could result in vehicles being driven for longer periods of time (Hayashi *et al.* 2001:135–8). For this reason, investment in technology ensuring that new vehicles create the lowest possible CO$_2$ emissions could be beneficial as these vehicles might be driven for longer.

A 'feebate' policy would involve both additional taxes and incentives. The additional taxes will discourage higher fuel consumption or CO$_2$ emissions and incentives will encourage lower fuel consumption and CO$_2$ emissions. From the results of the study performed in the USA by Greene *et al.* (2005:758), it is clear that a 'feebate' policy could be the most effective in reducing fuel consumption (which could also indirectly decrease CO$_2$ emissions). Greene *et al.* (2005:758–9) argued the merit of a 'feebate' policy and the importance of manufacturers' adoption of fuel economy technologies, which accounted for about 90 per cent of the overall increase in fuel economy. Peters *et al.* (2008:1364) suggest that the public acceptance of a 'feebate' policy in Europe is comparatively high and that when the changes were considered within a disaggregated car fleet a reduction in CO$_2$ emissions prevailed.

The 'feebate' policy should preferably also be revenue-neutral as far as government is concerned. This means that all the additional taxes collected by government would be allocated as incentives. If the 'feebate' policy were to be transparent and revenue-neutral, it could result in increased taxpayer confidence in the policy, as it would not be perceived as simply being an income-generating exercise from government (Greene *et al.* 2005:757).

The incentives could be provided to either consumers or vehicle manufacturers. Providing incentives to consumers could potentially not be as effective, as consumers might not fully value the benefit of fuel economy and the impact of CO$_2$ emissions (Greene *et al.* 2005:758; Kunert and Hartmut 2007:315).

Government could therefore consider implementing incentives for automobile manufacturers to encourage the development of fuel economy technologies to improve fuel consumption and reduce CO$_2$ emissions. The vehicle emissions tax recovered could then be earmarked to fund such incentives.

5.2   Increasing Fuel Levies

Fuel levies would be classified as usage dependant taxes which could be the most effective in reducing CO_2 emissions (Hayashi *et al.* 2001:135).

In the Budget Tax Proposal, SARS confirmed the importance of maintaining a strong price signal to limit fuel consumption, road congestion and environmental impact, and therefore proposed increasing the general fuel levy on petrol and diesel by 23 and 24 cents per litre respectively from 1 April 2009 (SARS 2009:15). The impact of further increases as an alternative for reducing CO_2 emissions should, however, be considered carefully.

From a socio-economic perspective, fiscal reform in South Africa should ensure that the environmental instruments would be pro-poor wherever possible, or at least should not place an unreasonable burden on lower-income groups. In the current economic climate, consumers are already struggling with high interest rates and petrol and diesel prices that have increased significantly over the past few years. This means that further increases in fuel levies may not be the most feasible alternative for reducing CO_2 emissions.

6   DEDUCTIBILITY IN TERMS OF THE SOUTH AFRICAN INCOME TAX ACT

The purpose of the vehicle emissions tax is to discourage the purchase of vehicles that emit higher CO_2 emissions. If the taxpayer could obtain a tax benefit (for example, in the form of a tax deduction), this could mitigate the effect of the vehicle emissions tax to act as a deterrent. According to Nieuwoudt (2001:45), legislation would influence fiscal policy and planning as well as the effectiveness of the tax base or instruments used. The following is apparent, based on the results of this study:

- the current provisions of the Act do allow for a deduction for the vehicle emissions tax to certain categories of taxpayers; and
- not all taxpayers would be allowed tax deductions, so certain taxpayers could be in a more advantageous position than others (although the benefits might be marginal if considered quantitatively).

7 CONCLUSION

7.1 Prospects of the Vehicle Emissions Tax Achieving its Purpose

The South African vehicle emissions tax can be classified as a purchase tax (see section 3.1). Hayashi *et al.* (2001:135–8) suggested that purchase taxes, which includes the vehicle emissions tax, were not particularly effective in reducing CO_2 emissions by influencing consumers' decisions relating to purchasing and/or driving patterns. An increase in purchase taxes is likely to result in longer lifetimes over which vehicles are used. If vehicles are used for longer periods the CO_2 emissions could be reduced by improving the fuel economy technology of more up-to-date vehicles. Consumers should then be encouraged to buy later models and to scrap older ones. The South African National Treasury (2006:70) included comments on providing increased scrapping rates for older vehicles. Based on information in the study performed by Hayashi *et al.* the design of the vehicle emissions tax as purchase tax could result in it not being particularly effective in reducing CO_2 emissions.

The fact that similar taxes have been implemented in EU countries and the USA mitigates any risks associated with unilateral implementation (Ashiabor 2005:300). Based on comparative study performed with regards to purchase taxes (see Table 11.3) it was noted that some purchase taxes introduced in EU countries and the USA incorporate environmental concerns in their assessment bases. In South Africa the vehicle emissions tax is currently the only direct purchase tax which takes into account CO_2 emissions. The purchase taxes considered in this chapter were also comparatively lower than the purchase taxes in EU countries and the USA, which might indicate possible room for alternatives in expanding vehicle green taxes.

The prospects of the vehicle emissions tax achieving its purpose could also be negatively affected by the focus on consumers. This concern could, however, be addressed through the implementation of a 'feebate' policy (see section 5.1) which might be even more effective in reducing CO_2 emissions. A 'feebate' policy also has the added benefit of providing continuous incentives for vehicle manufacturers to invest in fuel economy technology.

7.2 Deductibility of the Vehicle Emissions Tax in Terms of the Act

The purpose of the vehicle emissions tax is to affect consumer purchasing decisions so that they are likely to result in reduced CO_2 emissions. The impact of the emissions tax could be neutralised if the taxpayers were entitled to deduct the additional costs incurred for tax purposes. For this reason, due consideration should be given to possible amendments to section 23 of the Act to prohibit the deduction of the vehicle emissions tax if it were to be incurred.

7.3 Final Comments

It is not only the government's responsibility to address environmental concerns, but also that of every citizen. However, because citizens (as consumers) are not always fully aware of their 'carbon footprint', it would seem that the government has no alternative but to take the necessary steps in fiscal reform. If the initiative in proposing the vehicle emissions tax were to succeed only in making consumers more aware of their 'carbon footprint' it might have already achieved its purpose. In creating awareness it could result in consumers taking responsibility for their actions and possibly changing their behaviour and choices in order to be more environment-friendly.

At the end of the day the most effective fiscal reform initiative in reducing CO_2 emissions and conserving the environment might not be one that forces people to contribute, but rather one which encourages people to contribute and then rewards them if they do (Nel 2009:76). With the vehicle emissions tax initiative, as with any new fiscal reform initiative, a few 'teething problems' could be expected which could be resolved by public participation and discussions among the different stakeholders (government, taxpayers and the motor industry).

REFERENCES

Anjum, Nabilah (2008), 'Prospect of green-taxes in developing countries', *Business & Finance Review*, 28 April.
Ashiabor, Hope (2005), 'Fostering the development of renewable energy through emissions tax and other instruments', *IBFD Bulletin*, July, 295.
Atson, L. and C. Smith (2007), 'We'll toyi-toyi with our 4x4s', available at: www.fin24.com/articles/default/display_article.aspx?ArticleId=1518–1796_2232538 (accessed 3 May 2008).
Donnelly, Lynley (2009), 'For the good of green', available at: www.mg.co.za/printformat/single/2009-03-02-for-the-good-of-green (accessed 2 March 2009).
Energy Information Administration (2009), 'What we pay for in a gallon', available at: http://tonto.eia.doe.gov/oog/info/gdu/gasdiesel.asp (accessed 18 June 2009).
Gauteng (South Africa) (2009), 'Notice 692 of 2009', *Provincial Gazette Extraordinary*, **52**, 7.
Greene, D. L., P.D. Patterson, M. Singh, *et al.* (2005), 'Feebates, rebates and gas-guzzler taxes: a study of incentives for increased fuel economy', *Energy Policy*, **33**, 757–75.

Hayashi, Y., H. Kato and R.T. Val (2001), 'A model system for the assessment of the effects of vehicle and fuel emissions tax on carbon dioxide emissions', Transportation Research Part D6, 2001, pp. 123–39.

Idaho Transportation Department (2008), 'State-by-state comparison of annual motor vehicle registration fees and fuel taxes', available at: http://itd.idaho.gov/econ/MiscReports/ComparisonofAnnual MotorVehicleOperatingCosts2008.pdf (accessed 19 June 2009).

Internal Revenue Services (2005), 'Excise tax forms and publications – Form 6197', available at: www.irs.gov/pub/irs-pdf/f6197.pdf (accessed 22 June 2009).

Kunert, U. and K. Hartmut (2007), 'The diverse structures of passenger car taxation in Europe and the EU Commissions proposal for reform', *Transport Policy*, **14**, 306–16.

Nel, Rudie (2009), 'Proposed vehicle green taxes in South Africa: What are the prospects of it achieving its purpose?', Magister taxation thesis, South Africa, University of Pretoria.

New York Department of Motor Vehicles (2009), 'Vehicle safety, inspection, repairs and dealers', available at: www.nysdmv.com/vehsafe.htm (accessed 19 June 2009).

Nieuwoudt, Margaret J. (2001), 'Green charges or taxes and related income tax and value-added tax issues', *SA Journal of Accounting Research*, **15**(1), 45–63.

Peters, A., M.G. Mueller, R. de Haan, *et al.* (2008), 'Feebates promoting energy-efficient cars: design options to address more consumers and possible counteracting effects', *Energy Policy*, **36**, 1355–65.

Philander, Hailey (2007), 'Green car tax: SA sees red', available at: www.wheels24.co.za/News/General_News/Green-car-tax-SA-sees-red-20070524 (accessed 3 May 2008).

SARS, see South African Revenue Service.

South Africa (2008), Income Tax Act, No. 58 of 1962. *SAICA Legislation book 2007/2008*, Durban, Lexis Nexis Butterworths.

South African National Treasury (2006), 'A framework for considering market-based instrument to support environmental fiscal reform in South Africa'. Pretoria, National Treasury.

South African Reserve Bank (2009), 'Current market rates', available at: www.resbank.co.za/sarbdata/rates/rates.asp?type=cmr (accessed 9 July 2009).

South African Revenue Service (2009), 'Budget Tax Proposal 2009/10', available at: www.sars.gov.za (accessed 2 March 2009).

South African Revenue Service (2010), '2010 Budget Review', available at: www.sars.gov.za (accessed 10 May 2009).

Speck, Stefan (2008), 'Possibilities of environmental fiscal reform in developing countries', City for Bank Indonesia Publications, available at: www.bi.go.id/NR/rdonlyres/57BF6537–1BEA-4D42-B476–209DC56F11DA/14255/StefanSpeckdoc.pdf (accessed 15 June 2009).

Tax Foundation (2008), 'Sales tax map', available at: www.taxfoundation.org/UserFiles/Image/Blog/salestaxmap.jpg (accessed 15 June 2009).

Western Cape (South Africa) (2003), 'Notice 40 of 2003', *Western Cape Provincial Gazette*, 5980, 7 February.

Williams, John (2002), 'Survey of state and local gasoline taxes', Minnesota House of Representatives Research Department: Information Brief, available at: www.house.leg.state.mn.us/hrd/pubs/gastax.pdf (accessed 13 July 2009).

World Resources Institute (2000), 'World greenhouse gas emissions flow chart', available at: www.wri.org/chart/world-greenhouse-gas-emissions-flow-chart (accessed 25 April 2009).

12. Australian tax reform for sustainable transportation

Prafula Pearce

INTRODUCTION

This chapter examines whether there is a harmonious relationship between the transportation and tax policy in Australia and whether a change in tax policy is required to promote the use of more fuel-efficient vehicles and vehicles using cleaner fuels, a reduction in the use of vehicles and a reduction in congestion.

In this chapter a case is made for the introduction of tax measures in Australia that affect sustainable energy use in the transport sector, particularly passenger vehicles in the road transport industry. The tax should relate to the power and weight of the vehicle and its use and not where the vehicle is manufactured. A new way of thinking is required as the world resource of liquid fuel is being depleted. It takes millions of years for our planet to produce liquid fuel, but it takes an instant to burn it, and once burnt, it is irrecoverable. Therefore the Australian government should take responsibility and implement appropriate taxation policies to promote the efficient movement of people and goods with the least consumption of liquid oil.

THE LIQUID FUEL PROBLEM

Australia's energy management policy needs to focus on the liquid fuel problem, and in particular the passenger vehicles within the road transport industry, being the greatest consumer of liquid oil. Australia is the world's ninth largest energy producer accounting for around 2.4 per cent of world's energy production. It has 38.2 per cent of the total world resource of uranium; 18.5 per cent of the total world resource of coal; 1.4 per cent of the total world resource of gas; and only 0.3 per cent of the total world resource of petroleum. Petroleum is the generic term used for all hydrocarbon oils and gases including refined petroleum products. Although Australia is a net energy exporter, it is a net importer of crude oil and refined petroleum products (Australian Government, Department of Resources Energy and Tourism 2010).

The Australian Energy Resource Assessment (Geoscience Australia and ABARE 2010) states that in the year 2007–08, Australia's primary energy consumption was 5772 petajoules (PJ) (one joule is defined as the amount of work done by a force of one newton moving an object through a distance of one metre), of which 40 per cent was coal, 34 per cent was petroleum products and 22 per cent was gas. Petroleum products are hydrocarbons used directly as fuel and include liquefied petroleum, automotive gasoline, automotive diesel, aviation gasoline, fuel oil and kerosene. Liquid fuels are all liquid hydrocarbons, including crude oil, condensate, liquefied petroleum gas (LPG) and other refined petroleum products.

Of the 5772 PJ of energy in 2007–08, only 3917 PJ was available for disposal as 1856 PJ was required for conversion of energy to usable form. Table 12.1 shows that road transport was the largest consumer of energy in Australia in year 2007–08.

Table 12.1 Energy consumption in Australia 2007–08

	PJ
Agriculture	92.6
Mining	449.7
Food, beverages, textiles	212.1
Wood, paper and printing	75.1
Chemical	202.3
Iron and steel	117.4
Non-ferrous metals	461.5
Other industry	150.4
Construction	26.4
Road transport	1027.5
Rail transport	37.5
Air transport	226.3

	PJ
Water transport	70.6
Commercial services	278.9
Residential	425.7
Lubes, bitumen, solvents	62.9
Total	**3916.9**

Source: Australian Government, Department of Resources Energy and Tourism 2010.

A further examination of energy consumption within the road transport industry reveals that passenger vehicles consumed 61.7 per cent of the total consumption in 2006–07, as shown in Table 12.2.

Table 12.2 Road fuel consumption in Australia by type of vehicle 2006–07

	Percentage
Passenger vehicles	61.7
Buses	2.2
Motorcycles	0.4
Light commercial vehicles	15.8
Other trucks	0.2
Articulated trucks	12.0
Rigid trucks	7.7
Total	**100.0**

Source: Australian Government, Department of Resources Energy and Tourism 2010.

The energy used in Australian road transport comes mainly from automotive gasoline and automotive diesel oil as shown in Table 12.3.

Table 12.3 Consumption of petroleum products in Australia 2008–09

	Million litres
LPG	3996
Automotive gasoline	18 734
Avgas	96
Turbine fuel	6173
Kerosene	25
Heating oil	7
Automotive diesel oil	18 587
Industrial diesel fuel	16
Fuel oil	1423
Lubes and grease	437
Bitumen	809
Other	311
Total	**50 614**

Source: Australian Government, Department of Resources Energy and Tourism 2010.

Of the consumption of 50 614 litres of petroleum products, 78 per cent or 39 546 litres came from the petroleum refining industry in Australia. But 80 per cent of the 38 808 million litres of crude oil and condensate consumed by the Australian refineries was imported. This is partly because the Australian crude oil is generally light and getting lighter and the Australian refineries require the heavier crude oils. This means that Australia is very dependent on imported crude and petroleum products (liquid fuel).

Since Australia is dependent on imported liquid fuel, it is necessary to examine the world resource of liquid fuel on which it depends. The estimates of known oil reserves in the world, being reserves that can be recovered with reasonable certainty from known reservoirs under existing economic conditions, vary from one reporting agency to another as some are optimistic whereas others are pessimistic. Known oil reserves from selected agencies have been reported as shown in Table 12.4.

Table 12.4 Oil reserves reported from selected agencies

Reporting Agency	Timing	Billion barrels (Gb)*
Oil and Gas Journal	January 2009	1342
World Oil	Year end 2007	1184
Energy Information Administration	2008	1241
BP Statistical Review	June 2009	1258
Australian Bureau of Agriculture and Resource Economics	End 2008	1408

* One barrel = 158.987 litres oil.

Source: Owen, Inderwildi and King (2010).

The recent Geoscience Australia and ABARE report (2010, pp. 47–8) states that at current levels of world production the estimated proven oil reserves in the whole world are only enough to last for around 42 years. This creates a liquid fuel problem, not an 'energy crisis'. Hirsch, Bezdek and Wendling (2005) argue that technology has not developed engines that commonly use renewable energy such as solar, wind, photovoltaic, nuclear, geothermal or fusion. Motor vehicles, ships and aeroplanes are still commonly run by oil.

In order to prevent Australian dependency of foreign liquid fuel, it is necessary to examine the Australian transport policy and the growth of private vehicles in Australia and to determine whether a change in taxation policy is required to steer the energy management policy in this area.

AUSTRALIAN TRANSPORT POLICY AND THE GROWTH OF PRIVATE VEHICLES

Australia does not have a national transport policy, as transportation falls within the jurisdiction of the States. However in February 2008, the Australian Transport Council ministers began the process of developing a National Transport Policy Framework. The policy framework objectives include the promotion of efficient movement of people and goods in order to support sustainable economic development and prosperity, and the minimisation of emissions and consumption of resources and energy

(National Transport Commission 2009). The following examination of transportation data indicates that these desired policy objectives are not currently being met as Australians continue to rely on private motor vehicles that have high power and high power to weight ratios for personal transportation.

Since the end of the Second World War, Australian cities have grown, with expanding suburban areas. A rapid increase in motor vehicle owner-ship has encouraged the improvement and spread of the road system, thereby influencing the urban land use. In the 1920s, Australia had only 76 000 registered cars and station wagons, compared with 769 000 in 1950 and 10.4 million in 2003 (Australian Bureau of Statistics 2005). In 1995, private road vehicles represented 95 per cent of city passenger transport. In March 2009, 92 per cent of Australian households kept at least one registered motor vehicle at home. The proportion of households with two or more registered vehicles increased from 51 per cent in 2006 to 56 per cent in 2009 (Australian Bureau of Statistics 2010, p. 84). In 2009, 80 per cent of people in Australia used private motor vehicles to travel to work or full-time study, 14 per cent took public transport, 4 per cent walked and 2 per cent cycled. Ninety-four per cent of people who used a private motor vehicle to travel to work or full-time study did so as a driver or rider and only 6 per cent travelled as a passenger. The most common reasons for Australians not using public transport are: lack of service at right or convenient time; convenience, comfort and privacy; travel time too long; and own vehicle needed (Australian Bureau of Statistics 2010, p. 85).

A Senate inquiry on Investments of Commonwealth and State funds in public passenger transport infrastructure and services reported in August 2009 that metropolitan travel passenger-kilometres is about 85–90 per cent by car, 10 per cent by public transport and the rest by cycling and walking. The most prominent comment in the submissions was the need for improvement to public transport service and to encourage public transport use. A number of recommendations were made which included that the government should investigate options for tax incentives for public trans-port and that the government should support behavioural change pro-grammes (Parliament of Australia 2009).

Before examining how the Australian taxation policy can be changed to influence the choice of motor vehicles for personal transportation, it is worth noting that even though the engines powering our vehicles have become more efficient at extracting energy from liquid fuels, this has not resulted in fuel saving. The reason for this is that manufacturers have increased the power output of the motor vehicles as a selling aid to attract customers, as customers are demanding larger and more powerful motor vehicles.

Greater power output has had a real term net gain in vehicle weight, as shown in Table 12.5. For example, the Holden's first family motor vehicle, the Holden FJ, produced in 1953 had a 2.15 litre engine and power output of 45 kilowatt (kW), but the vehicle weighed only 1018 kilograms (kg), which gave a power to weight ratio of 44.46 kW per tonne. However, the average family car in 2008, for example, the Holden Commodore VE, has power output of 180kW, weighs 1700 kg and has a power to weight ratio of 105.88 kW per tonne (Holden Specifications 2008). If a 45kW output engine was produced today, it would not require a 2.15 litre engine, but would only require an approximately 855 cc engine with a much lower weight and fuel consumption, and the vehicle would be able to accelerate from 0 to 100 km per hour in approximately 12 seconds. This is based on 0.052 kW per cubic centimetre capacity, as demonstrated by Schefter (2008) that the 'Smart Fortwo' has a 1 litre engine producing 52 kW power and accelerates from 0 to 100 km in 12.8 seconds. This would be more than adequate to drive on most roads.

Table 12.5 Specifications of Holden family car 1948–2008

Car model	Year introduced	Engine size (litre)	Power (kW)	Weight (kg)	Power: weight ratio (kW per tonne)	Performance 0–100 km/h (seconds)
Holden48–215 (FX)	Nov. 1948	2.15	45	1012	44.46	20.0
Holden FJ	Oct. 1953	2.15	45	1012	44.46	20.0
Holden FE	July 1956	2.15	53	1080	49.07	20.4
Holden FC	May 1958	2.15	53	1084	48.89	19.5
Holden FB	Jan. 1960	2.26	56	1122	49.91	20.8
Holden EK	May 1961	2.26	56	1121	49.95	20.8
Holden EJ	July 1962	2.26	56	1130	49.56	18.0
Holden HD	Feb. 1965	2.45	86	1216	70.72	13.2
Holden HR	Apr. 1966	2.45	86	1217	70.66	15.3
Holden HK	Jan. 1968	2.65	85	1300	65.38	15.2
Holden HT	May 1969	2.65	85	1300	65.38	10.1
Holden HG	July 1970	2.65	85	1300	65.38	12.8

Car model	Year introduced	Engine size (litre)	Power (kW)	Weight (kg)	Power: weight ratio (kW per tonne)	Performance 0–100 km/h (seconds)
Holden HQ	July 1971	3.3	101	1338	75.48	13.1
Holden HJ	July 1974	3.3	96	1338	71.75	13.1
Holden HX	July 1976	3.3	82	1330	61.65	16.4
Holden HZ	Oct. 1977	3.3	81	1342	60.35	16.8
Holden VB	Oct. 1978	3.3	71	1220	58.20	16.4
Holden VC	Mar. 1980	2.85	76	1158	65.63	13.9
Holden VH	Oct. 1981	2.85	76	1152	65.97	10.2
Holden VL	Mar. 1986	3.0	114	1250	91.20	7.04
Holden VP	Sept. 1991	3.8	125	1332	93.84	8.1
Holden VT	Aug. 1997	3.8	147	1512	97.22	9.1
Holden VX	Sept. 2000	3.8	147	1519	96.77	9.1
Holden VY	Oct. 2002	3.8	152	1522	98.55	9.0
Holden VZ	Aug. 2004	3.6	180	1700	105.88	8.6
Holden VE	July 2008	3.6	180	1700	105.88	8.6

Source: Holden Specifications 2008.

Based on the data in Table 12.5 it can be concluded that from 1948 to 2008, the average family vehicle has progressively increased in weight, power and performance. The extraction of power per cubic centimetre of engine capacity in 1948 was 0.021 kW (45 kW/2150 cc) compared with 0.05 kW (180 kW/3600 cc) in 2008, an increase of 138 per cent. However, this power could have been better utilised by producing a smaller and lighter motor vehicle that would save energy and reduce consumption. Lighter vehicles do not have to sacrifice on safety as demonstrated by racing Formula 1 cars, which are lighter and yet safe.

The question this raises is whether the current Australian tax policy has the potential to bring about the changes required in the attitude towards the choice and usage of motor vehicles for personal transportation.

AUSTRALIAN TAXATION POLICY AND ITS INFLUENCE ON PERSONAL TRANSPORTATION CHOICES

In order to determine whether reform of motor vehicle transportation taxation is required in Australia to promote the efficient movement of people and goods with the least consumption of liquid oil, it is first necessary to analyse if existing tax policies play a role in determining a person's attitude towards the choice of motor vehicle for personal transportation. The transport sector in Australia is heavily taxed, involving crude oil excise and royalties, fuel excise, goods and services tax (GST), fringe benefits tax (FBT), luxury car tax (LCT), tariffs on imported vehicles, taxes on insurance, stamp duty on motor vehicles and licence and registration fees.

The tax revenues from the transportation sector are summarised in Table 12.6.

Table 12.6 Australian tax revenues from transportation taxes

Tax	Revenue
Commonwealth taxes	*Year 2007–08 ($ million)*
Fuel excise on petrol and diesel	13 633
Import tariff on passenger motor vehicles	1400
Luxury car tax	464
Fringe benefits tax	< 3796
State taxes	*Year 2006–07 ($ million)*
Motor vehicle registration duty on transfer	1989.7
Annual motor vehicle registration fees and taxes	3806
Surcharge and levies on compulsory third party insurance	222.6

Source: Clarke and Prentice 2009.

The Australian federal government also imposes GST and excise on petroleum products, including commonly used fuels. For every litre of petrol or diesel, whether imported from overseas or produced in Australia, an excise of $0.3814 per litre is imposed. However, an increase in fuel excise by the government is unlikely to affect the consumption of fuel as it has been noted in various studies that the consumption of fuel is inelastic. The reason for this is that people have a need to drive. It is difficult to reduce demand for fuel without changing habits, for example, purchasing a smaller, lighter vehicle that consumes less fuel, using more public transport or driving less. Moreover there is no readily available substitute of liquid fuel which can be used without making major alterations to the current design of vehicles. At the Senate Select Committee on Fuel and Energy (2009, pp.184 and 185), RACQ Insurance Limited argued that in the short term, car fuel use declines about 1.5 per cent with any 10 per cent concurrent increases in the price of fuel.

Taxes such the FBT and the LCT also do not have any impact on motorists' purchasing or driving habits. The FBT in fact encourages more driving as the greater the distance travelled, the lower is the taxable value. The reason for this is that the government assumes that if the distance travelled is greater, the proportion of private use is lower and therefore the FBT should be reduced. However, a lower FBT acts as an incentive to drive more rather than less and wastes our precious resource of oil. The LCT is also unlikely to change behaviour as the purpose of the LCT was to prevent luxury cars becoming cheaper with the introduction of the GST. However, the purpose should have arguably been to encourage people to purchase smaller, lighter and low emission vehicles.

The need for a tax to change behaviour and to drive less in more fuel efficient motor vehicles was recognised by the Australian government and referred to the review of Australia's Future Tax System commonly known as the 'Henry Tax Review' (Commonwealth of Australia 2008a).

Around 1500 formal submissions were received and some of the key messages from the submissions were: use of motor vehicles imposes costs on society; registration, insurance and fuel charges should be replaced by charges that reflect vehicle mass, distance travelled and location of use; taxes on the purchase of motor vehicles should promote fuel efficiency; and the fringe benefits tax treatment of motor vehicles leads to their overuse (Commonwealth of Australia, 2008b).

The Henry Review made recommendations to the government: to abolish the luxury car tax; that vehicle registration taxes be replaced by more efficient road user charges; and congestion tax should be introduced to change societal behaviour as the tax could be avoided by cutting down unnecessary trips and using public transport where possible (Common-wealth of Australia, 2010). These recommendations, if implemented, would satisfy some of the objectives of the Australian national transportation policy. However, a tax that should be introduced in Australia would encourage the purchase and use of motor vehicles that are lower in power to weight ratio; reduce the kilometres driven; and reflect the choice of a vehicle from the initial acquisition to its time-spanned recycling point. The next section explores the tax policy changes made by other countries and the lessons that Australia can learn.

TAX POLICY CHANGE

Many countries around the world are changing their transportation tax policy for a number of reasons, including the increasing reliance on imported fuel, climate change, congestion and forecasted drop in revenue from excise. If Australia is to change its transport tax policy, then it should take into consideration that motor vehicles have increased in power and weight. Motor vehicles for transportation should be designed and used as a means of transporting a person safely from one place to another with the least consumption of fuel. The tax imposed and collected on transportation does not have to be more, but its design criteria should serve other policy aims including environmental goals and not just the raising of general government revenue. The normal traditional bases for taxation, being income, consumption or wealth, cannot affect environmental goals such as preserving a limited resource of fossil fuel. Environmental goals require a specific, targeted tax.

Many countries tax motor vehicles on their initial purchase, their annual registration and their use in terms of fuel. Countries including Australia charge a higher tax on larger engine capacities of motor vehicles. Many countries around the world have either changed their tax policies or have carried out studies of how to change their transportation tax policies in the future to not only make transportation more sustainable, but to maintain the government revenue base in the years to come.

As from April 2010, the UK has introduced 13 bands of car purchase tax for cars registered on or after 1 March 2001 based on CO_2 emissions (HM Government 2010). In the UK, the concept of a generalised road user charge was supported by the House of Commons Transport Select Committee (2008–09), but has not been implemented. A similar car purchase tax based on CO_2 emissions has also been introduced in Ireland as from January 2009 (Department of Environment, Heritage and Local Government 2009).

The Dutch had planned to introduce a mileage tax. In November 2009, the Dutch cabinet approved a new road tax bill that would eliminate their current 25 per cent car sales tax and current road taxes and replace them with a charge per kilometre driven tax (Green Car Congress 2009). However, following a change in government, the implementation of this tax has been put on hold. Under the proposed mileage tax, different vehicle types had different base rates, determined by CO_2 emissions or weight. Higher charges were to be levied during the rush hour and for travelling on congested roads. Also bigger cars emitting more CO_2 were to be assessed at a higher rate, while smaller cars were expected to pay less. Each vehicle was required to be equipped with a GPS device that tracks the number of kilometres that are driven and when and where they are driven and a central agency was to collect this information. Starting in 2012, drivers were expected to be charged €0.03 (US$0.07) per kilometre driven, slowly increasing to €0.067 (US$0.16) per kilometre by 2018.

It is not only the European countries that are in the forefront to transform their transportation tax policies: the State of Oregon in the USA is in the process of developing a 'road user fee' (Oregon Department of Transport 2007). Unlike the Netherlands model, the Oregon model does not recommend a centralised collection agency, but fuel pump stations as collecting agents as part of the fuel purchase.

The Oregon concept involves the fitting of a device in the vehicle that records the number of miles driven by a vehicle within various pre-identified zones. At the fuel pump station, the stored miles driven in each zone are electronically transferred to the station's point of sale system for application of the mileage fee rates. The final receipt presented to the motorist at the fuel pump station would display each amount involved in the mileage fee transaction separately. Once payment is made, the central database is updated with the last mileage reading, the amount of fuel purchased and the total mileage fee assessed.

The Oregon's road user fee pilot programme indicates the extent to which governments are prepared to go to change their motor vehicle taxation regime. The lesson for Australia should be to focus on liquid fuel being a luxury, and vehicles that are heavier and more powerful should bear more tax. The tax design for Australia should incorporate the following four factors of a motor vehicle: weight; engine capacity; power output; and CO_2 emissions. The focus should be to change people's perception of the car, as it has evolved from an expensive luxury for a few to an important tool for the everyday lives and employment of the majority of people, a status symbol and a hobby. The vehicles have become bigger and heavier as technological efficacies are not utilised to save fuel and emissions.

The momentum is building for Australia to reform its transportation taxes. Instead of just following the examples of other countries and adding on congestion taxes and road user charges, the Australian government should take the lead and replace the transportation taxes with a luxury energy tax (LET), not only to bring about an awareness of the limited resource of fossil fuel, but also to influence consumers to change their perception of ownership and use of motor vehicles and for the manufacturers to change their vehicle design considerations from selling dreams to selling sustainable vehicles.

The purpose of the LET should be the imposition of a tax that would impact on a person's decision to purchase a vehicle that consumes less fuel, impact on its use and its ongoing upkeep up until its appropriate time-spanned recycling point. The tax should be imposed at four taxing points based on the vehicle's gross weight, engine capacity, power output and CO_2 emissions. These characteristics should be reflected at each of the four taxing points, which are: initial purchase of the vehicle; road registration; fuel consumption; and repairs and maintenance. There is enough technology available to enable a tax design to impose tax at four taxing points as demonstrated by systems in place in other countries. Such a tax is required as the four taxing points would work together to educate that larger engine capacities mean larger power output from the vehicles, which brings about heavier vehicles that consume more fuel and emit more emissions. The taxation at the four levels would also discourage extra power being added to smaller engines by other means such as turbo- or supercharging and adding nitrous oxide injections. Taxation has to be used as a means of promoting redesign of motor vehicles as it is not necessary to have such weight and power to move a person from one place to another for personal transportation.

The purpose of LET should be to educate the user and indirectly the manufacturer of motor vehicles that liquid fuel is a luxury and should be paid for if the use is so desired.

CONCLUSION

Since Ford's invention of the constant moving assembly line in the early part of the 20th century, motor vehicles have become bigger and more powerful and consume more fuel. This has created the problem of diminishing a finite resource of liquid fossil fuel. The world's energy resource is not just for the people of today, but for future generations and all mankind to share. In this chapter a case is made for the introduction of tax measures in order to lead to a new way of thinking about energy. The tax should relate to the power and weight of the vehicle and its use and not where the vehicles are manufactured. A new way of thinking is required as it takes millions of years for our planet to produce fossil fuel, but it takes an instant to burn it, and once burnt it is irrecoverable. Therefore the Australian government should take the responsibility and implement appropriate taxation policies such as the LET to promote its transportation policy of efficient movement of people and goods with the least consumption of liquid oil.

REFERENCES

Australian Bureau of Statistics (2005), *Yearbook Australia 2005: Use of Urban Public Transport in Australia*, Canberra, Australian Bureau of Statistics, available at: www.abs.gov.au (accessed 6 May 2010).

Australian Bureau of Statistics (2010), *Yearbook Australia 2009–10*, Canberra, Australian Bureau of Statistics, available at: www.abs.gov.au (accessed 6 May 2010).

Australian Government, Department of the Environment, Water, Heritage and the Arts (2005), 'TravelSmart snapshot', available at: www.environment.gov.au/settlements/transport/publications/travelsmart-snapshots.html (accessed 25 June 2010).

Australian Government, Department of Resources Energy and Tourism (2010), *Energy in Australia 2010*, Canberra, Commonwealth of Australia.

Clarke, H. and D. Prentice (2009), 'A conceptual framework for the reform of taxes related to roads and transport', commissioned research paper prepared for Australia's future tax system, available at: www.taxreview.treasury.gov.au/content/Content.aspx?doc=html/commissioned_work.htm (accessed 1 June 2010).

Commonwealth of Australia (2008a), 'Architecture of Australia's tax and transfer system', available at: www.taxreview.treasury.gov.au/Content/downloads/report/Architecture_of_Australias_tax_and_transfer_system_revised.pdf (accessed 12 November 2008).

Commonwealth of Australia (2008b), 'Australia's future tax system: consultation paper', available at: http://taxreview.treasury.gov.au/content/ConsultationPaper.aspx?doc=html/publications/Papers/Consultation_Paper/section_12.htm (accessed 1 June 2010).

Commonwealth of Australia (2010), 'Australia's future tax system: final report – detailed analysis', available at: http://taxreview.treasury.gov.au/content/FinalReport.aspx?doc=html/Publications/Papers/Final_Report_Part_2/Chapter_e.htm (accessed 1 June 2010).

Department of Environment, Heritage and Local Government, Ireland (2009), 'Motor tax rates based on CO2 emissions – effective from 1st January 2009', available at: www.environ.ie/en/LocalGovernment/MotorTax/MotorTaxRates/MotorTaxRatesbasedonCO2EmissionsEffectivefromthe1jan2009 (accessed 3 September 2010).

Geoscience Australia and ABARE (2010), 'Australian energy resource assessment', Canberra, available at: www.abare.gov.au/publications_html/energy/energy .../ ga_aera.html (accessed 6 May 2010).

Green Car Congress (2009), *Dutch Cabinet Approves Mileage Tax*, available at: www.greencarcongress.com/2009/11/dutch-cabinet-approves-mileage-tax-in-effect-in-2012-if-approved-by-parliament.html (accessed 16 September 2010).

HM Government (2010), 'The cost of vehicle tax', available at: www.direct.gov.uk/en/Motoring/OwningAVehicle/HowToTaxYourVehicle/DG_4022118 (accessed 3 September 2010).

Hirsch, R.L., R. Bezdek and R. Wendling (2005), 'Peaking of world oil production: impacts, mitigation and risk management', available at: www.netl.doe.gov/publications/others/pdf/oil_peaking_netl.pdf (accessed 6 May 2010).

Holden Specifications (2008), richardlewis.org, available at: http://homepages.paradise.net.nz/richa306/holdenspecs.html (accessed 24 July 2008).

House of Commons Transport Committee (2008–09), 'Taxes and charges on road users: Government response to the Committee's Sixth Report Session', available at: www.publications.parliament.uk/pa/cm200809/cmselect/cmtran/995/995.pdf (accessed 3 September 2010).

National Transport Commission (2009), 'National transport policy framework', available at: www.ntc.gov.au/viewpage.aspx?AreaId=34&DocumentId=1750 (accessed 1 July 2010).

Oregon Department of Transport (2007), 'Oregon's mileage fee concept and road user fee pilot program final report', available at: www.oregon.gov/ODOT/HWY/RUFPP/docs/RUFPP_finalreport.pdf (accessed 3 September 2010).

Owen, N., O. Inderwildi and D.A. King (2010), 'The status of conventional oil reserves – hype or cause for concern?', *Energy Policy*, **38**, 4743–9.

Parliament of Australia (2009), 'Senate Rural and Regional Affairs and Transport Committee: executive summary and recommendation', available at: www.aph.gov.au/senate/committee/rrat_ctte/public_transport/report/b01.htm#anc2 (accessed 25 May 2010).

Schefter, K (2008), 'Smart car offers drivers new high MPG option, top crash rating', available at: www.greencar.com/articles/smart-car-offers-drivers-new-high-mpg-option-top-crash-rating.php (accessed 1 July 2010).

Senate Select Committee on Fuel and Energy (2009), 'The CPRS: economic cost without environmental benefit', Parliament of Australia, Senate, available at: www.aph.gov.au/senate/committee/fuelenergy_ctte/interim_report/report.pdf (accessed 30 April 2010).

Tax Laws Amendment (Luxury Car Tax) Act 2008 (Cth).

PART IV

Environmental Taxation in Australia

13. The political economy of Australia's proposed resource rent taxation regime*

Hope Ashiabor and Moira Saccasan

INTRODUCTION

The seminal work, the *Brundtland Report*,[1] couched the notion of sustainable development in terms of inter-generational equity. The report defined sustainable development with reference to paths of progress that meet the needs and aspirations of the present generation without compromising the ability of future generations to meet their needs. The report went further to state that this ability of future generations to meet their own needs could be compromised as much by affluence – the excesses of industrial and technological development – as by environmental degradation and underdevelopment. In presenting the report to the United Nations Environment Programme's 14th Governing Session, the chairman said:

> At the same time as we call for a revival of economic growth, we urge that the quality of growth be changed. Growth must promote a fair distribution of income. It must be soundly based on the stock of natural capital that sustains it, instead of overusing it. It must respect limits to environmental resources such as clean air and water, forests and soils; it must maintain genetic diversity; it must be based on more effective uses of energy and raw materials. The environment must become an ally, not a victim of development.[2]

In most countries (including Australia) that are rich in non-renewable resources, these concerns have come into focus on a number of fronts. The first relates to managing the devastating environmental degradation that is often left in the wake of the exploitation of these non-renewable resources. As most countries have devised comprehensive protocols for managing this environmental degradation, a discussion of it falls outside the chosen focus of this chapter.[3]

The second concern stems from the conditions for a two-speed economy which is often left in the wake of resource booms. The challenges that non-renewable resource-exporting countries have had to grapple with in this context have been ensuring that their overall economies and future generations reap the dividends of the windfall profits generated by the boom conditions in the resources sector. Closely intertwined with issues of managing the boom are the challenges of devising appropriate mechanisms to charge for the exploitation of non-renewable resources and the stewardship of revenue flows from resource charges.[4] These developments have brought the efficacy of conventional royalty arrangements into question.

These issues came to a head in May 2010, when at the time of the release of the Henry Review's report on Australia's Future Tax System, the federal government flagged its proposal to introduce a resources super profits tax (RSPT) from 2012. The RSPT will apply to all mining activity, coupled with a refunding to mining companies of capped royalties paid to state or territory governments. These measures are sometimes referred to as 'the proposed tax package' in this chapter.[5] The backlash unleashed from the mining sector in the wake of the announcement and community disquiet generated was tantamount to opening up the proverbial Pandora's box.

This chapter critically evaluates the tortuous trajectory that the proposed measure was subjected to after it was unveiled. It also evaluates the adequacy of the mechanisms incorporated into the proposed tax package in rebalancing the impacts of the resources boom on the Australian economy. In addition, the chapter examines the issue of the extent to which resource rent tax regimes effectively tackle the issue of intergenerational equity that was raised in the Brundtland Report. The proposed tax measure has also run into legal and constitutional headwinds over the Commonwealth's authority to encroach into an area that has historically been within the regulatory competence of the states. Consequently, the chapter will examine the nature of the issues and problems that result from the fact that more than one level of government asserts an interest and responsibility in this area that the federal government wants to encroach into. Lessons drawn from this experience are then extrapolated and contextualized in a comparative setting in an attempt to unfold the extent to which any basis can be established in building consensus when it comes to the implementation of fiscal measures that adversely impact on powerful sectional interests. The chapter will also analyze the wider implications to be drawn from this experience in the formulation of a framework for setting a price on carbon or environmental taxes generally. To set the framework for the analysis, the chapter starts off with a cursory discussion of Australia's non-renewable resources potential and the conditions presented by the two-speed economy.

SETTING THE CONTEXT

Australia is endowed with substantial deposits of non-renewable resources. It has the world's largest economic demonstrated reserves (EDRs) of brown coal, lead, mineral sands (rutile and zircon), nickel, silver, uranium and zinc; and the second largest reserves of bauxite, copper, gold and iron ore.[6] Its proven oil reserves are the 26th largest in the world; its natural gas reserves are the 14th largest in the world under current production rates, and could continue to be exported for the next 65 years.[7]

For the past 50 years, Australia has been able to harness its good fortune of having abundant, high-quality reserves of an extensive range of mineral commodities, particularly of the key steel-making raw materials, iron ore and coal, and of being strategically located close to the world's fastest-growing markets for those materials – first in Japan, Korea and Taiwan, and subsequently in China and India.

A major challenge encountered by countries that are experiencing mining booms is the risk they run of contracting the 'Dutch disease'.[8] In the Australian context, the mining boom has skewed the economy. Industries outside the resources sector have found it more difficult to attract skills and investment. These industries also run the risk of facing credit squeezes in the future as the capital markets focus on resources. Given estimates that almost $AU300 billion is needed to fund Australia's mining expansion, this inevitably will result in a focus on capital raising in this sector.[9] The other issue that industries outside this sector will have to contend with is the upward pressure on the dollar that is a result of Australia's being an exporting nation. A stronger Australian dollar means that for other export industries and local firms competing with imports, their products will become relatively less competitive than before. In countries experiencing resource booms this invariably leads most manufacturers to abandon exporting.

The challenge for governments and regulators is one of working out how the profits from this once-in-a-lifetime boom can be harnessed to ensure Australia has a multi-speed economy with sectors that can drive growth once the boom ends. If this is not properly managed, then, as the Brundtland Report put it, when countries export: 'We borrow environmental capital from future generations with no intention or prospect of repaying.'[10] The report then made the cautionary observation that such practices amounted to 'drawing too heavily and too quickly on already overdrawn environmental resource accounts to be affordable far into the future …' and risked 'bankrupting those accounts'.[11]

EXISTING REGIME – ROYALTY ARRANGEMENTS

Investments in non-renewable resources are generally subject to corporate income tax and royalty regimes. From a jurisdictional perspective, taxes are levied at the federal or state level. However, by virtue of its federal constitutional arrangement, the collection of royalties with respect to onshore resources in Australia has historically been a matter within the jurisdictional competence of the states.[12] The royalties levied are generally specific, as they are either charged per unit of output or as a proportion of the revenue received (on *ad valorem* rates). The prevailing state-based royalty rates are set at between 2 per cent and 10 per cent of revenue.

Royalty regimes have traditionally been criticized on the grounds that they tend to distort mining investment decisions. Onshore mining, which is largely subject to state royalties, typically applies *ad valorem* rates to output or revenues, regardless of costs of exploration and production. This feature of royalties discriminates against marginal projects with higher costs, such as some of the more risky deposits or those that are more difficult to develop. It also has the potential of deterring investment decisions in marginal projects.

Certain rigidities built into the royalty system mean that they only capture a small share of the economic rent earned by mines and wells endowed with huge deposits of natural resources, and the windfall profits earned during mining booms. When profitability is low, these royalties collect a greater share of the returns; when profitability is high a smaller share of the returns is collected.

As shown in Figure 13.1, the effect of these inbuilt rigidities meant that, as profits increased over time, and due to higher demand, the percentage of profits collected as royalties by the states fell dramatically. In real terms, the effective resource charge more than halved from an average of around 34 per cent over the first half of this decade to less than 14 per cent in 2008–09, due to unresponsive royalty regimes.[13] As demonstrated in Figure 13.1, these taxes and charges only delivered a small share of the increased value of resource deposits. Resource profits were over AU$80 billion higher in 2008–09 than in 1999–2000, but governments only collected an additional AU$9 billion through resource taxes and charges.

The overall effect therefore has been that state governments have been collecting inefficiently designed royalties that were substantially less than profits.

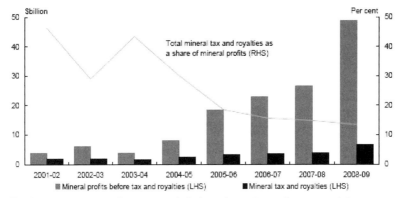

(a) Mineral profits before tax and royalties are measured using income less an allowance for corporate capital.
Source: Australian Treasury estimates.

Source: Australia's Future Tax System, Report to the Treasurer, December 2009, Part Two, Detailed Analysis, volume 1 of 2.

Figure 13.1 Mineral tax and royalties as a share of mineral profits[a]

RESOURCE RENT TAXES GENERALLY[14]

The finite supply of non-renewable resources allows their owners to earn above normal profits (economic rents) from exploitation. Rents occur where the profits from the sale of resources exceed the normal return to capital invested in the project.

Resource rent taxes are a mechanism for pricing the resource from which mining companies earn their profits, by transforming the resource in the ground to a saleable commodity. Unlike royalties, resource rent taxes are more flexible as they align the resource charge with the profitability of the project. As a result, revenues raised by a resource rent tax increase as profit levels increase, and similarly as profits decline there is a corresponding reduction to the tax obligations of the entity.

The taxation of super profits on resource projects is an issue that has long been discussed in the tax policy literature and has been put forward as a basis for policy reform. Table 13.1 lists Australian and overseas schemes which have adopted some elements of the taxation of resource super profits.

Table 13.1 International resource rent taxation regimes on mining and petroleum

Continent	Country	Sector	Years in force	Legislated or contractual
Africa	Ghana	Petroleum	Since 1984	Contractual
	Tanzania	Petroleum	Since 1984	Contractual
	Ghana	Mining	1985–2003	Legislated
	Madagascar	Petroleum and mining	1980s	Legislated
	Namibia	Petroleum	Since 1993	Legislated
	Zimbabwe	Mining	Since 1994	Legislated
	Angola	Petroleum	Since mid-1990s	Contractual
	Malawi	Mining	Since 2006	Legislated
	Liberia	Mining	Since 2008	Legislated
Asia-Pacific	Australia	Offshore petroleum	Since 1986	Legislated
	Papua New Guinea	Petroleum	Since 1977 (frontier areas exempt)	Legislated
		Mining	1978–2002	Legislated
	Timor-Leste	Petroleum	Since 2003	Legislated
	Solomon Islands	Mining (gold)	Since 1999	Contractual

Continent	Country	Sector	Years in force	Legislated or contractual
Europe	Denmark	Petroleum (profits-based tax)	Since 1982	Legislated
	Norway	Petroleum (profits-based tax)	Since 1975	Legislated
	Russia	Petroleum (Production Sharing Agreements)	Since 1994	Contractual
North America	Canada, British Columbia	Mining	Since 1990	Legislated
	US (Nevada)	Mining (metals, minerals, coal)**	2011	Legislated
	Saskatchewan	Mining (metals, minerals)*	Since 1986	Legislated
Eurasia	Azerbaijan	Petroleum	Since 1996	Contractual
	Kazakhstan	Petroleum	Since mid-1990s	Contractual

Notes:
* Percentage of taxable profits.
** Net super profit above threshold.
(a) Both Papua New Guinea and Ghana have discontinued the application of this tax on mining rents.
(b) Australia's petroleum resource rent tax (PRRT) levied on offshore petroleum projects is an example of a Garnaut and Clunies-Ross resource rent tax.

Source: Adapted from Land (2010), pp. 241–63.

The view among tax policy experts has been that taxes do not impact on investment decisions if they fall on the net cash flows. This is due to the fact that any investment behaviour that maximizes the net present value of the cash flows will also maximize the present value of before-tax cash flows. This type of tax is often referred to as a Brown tax (named after the American economist Carey Brown).[15] Alternative models of rent taxes are the Garnaut and Clunies-Ross rent tax,[16] and the Allowance for Corporate Capital.[17]

While a Brown tax is often seen as ideal for taxing resource profits, its major drawback is that the government is required to contribute additional investment immediately (that is, the government needs immediately to provide a rebate for all negative cash flows). This can impose significant pressure on government cash flows as such payments are not able to be foreseen by governments. It could also affect the government's ability to budget whenever the sector undertakes significant investment.

To counter the drawbacks of a pure Brown's tax, *Australia's Future Tax System* report recommended that the government should implement the Allowance for Corporate Capital model as the basis for its proposed RSPT. In this way, the proposed RSPT would achieve the same economic outcome as a Brown tax while providing policy stability as it allows the government better to plan for large expenses.

Under the proposed RSPT, the government provided a guaranteed tax credit for all expenditure. However, instead of recognizing expenditure at the time it was incurred, the government deferred recognition through depreciation and loss carry-forward arrangements. To ensure investors were not disadvantaged by this deferral, the government provided entities, through the proposed RSPT, with an uplift allowance that compensated for the delay in accessing the credit.

Like the Brown tax, the proposed RSPT only taxed the profits associated with the value realized from Australia's non-renewable resources. The normal return on invested capital (both domestic and foreign) was not taxed over time under the proposed RSPT. The company tax would remain, and would tax the normal return, but the effective tax rate on the normal return would be reduced by the proposed cut in the company tax rate.

AUSTRALIA'S FUTURE TAX SYSTEM REPORT – THE MAIN ISSUES IDENTIFIED

In May 2008, the Rudd Government commissioned the Review into Australia's Future Tax System. Its mandate was to undertake a comprehensive review into Australia's tax system and to propose the framework of a robust tax structure to enable Australia to deal with the social, economic and environmental challenges of the 21st century. The review extended to all federal and state taxes (except the goods and services tax) and their interactions with the transfer system.

Following an extensive period of public consultation, the review panel delivered its final report to the Treasurer in December 2009 (hereafter referred to as the AFTS report).[18] One of the most controversial aspects of the review panel's recommendations on business taxation was the tax treatment of mining. The recommendation proposed the replacement of the prevailing state-based royalties with a uniform tax on the economic rent component of mining returns.

The report put forward the views that:

- the rights to these resources are owned by the Australian community through the Australian and State governments;
- the proposed reforms would overcome the inefficiencies of royalty regimes, and ensure that mining profits were taxed in a way that supported the growth of the industry and the economy; and
- the measures would ensure that Australians received a fair return for the global demand for their natural resources.[19]

THE GOVERNMENT'S RESPONSE: THE RESOURCE SUPER PROFITS TAX

On 2 May 2010, the government released the final AFTS report and indicated its initial response to its 138 recommendations. This announcement occurred one week before the federal budget was due to be handed down. While several recommendations were not adopted, those relating to resource rents resulted in the announcement of the RSPT, which was to commence on 1 July 2012.

Some time later the government released a discussion paper that set out details of three consultation phases: the preliminary publication of an issues paper, a final design paper and an exposure draft legislation.[20]

The RSPT was to apply to all entities directly involved in the exploitation of non-renewable resources.[21] Existing resource projects were transitioned into the new scheme (with the exception of those already covered by the PRRT, which were given a choice as to which regime they wished to have their projects subjected to).

While the AFTS report recommended the exclusion of low value projects, the government decided otherwise. Its view was, *inter alia*, that such projects were likely to benefit the most from the shift from a royalty regime to the RSPT. Further, it was the government's view that exemptions would increase complexity of the law, require integrity mechanisms and increase compliance costs.[22]

The RSPT was to be charged at a rate of 40 per cent of assessable resource profits (measured as the difference between the revenues generated from resource extraction and associated costs). Losses could be used to offset an RSPT profit in subsequent years or transferred to other projects owned by the entity. Unlike the existing PRRT, most capital expenditures could be written off over time, and unutilized expenditure would be refundable. There would only be one uplift rate for all capital expenditure and that would be set annually at the ten-year government bond rate.

Unlike company income tax, the government guaranteed to refund mining companies 40 per cent of the losses that could not be offset against assessable future resource super profits. This would occur when, for example, a project closed and the loss could not be transferred to another project.

To avoid 'double taxation' a refundable credit was to be provided to resource entities for royalties paid to state governments following commencement of the RSPT. This meant that mining companies would initially be paying royalties on the resources extracted; they would then pay RSPT and receive a credit for the royalties that they had paid. RSPT payments would be deductible and refunds would be assessable for income tax purposes.

The revenues were to be split into thirds and earmarked for the following purposes:

- to assist directly the resources sector with a resource state infrastructure fund; and
- to provide for superannuation measures, saving for the future. Australia has an ageing population and that is of concern, so setting aside money for superannuation could offset the demands being made on the transfer system when the postwar baby boomers start to retire.

These two measures were designed to address the issues of intergenerational equity – to promote growth across the economy, addressing the risk of a two-speed economy by cutting the company tax rate by 2 percentage points from 30 per cent to 28 per cent. This would assist industry that was not necessarily involved in mining.

The retrospective application of the RSPT to existing projects was a primary cause for much of the acrimonious debate that occurred after the release of this announcement. The effect of the transitional rules amounted to a compulsory acquisition of a 40 per cent share of the 'good' projects (those that were ultimately able to make full use of the deductions).[23] The

AFTS report argued that existing projects had to be subject to the tax because a 'significant part of the expected growth in mining industry output is likely to come from the expansion of existing mines'. Leaving existing mines out would also have increased administrative costs by requiring multiple tax regimes to operate in parallel. Elaborating on the concerns underlying the mining industry's dissatisfaction with the RSPT's application to existing projects, one commentator noted that:

> The government may be paying market value for 40 per cent of the picks and shovels, as it were, but is not paying 40 per cent of the market value of the resources that they were designed to extract. The government's position, of course, is that these belong to the 'Australian people' whom it represents. The industry's position was that it was promised these resources (less royalties) and that it was on that basis that risky investments in the currently successful projects (and in those that were not successful) were made.[24]

It is an established principle of tax reform that changes are not to be retrospective. However, the dilemma facing the government is that, without applying the tax to existing projects as well as to new ones, it would not be able to raise anywhere near its projected revenues. The government would have to compensate existing investors if it sought to apply the tax to both existing and new projects.

The retrospective application of the minerals resource rent tax (MRRT) risks infringing the constitutional provisions that qualify the taxation power.[25] In the *Newcrest Mining* case, the High Court ruled that the Commonwealth could not include existing mining leases in Kakadu National Park (a World Heritage site, where mining is prohibited) as that would have amounted to an acquisition of property on unjust terms.[26]

THE FALLOUT

The mining industry cried foul, alleging that there was no prior consultation in the lead-up to the announcement. Although a consultation panel was convened to coincide with the announcement, the mining companies felt they had been ambushed. Media reports indicated that 80 mining stakeholders were being consulted; however, the taxing rate of 40 per cent and the uplift factor of the ten-year government bond rate were not negotiable. This degenerated into an acrimonious and vociferous advertising campaign between the industry and the government. The campaign was essentially coloured by false representations about the effects on new mining investments and had far-reaching ripple effects – it unnerved the financial markets, the public was very confused and media reports indicated that Australians were evenly divided on the issue. Some feared that the RSPT would lead to a loss of jobs; others were concerned about the effects of the tax on the value of their share portfolios in the mining companies; and yet others believed that the mining sector was trying to escape paying its way.

The opposition dutifully opposed, with its leader declaring that the tax would 'kill the goose that lays the golden egg', and assured a jittery electorate and an angry mining industry that, if elected into government, it would scrap the tax proposal.

MINERALS RESOURCE RENT TAX

On 24 June 2010, the Prime Minister, Kevin Rudd, was removed from office and replaced by the deputy Prime Minister Julia Gillard. The incoming Prime Minister immediately called a truce with the mining companies. The advertising campaigns were suspended while further negotiations took place behind closed doors with representatives from three of the largest mining companies operating in Australia – BHP, Rio Tinto and Xstrata. This culminated in the announcement of new taxation arrangements on 2 July 2010. Its features were as follows.

- From 1 July 2012, a new minerals resource rent tax (MRRT) would apply only to mined iron ore and coal; all other minerals were excluded. The PRRT was to be extended to include all onshore and offshore oil and gas projects.
- The rate of tax would be 22.5 per cent. There would be a 30 per cent tax applied to the taxable profit of the resource, on which a 25 per cent 'extraction allowance' would apply, bringing that down to 22.5 per cent.
- Unutilized expenditures would no longer be refundable.
- MRRT losses would be transferrable to other projects.
- There would be no MRRT liability for taxpayers' profit below $AU50 million and reduced liability for profits up to $AU100 million.
- All state and territory royalties would be creditable against MRRT liability.

The rate at which royalties would be credited under the MRRT was frozen at those rates in place or scheduled on 2 May 2010. It appears that this was not made clear during the negotiations with the big mining companies, as the negotiations did not resolve issues relating to royalties paid to the states. The miners maintained that during their secret negotiations with the government, they were promised that all state royalties including future increases would be refunded by the federal government. The government later hinted that it might not credit all future royalties as this would amount to writing a blank cheque for the states. The federal government plans to force the state governments to cap their royalties or face financial penalties.

Small and mid-tier mining groups were excluded from the MRRT negotiations and were dissatisfied with the outcome. They argued that the new rent tax would have a much more adverse impact on them than on the larger miners; the unutilized expenditures could be written off against other projects of the big miners, whereas projects undertaken by the smaller miners were not eligible.

To address these concerns, on 3 August 2010 the Policy Transition Group (PTG) was set up to advise on the technical design and implementation arrangements for the MRRT.[27] On 1 October 2010, the PTG released an issues paper which comprehensively set out topics for discussion and the different options that could be implemented.[28]

Following extensive consultations, the PTG handed a report in December 2010 outlining a much watered-down version of the resource rent tax. It recommended the government reimburse miners for any future increases in state royalties. The big mining companies welcomed this recommendation. The federal government is yet to respond, however.

A stalemate has been reached as the premiers of the mining-rich states of Queensland and Western Australia have refused to rule out future increases to mining royalties.[29] Despite pleas from the federal government to the states to cap future mining royalties to keep the industry competitive, the states were having no bar of it. South Australia announced increases in its royalty regime to take effect from July 2011. Western Australia indicated that it was prepared to launch a constitutional court challenge against the federal government to affirm its right to increase its royalty rates whenever it wished to do so. The situation has not been helped by the fact that, since the August 2010 federal election when the federal government was returned with a wafer-thin majority, changes have also occurred to the political landscape in the other mining states of Victoria and New South Wales to parties that are affiliated with the federal opposition. In the meantime, the mining industry is threatening to resume hostilities through its negative advertising campaign if the government is unable to get the states onside. These developments have raised questions about just how powerful the mining heavyweights have become.

OECD'S REACTION

In a 2010 report, the Organisation for Economic Co-operation and Development (OECD) commended Australia's proposed shift to a rent tax approach to non-renewable resources to replace the existing state-based royalties system. It went on to recommend that 'the resource rent tax be extended to all commodities and companies irrespective of their size', otherwise this focus on only parts of the resources sector could distort investment and would hurt the government's ability to raise revenues.[30]

LEGAL AND CONSTITUTIONAL MINEFIELD

Simmering beneath the tensions between the Commonwealth, on the one hand, and the states and the mining industry, on the other, are unresolved legal and constitutional issues that could unravel the entire tax proposal. Based on the government's explanation of how the tax would work, legal experts have warned that the High Court could strike out central planks of the proposed tax package as being unconstitutional.[31] The major constitutional obstacle to the introduction of a resource rent tax is that historically the direct constitutional responsibility for determining and administering the appropriate charging mechanism for the exploitation of mineral resources has been a state and territory government matter and not a Commonwealth one.

It is within the jurisdictional competence of the states and territories to determine how best to regulate and charge for the use of their property. However, the Commonwealth oversees the distribution of general government revenue to the states and territories via a formula that takes account of the capacity of those regions to raise their own revenue. An option that the Commonwealth could have pursued would have been for it to assess that capacity on the basis of what the states and territories could have raised, instead of what they chose to raise.

The idea of a Brown tax was originally mooted by the Industry Commission in 1991.[32] However, there were practical obstacles that stood in the way of any attempt by the states and territories to implement it. As Brown taxes require governments to take a silent equity stake in exploration and mining activity equal to the tax rate, states contemplating its introduction run the risk of exposing their fragile revenue base to a greater degree of instability and uncertainty than would otherwise be acceptable. This was more so the case in those states where the concentration of mining activity was quite high. Further, the states did not have the capacity to administer a Brown tax and the costs that it entailed as they did not have the institutional framework with the resource capabilities of central tax administrations that were accustomed to dealing with corporate income.[33]

Apparently, the private view held in Industry Commission circles at the time was that, without Commonwealth action to coordinate the implementation of a Brown tax and smooth fluctuations in state revenues, the recommendation was unlikely to see the light of day. It was hoped that the Commonwealth would consult with the states and territories on how its recommendations might be implemented, but the government of the day was reluctant to pursue the matter along those lines.[34]

The Commonwealth's failure to proceed with this line of consultation when the issue resurfaced in the 2009–10 before deciding how to implement the AFTS report's recommendations represented a missed opportunity, in spite of the fact that the possibility of such discussions delivering agreed policy outcomes on this matter could not be guaranteed. Consultation with the states would at least have given state governments an opportunity to understand the effects of the tax and be better prepared to assess the validity of the mining industry's assertions about the consequences for activity within their jurisdictions. Instead, the Commonwealth chose to go it alone by proposing to nullify the effects of state-based royalties. It did this by crediting the mining companies for royalties paid. The effect of the crediting up to the reimbursement limit was that royalties had no impact on mining company profitability or on the incentives to undertake exploration and mining investment.

Unless the state and territory royalties were capped, reimbursements to the miners presented the state and territory governments with a *carte blanche* to increase royalty rates at the Commonwealth's expense. To obviate this, the proposal sought to peg the extent to which the reimbursement would be granted conditional upon freezing the rates that either existed or were foreshadowed at the time of the RSPT announcement.

The crediting of royalties to the miners opens up a number of potential legal and constitutional issues. In its discussion paper, the government indicated that the intended impact of the crediting mechanism under the RSPT was to remove the effects that these royalties have on mining investment and production. Further, eligibility for crediting was conditional upon freezing the state-based royalty rates. Technically, these measures ran the risk of infringing section 118 of the Constitution which requires the Commonwealth to give 'full faith and credit' to the laws of the states.

Further, legal advice provided by the Australian Government Solicitor to the Treasury on 27 April 2010 with respect to the original RSPT highlighted 'a risk' that a scheme that enabled a company to claim a tax credit for royalties paid would contravene the constitution by applying differently in different States.[35] The Government Solicitor's advice released under freedom of information laws warned that a tax law that provides a credit for royalties paid would 'on its face' appear discriminatory because a miner could receive a different refund depending on which state it was in. The advice also cautioned that a cap on royalty rates at the time of the RSPT announcement – as proposed – could be outside the taxation powers and discriminatory. This is because it would set a different cap on the refund amount available in relation to each state; that cap would be frozen at a particular point in time.

The arrangement for reimbursing royalties which was integral to the proposed tax package also ran the risk of being declared unconstitutional, if the legislation was enacted on the grounds that the Commonwealth could be acting outside its constitutional powers.[36] The states could either argue that the arrangements amounted to a federal attempt to tax its property (by arguing that the Commonwealth's purported investment in its exploitation was tantamount to taxation) or interfering with the rights of the states themselves to regulate and charge for the use of that property (by arguing that the intended effect of royalties is to discourage activity and that the Commonwealth's reimbursement of them frustrates that intent).

In addition, the fact that the proposed tax also committed the government to taking on a proportion of the losses on resource projects in principle infringed section 55 of the constitution, which expressly provides that laws that impose taxes can be used to achieve only one purpose – taxation.

The foregoing underscores the complications in the gestation period of the proposed resources rent tax. To forestall a stillbirth of the tax, the consensus among constitutional law experts is that a delicate job would be needed in drafting the bill. Finally, while it may have been sensible for the Commonwealth to take the initiative in reforming the means of charging for mineral resource depletion, its failure in seeking out a workable consensus with the states and territories has placed the viability of the entire mining tax package in jeopardy. Consultation and agreement with the states is ultimately necessary to generate a stable rationalization of this charging mechanism.

CONCLUDING OBSERVATIONS

This chapter has highlighted the practical difficulties that federal jurisdictions encounter when the purported exercise of their regulatory powers in matters of national interest encroaches into areas that are traditionally within the jurisdictional competence of the constituent states. The flash-point often occurs in matters relating to the stewardship of the commons for the community as a whole, including future generations. Superimposed on the complexities of the intergovernmental demarcation issues is the stranglehold that powerful sectional interests have on public policy formulation, as demonstrated in the case of the resource rent tax proposal. In a speech to mining executives at the Melbourne Mining Club in London the chief executive officer of the mining giant Rio Tinto issued a not-too-subtle warning about the events in Canberra. The warning was directed to Australian politicians as well as those of other nations who might be attracted to the idea of 'resource nationalism' by increasing taxes on mining profits to think carefully through any such highly risky actions before announcing them.[37] He then added:

> Policy makers around the world can learn a lesson when considering a new tax to plug a revenue gap, or play to local politics. And that's the importance of fully considering the broader economic consequences and continued investment impacts. Such decisions must be made taking in a wide range of views, in a spirit of consultation and engagement.

He went on to say that the point missed by Australian bureaucrats and government is that, even though Australia's relative position in the world is special, it is by no means unique, as other parts of the planet also have the same resources that Australia possesses. He stated that those governments that encourage mining through their tax and legal systems can and will compete with Australia. Consequently, if the return on capital is better elsewhere, there will be a relative dearth of capital to maintain growth in countries that seek to introduce policies that are unfriendly to the mining sector.

The powerful sectional interests have also capitalized on free riding as a perfect cloak to disguise their pursuit of the status quo. This has been evident in the failed attempts in several countries to introduce a pricing mechanism on carbon emissions in the global fight to stem the tide of climate change. As evidenced in Australia the integrity of the draft legislation of its ill-fated carbon pollution reduction scheme was undermined when in late 2009 the government caved in to lobbying from the emissions-intensive trade exposed industries by granting them overgenerous compensation arrangements. These concessions created an anomalous situation in which the Australian government's proposed emissions trading scheme would have ended up in paying the polluter to pollute instead of making the polluter pay.

Emboldened by its success, the mining sector is insisting that the government consider the sector's acceptance of the watered-down proposed resource rent tax as being conditional on their being exempted from the proposed carbon pricing regime.

Addressing the major environmental degradation challenges of our time will require a paradigm shift – and taxes and market instruments will play a pivotal role in the policy mix. Acceptance building is one of the major challenges to environmental tax reform. To ensure that public policy in this area maintains its legitimacy in the community, all stakeholders must be fully engaged in the policy formulation process through effective public education programs and consultations that are conducted in good faith. The need for transparency in such situations is paramount as it avoids secret deals which, when they eventually leak out, heighten public cynicism.

Evaluating the revised resources rent tax proposal in the context of the foregoing, it becomes increasingly apparent that the prospect of it achieving its dual objectives – tackling intergenerational equity as well as the two-speed economy – is not promising. With respect to the former, the weak link in the policy relates to the management of revenues from non-renewable resources. The government proposes to spend all the expected higher budget revenues from resource taxation. This essentially implies that the price increases are assumed to be permanent, and to that extent risks a costly reversal of some spending should prices fall again. This differs from the approach adopted by countries with broadly similar circumstances – for example, Norway and Chile – which have established sovereign funds financed by revenue from the taxation of non-renewable resources.[38] Even though the motivations of these two funds are not identical, they do perform the same functions, such as shielding fiscal policy from commodity price fluctuations and limiting the risks that policy will be pro-cyclical. There have been calls from several quarters to deploy the super profits from the mining boom into sovereign wealth funds so that future generations may also benefit from this once-in-a century boom. The former Finance Minister Lindsay Tanner said in November 2010 that the government might consider the idea, but only once the budget was back in surplus.[39] This is in spite of the conclusions of a Treasury report, which examined the issue of sovereign funds, that Australia did not have a public debt issue and that the community should be less concerned about running budget deficits, as long as day-to-day operations are met.[40]

In the case of the latter objective of the proposed tax package, it is unlikely to address the challenges of the two-speed economy, as the changes in the watered-down version are not neutral. Rather, it will end up distorting investment decisions. Not only has its scope in terms of the coverage of minerals been severely curtailed, thereby favouring some types of mining projects over others, but the writing-off of cost deductions is too generous as the costs are carried forward at a discount rate that is too high. Even among the projects which will be subject to the tax, it only applies to those earning more than AU$50 million a year. This makes it doubtful whether the tax package would raise the projected revenue streams being bandied around by government and Treasury.

In this respect, it is quite instructive to note that in May 2010, when the then Prime Minister Kevin Rudd announced the super profits tax, he said it would raise AU$12.5 billion. Following the breakthrough agreement on 2 July 2010 after his removal from office, incoming Prime Minister Gillard said the revised tax would raise AU$10.5 billion. The Treasury Secretary confirmed this three days later, saying that the estimate was supported by raised commodities price assumptions. Then on 9 November 2010, the Treasury cut revenue estimates to AU$7.4 billion, blaming the strong Australian dollar.[41]

Further, the 1 per cent reduction in corporate taxes is unlikely to benefit most small businesses in the country as they do not conduct their operations through the corporate structure. It is these businesses that are experiencing the worst effects of wage pressures brought on by available labour and skills being absorbed by mining companies.

Finally, as pointed out in the paper, the entire proposed tax package is based on shaky constitutional foundations, and if the government is to avoid a potentially damaging constitutional challenge, it will need to take great care in the way that the text of the legislation is drafted.

NOTES

[*] Moira Saccasan was involved in the early stages of the development of this chapter. However, Hope Ashiabor has been responsible for its preparation.
[1.] See World Commission on Environment and Development (1987).
[2.] See Brundtland (1987), p. 7.
[3.] Some of the protocols include a mandatory requirement for industries to undertake environmental impact assessments prior to the commencement of the projects; other countries (Australia, Canada), for instance, provide tax incentives to foster the rehabilitation of mining sites; the US uses the superfund tax system to achieve this end.
[4.] See Australia's Future Tax System Review Panel (2009), p. 217.
[5.] See Swan (2010).
[6.] See Geoscience Australia (2008).
[7.] See BP (2009).
[8.] This phrase was first coined by *The Economist* in 1977 to describe how Holland's North Sea oil discoveries in 1959 coincided with a decline in Dutch manufacturing. See *The Economist*, print edition (2010).
[9.] See *Business Review Weekly* (2010).
[10.] See World Commission on Environment and Development (1987), p. 8.
[11.] See *ibid.*

12. Australia has a potpourri of royalty regimes characterised by wide variations in the rate thresholds and royalty bases. For example, the states implement an output-based royalty system, while the federal government implements a profit-based royalty regime in the Northern Territories and a rent-based royalty regime to the Barrow Island project. Offshore resources (currently petroleum) are subject to the overgenerous PRRT regime which is based on cash lows.
13. See Australia's Future Tax System Review Panel (2009), p. 226.
14. Information from this section has been drawn from Commonwealth of Australia (2010), pp. 23–7; Australia's Future Tax System Review Panel (2009), pp. 221–3, 233–6.
15. See Brown (1948).
16. See Garnaut and Ross (1975).
17. See Boadway and Bruce (1984).
18. See Australia's Future Tax System Review Panel (2009).
19. *Ibid.*, p. 220.
20. See Commonwealth of Australia (2010).
21. The coverage of the RSPT was to apply to onshore petroleum drilling, uranium, black coal, iron ore, gold, silver, copper, lead, nickel, tin, zinc, bauxite, diamonds, other precious stones and mineral sands. Brown coal was to be further considered.
22. See Commonwealth of Australia (2010), pp. 29–30.
23. See Evans, Krever and Mellor (2009), pp.379–80.
24. Ben Smith, Chapter 15, 'Charging for non-renewable resource depletion, or slimming the goose: Less *foie gras* but more golden eggs?', in Evans, Krever and Mellor (2009), p. 380.
25. The taxation power under section 51(ii) of the Constitution is qualified by section 51(xxxi), which imposes a condition on the Commonwealth's power to make laws with respect to the acquisition of property, except on just terms.
26. See *Newcrest Mining (WA) Ltd* v. *Commonwealth* (1997) 190 CLR 513, (1997) 147 ALR 42, available at: www.aph.gov.au/library/pubs/rn/1997–98/98rn06.htm.
27. Policy Transition Group Membership and Terms of Reference, www.alp.org.au/federal-government/news/policy-transition-group-membership-and-terms-of-re/ (accessed 14 December 2010).
28. Commonwealth of Australia, Policy Transition Group (2010).
29. Queensland announced a raft of royalty increases in the 2008–09 year, some of which will take effect from 1 January 2011.
30. See OECD (2010), pp. 15, 69–72.
31. Merritt (2010).
32. Industry Commission (1991).
33. See Ben Smith, Chapter 15, in Evans, Krever and Mellor (2009), p. 384.
34. *Ibid.*
35. The Constitution gives the Commonwealth the power to make laws but so 'as not to discriminate' between states. It also prevents the Commonwealth from making laws regulating trade or commerce that gives 'preference to one State'.
36. Section 114 of the Constitution prevents the Commonwealth and the states from imposing 'any tax' on their respective 'property of any kind': Merritt (2010).
37. Albanese (2010).
38. OECD (2010), p. 75; Australia's Future Tax System Review Panel (2009), p. 224; Osmundsen (2010).
39. Martin (2010).
40. See Australian Government, The Treasury (2010).
41. Probyn (2010).

REFERENCES

Albanese, T., Chief Executive Officer, Rio Tinto (2010), 'Mining issues, a global view', presented at the Melbourne Mining Club in London, 8 July. The full text of the speech can be accessed at: www.riotinto.com/media/18435_presentations19361.asp.

Australia's Future Tax System Review Panel (December 2009), *Australia's Future Tax System: Report to the Treasurer* (Henry Review; AFTS report).

Australian Government, The Treasury (2010), *Economic Roundup*, Issue 1, 2010, 'Managing manna from below: sovereign wealth funds and extractive industries in the Pacific'.

Boadway, R., and N. Bruce (1984), 'A general proposition on the design of a neutral business tax', *Journal of Public Economics*, **24**(2), 231–9.

BP (2009), *BP Statistical Review of World Energy*, June, available at: www.bp.com/statisticalreview.

Brown, E.C. (1948), 'Business-income taxation and investment incentives', in L.A. Metzler, *Income, Employment and Public Policy: Essays in Honour of Alvin H Hansen*, New York, Norton, pp. 300–316.

Brundtland, G.M., Chairman, World Commission on Environment and Development (1987), 'Presentation of the Report of the World Commission on Environment and Development to UNEP's 14th Governing Council Session', Nairobi, Kenya, 8 June.

Business Review Weekly (October 21–27 2010), 'Cover Story: Ride the Boom', **32**(41), 22 at 24.

Commonwealth of Australia (2010), *The Resource Super Profits Tax – A Fair Return to the Nation*, Canberra, Australian Government.

Commonwealth of Australia, Policy Transition Group (2010), 'Technical design of the minerals resource rent tax, transitioning existing petroleum projects to the petroleum resource rent tax, and policies to promote exploration expenditure', issues paper, 1 October.

Economist, The, print edition (2010), 'A special report on Latin America: it's only natural: commodities alone are not enough to sustain flourishing economies', 9 September, available at: www.economist.com/node/16964094.

Evans, C., R. Krever and P. Mellor (2009), *Australia's Future Tax System: The prospects after Henry (Essays in honour of John W Freebairn)*, Sydney, Thomson-Reuters, pp. 379–80.

Garnaut, R., and A.C. Ross (1975), 'Uncertainty, risk aversion and the taxing of natural resource projects', *Economic Journal*, **85**(338), 272–87.

Geoscience Australia (2008), *Australia's Identified Mineral Resources 2008*, Canberra, Geoscience Australia, available at: www.ga.gov.au.

Industry Commission (1991), *Mining and Minerals Processing in Australia*, Report No. 7.

Land, B.C. (2010), 'Resource rent taxes – a re-appraisal', in P. Daniel, M. Keen and C. McPherson, *The Taxation of Petroleum and Minerals: Principles, Problems and Practice*, Oxford, Routledge, pp. 241–63.

Martin, Peter (2010) (2010), 'Treasury probes sovereign wealth funds', *The Sydney Morning Herald*, 10 April, Business Day liftout, available at: www.smh.com.au/business/treasury-probes-sovereign-wealth-funds-20100409-ryxo.html (accessed 21 January 2011).

Merritt, Chris, legal affairs editor (2010), 'How to kill the resource tax', *The Australian*, 21 May, pp. 33–4.

Newcrest Mining (WA) Ltd v. *Commonwealth* (1997) 190 CLR 513; (1997) 147 ALR 42, available at: www.aph.gov.au/library/pubs/rn/1997–98/98rn06.htm.

Organisation for Economic Co-operation and Development (OECD) (2010), *OECD Economic Surveys: Australia*

Osmundsen, P. (2010), 'Time consistency in petroleum taxation: lessons from Norway', in P. Daniel, M. Keen and C. McPherson, *The Taxation of Petroleum and Minerals: Principles, Problems and Practice*, Oxford, Routledge, pp. 425–44.

Policy Transition Group Membership and Terms of Reference, available at: www.alp.org.au/federal-government/news/policy-transition-group-membership-and-terms-of-re/.

Probyn, Andrew (2010), 'Mining tax estimate tumbles' *The West Australian*, 24 December, available at: http://au.news.yahoo.com/thewest/a/-/newshome/8559902/mining-tax-estimate-tumbles/ (accessed 17 February 2011).

Swan, Hon. Wayne, Treasurer (2010), 'A stronger economy and a fairer share for all Australians', ministerial statement, House of Representatives, Canberra, 24 May, available at: http://ministers.treasury.gov.au/DisplayDocs.aspx?doc=speeches/2010/013.htm&pageID=005&min=wms&Year=&DocType=1 (accessed 30 July 2010).

World Commission on Environment and Development (1987), *Our Common Future*, Oxford, Oxford University Press.

14. Australia's proposals to tax coal super profits: a cautionary tale for the environment

Bill Butcher

INTRODUCTION

Coal is a vital resource, producing 27 per cent of the world's energy and 42 per cent of global electricity.[1] For Australia, it is especially critical, given that it produces 76 per cent of Australia's electricity and is a vital major export commodity.[2] As is well known, these benefits do not come without a cost, the great disadvantage being the damage the consumption of coal causes to the global environment, particularly in the generation of electricity. Coal accounts for up to 37 per cent of Australia's greenhouse gas emissions,[3] and about 20 per cent of global emissions.[4]

This chapter examines the treatment of coal under the Australian taxation system. It considers the current regime for taxing the extraction and sale of coal, examines recent proposals for major reform of mineral tax policy, and concludes with observations on the place of green issues and imperatives within that regime.

THE CURRENT AUSTRALIAN SYSTEM

Any discussion of coal taxation must start with the understanding that minerals in the ground belong to the state, which may grant, through licensing or some other means, the right to extract and sell those minerals. Naturally, the entity to which that right is granted must pay for it, usually in addition to the normal income tax imposed on any profits generated through its business activities. In Australia, as in many countries, the payment for the right to extract and sell coal takes the form of royalties. The Australian Federal Constitution preserves in the states this right to impose and collect mineral royalties to the states, rather than granting it to the federal government.

Royalties are deductible for income tax purposes, resulting in an effective transfer of revenue from federal government to state governments (income tax being a federal impost). Any increase in royalties collected by states means a reduction in the income tax that can be collected by federal government. As will be discussed later in this chapter, this is an issue at the heart of the current controversy over the proposed new federal mining tax.

States are free to set their own rates for royalties. Table 14.1 provides a comparison of selected Australian state royalty regimes.[5]

Table 14.1 Selected Australian state royalty regimes

State	Royalty rate	Basis of calculation	Last review/change
QLD	7% where the value of the coal produced does not exceed $100/tonne 10% on the value of the coal exceeding $100/tonne	*Ad valorem*	2008 – Mines and Energy Legislation Amendment Regulation (No. 2) 2008
NSW	Open cut mining 8.2% Underground mining 7.2% Deep underground mining 6.2%	*Ad valorem*	2008 – State Revenue and Other Legislation Amendment (Budget Measures) Act 2008
VIC	Brown coal $0.0588 per GJ, adjusted in accordance with the consumer price index Other than brown coal 2.75%	*Ad valorem* with quantum rate for brown coal	2006 – Mineral Resources Development (Amendment) Regulations 2006
WA	If exported 7.5% If not exported $1/tonne (adjusted each year on 30 June in accordance with comparative price increases)	*Ad valorem* and quantum rate	2000 – Mining Amendment Regulations (No. 4) 2000
SA	3.5%	*Ad valorem*	2005 – Mining (Royalty No 2) Amendment Act 2005

From an environmental tax perspective, two features stand out from Table 14.1.

First, New South Wales has differential rates according to whether the coal is extracted through open cut mining, underground mining and deep underground mining. This might be seen as a form of green taxation, where the more damaging the activity is to the surface environment, the higher the royalty. On the other hand, it can also be explained economically in two ways: since underground mining involves greater risk and expense, the New South Wales government may be concerned to minimize the disincentives to such endeavours; and coal situated deep underground, being harder to extract, has a lower value than coal nearer the surface and hence should bear a lower royalty to reflect that lower value.

Second, Victoria, the only state that produces the far less efficient and more environmentally damaging brown coal (or lignite), taxes it based on its energy yield, unlike the more typical *ad valorem* method. Effectively, this is the opposite of a green tax in that it imposes less tax on the ore which is least efficient and which produces the most carbon dioxide per unit of electricity produced. In Pigouvian terms, this is a situation where that which has the greatest negative externalities is taxed the least, when the reverse should be the case.[6] It is also noteworthy that black coal, along with all other minerals (apart from brown coal), is taxed in Victoria at the relatively low rate of 2.75 per cent.

THE PROBLEM WITH ROYALTIES

Royalty-based systems of mineral taxation calculate imposts according to the quantity or value of coal produced and are levied irrespective of the cost of production. They take no direct account of the amount of any profit is being made.[7] This discourages miners from extracting lower-grade minerals which generate lower profits and, while this itself has environmental benefits, it unfavourably distorts investment decisions. A wide ranging report into the Australian taxation system, *Australia's Future Tax System* (known colloquially as the Henry Review) released in 2010 stated that: 'Australia's current resource charging arrangements and the mechanisms for allocating exploration permits distort investment and production decisions, further lowering the community's return from the exploitation of its non-renewable resources.'[8]

Moreover, revenue impositions under the current royalty-based system do not reflect windfall profits that occur when commodity prices rise above the levels anticipated by miners when calculating their expected rate of return before investing in a project. A high level policy group tasked in late 2010 to examine resource taxation commented on the inefficiency of the royalty-based system in these terms: 'royalty regimes are inherently less flexible during a downturn and can unnecessarily damage the industries and prevent optimal resource extraction. Further, by their nature the royalty regimes do not capture the economic rents during a boom period.'[9] Who should benefit from these 'rents'[10] – the state, which owns the minerals, or the mining companies that took the risks and provided the investment to extract them? Under the royalty-based system most of the benefit falls to the miners, and there is a growing view that this should be shared more evenly with the state. This was the view taken by the Henry Review.

PROPOSAL FOR A NEW RESOURCE TAXATION SCHEME

Among the Henry Review's 138 recommendations was a proposal for a federal tax on mining profits. Recommendation 45 proposed:

> The current resource charging arrangements imposed on non-renewable resources by the Australian and State governments should be replaced by a uniform resource rent tax imposed and administered by the Australian government that:
>
> (a) is levied at a rate of 40 per cent, with that rate adjusted to offset any future change in the company income tax rate from 25 per cent, to achieve a combined statutory tax rate of 55 per cent;
>
> (b) applies to non-renewable resource (oil, gas and minerals) projects, except for lower value minerals for which it can be expected to generate no net benefits. Excepted minerals could continue to be subject to existing arrangements if appropriate;
>
> (c) measures rents as net income less an allowance for corporate capital, with the allowance rate set at the long-term Australian government bond rate;
>
> (d) requires a rent calculation for projects;
>
> (e) allows losses to be carried forward with interest or transferred to other commonly owned projects, with the tax value of residual losses refunded when a project is closed; and
>
> (f) is allowed as a deductible expense in the calculation of income tax, with loss refunds treated as assessable income.

State royalties paid would generate a credit against the resource rent tax. As will be seen later in the chapter, this creates a new transfer of revenue from federal to state governments and has become a major sticking point to the introduction of a new resource tax.

The Henry Review left open the issue of whether brown coal should be subject to the resource rent tax, indicating that given its greater polluting effect, brown coal might be subject to higher tax levels and stating:

'Whether brown coal should be subject to the resource rent tax merits further consideration.'[11]

THE FIRST GOVERNMENT RESPONSE – THE RESOURCE SUPER PROFITS TAX (RSPT)

The Henry Review recommendation for a rent tax on mining was one of the few taken up, albeit in a modified form, by the Australian government. The government proposed a RSPT to be introduced with effect from 1 July 2012.[12] This was to be imposed in addition to (and interacting with) the royalties payable to the states, and federally levied income tax.

The main features of the RSPT were:

- a 40 per cent tax rate on assessable resource profits;
- the tax to be imposed on revenue less deductions with an allowance for capital expenditure;
- the tax to be imposed on profits above the 'normal' rate of return – determined as 6 per cent, being the 'risk free' long-term bond rate (LTBR); and
- to compensate for the higher risk involved in mining ventures, losses on abandoned projects were to be refunded at the mirror rate of 40 per cent of the loss suffered.

Effectively, the government would be a 40 per cent 'partner' in any venture, sharing the risk as well as any 'rent' profits.[13] This contrasted with the petroleum resources rent tax (PRRT) levied since 1988 on profits from the sale of offshore oil and gas, which sets a 'normal' rate of return at 11 per cent (the LTBR plus an uplift of 5 per cent in recognition of the higher business risk involved) but allows no refund in the event of a loss.

The RSPT was to be deductible in the calculation of income for federal income tax purposes, and to be reduced by any royalties paid to state governments.

The RSPT was vigorously opposed by the mining industry in a campaign which contributed to the replacement of the sitting Prime Minister, Kevin Rudd. Miners objected to their exclusion from the decision-making process and argued that the tax was imposed on profits, rather than 'super' profits (given the absence of any uplift above the government bond rate). Concerns were forcefully expressed that the potential effective tax rate of up to 58 per cent (adding together income tax and the RSPT) and the sovereign risk involved in the potential for unpredictable taxes would discourage investment, thereby damaging the Australian mineral industry, resulting in a loss of employment and endangering Australia's recovery from the global financial crisis.[14]

SECOND GOVERNMENT RESPONSE – MINERAL RESOURCE RENT TAX (MRRT)

Following consultation with the mining industry, particularly the larger miners, the government abandoned the RSPT[15] and announced a new proposal for the taxation of 'super' mining profits – the MRRT. It differs from the RSPT in a number of respects, as follows.

- Unlike the RSPT, which had a much wider reach, the MRRT is to tax only iron ore and coal and will not be imposed on smaller producers (those whose MRRT assessable profits are less than $50 million per annum).
- The nominal tax rate is 30 per cent, rather than the RSPT's 40 per cent, and due to a 25 per cent 'extraction allowance', the effective MRRT rate is 22.5 per cent. The extraction allowance is to compensate miners for the extra returns from items like managerial expertise, entrepreneurship and technical innovation that will be captured by the tax. This is to 'focus the tax on the value of the resource rather than the value added through mining expertise'.[16] This means, when income tax is added, the effective combined tax rate for companies affected by the MRRT will be between 42 per cent and 45 per cent, rather than the potential 58 per cent under the RSPT.
- The MRRT is levied on the operating margin (revenue less operating and investment costs) less the extraction allowance and the 'MRRT allowance'. The MRRT allowance is the LBTR plus 7 per cent. The additional uplift of 7 per cent is to recognize the risk involved in mining investments. Because that risk is now being recognised at the calculation stage, losses will not now be refundable by the government.
- Unutilised losses can be carried forward at the LTBR plus 7 per cent.

As under the RSPT, the MRRT is deductible for income tax purposes and allows a credit for state royalties (with unused royalty credits to be uplifted at LTBR plus 7 per cent).

THE MRRT – A WORKED EXAMPLE

This example is taken from the Government Fact Sheet on MRRT[17]

The example presents outcomes for a single project company with an equity financed mine that operates for five years. The company is assumed to invest $1 billion in the first year of the project. Over the life of the project the pre-tax rate of return (revenue less operating and investment costs) is 50 per cent.

The MRRT is levied at a rate of 30 per cent of the operating margin (revenue less operating and investment costs) less the MRRT allowance and the extraction allowance. The MRRT allowance is calculated as the value of unused losses uplifted by an allowance rate equal to the LTBR plus 7 percentage points. The extraction allowance provides a 25 per cent discount to the MRRT liability to focus the tax on the value of the resource rather than the value added through mining expertise.

State royalties are assumed to be equal to 7.5 per cent of sales revenue and are credited against the MRRT liability to produce the net MRRT liability. Where royalty payments exceed the MRRT liability in any one year, the balance is uplifted at the allowance rate to be offset against future MRRT liabilities. The total resource charge is the sum of royalties paid in the year and the net MRRT liability.

In this example the average tax rate over the life of the project (total tax as a percentage of total profit before tax) is 42.3 per cent.

Table 14.2 Average tax rate over the life of the project

	Year 1	Year 2	Year 3	Year 4	Year 5	Year 6
Resource charge	$m	$m	$m	$m	$m	$m
Revenue	0	520	830	910	1090	1100
Operating expenses	0	130	210	230	270	280
Depreciation	1000	0	0	0	0	0
MRRT allowance @ 13%	0	130	96	28	0	0
MRRT unutilised losses	0	1000	740	216	0	0
MRRT profit/loss	–1000	–740	–216	436	820	820
MRRT @ 30%	0	0	0	131	246	246

	Year 1	Year 2	Year 3	Year 4	Year 5	Year 6
Extraction allowance @ 25%	0	0	0	33	62	62
MRRT after extraction allowance	0	0	0	98	185	185
Royalty @ 7.5%	0	39	62	68	82	83
Uplifted royalty offset	0	0	44	120	102	0
Net MRRT	0	0	0	0	1	102
Total resource charge	0	39	62	68	82	185
Company tax						
Revenue	0	520	830	910	1090	110
Operating expenses	0	130	210	230	270	280
Depreciation	0	200	200	200	200	200
Total resource charge	0	39	62	68	82	185
Company taxable income	0	151	358	412	538	436
Company tax @ 29%	**0**	**44**	**104**	**119**	**156**	**126**
Profit before tax	0	190	420	480	620	620
Total tax	0	83	166	188	238	311

CONSTITUTIONAL PROBLEMS WITH THE MRRT

The validity of the MRRT has been questioned on constitutional grounds. The primary argument stems from the principle that under the Australian Constitution, federal government has only the powers delegated to it by the states upon federation in 1901. These do not include ownership or control of mining land, which belong to the states where the land is located. Hence the federal government has no taxing power over that land or the minerals contained in it. Consequently, the federal government has no power to impose the MRRT, since it can be regarded as a tax on minerals. Moreover, s. 114 of the Australian Constitution forbids the federal government from taxing state government property. The federal response is that the MRRT is a tax on profits, which is within its powers, and is not a tax on the land or the minerals themselves.

Another constitutional question arises over the crediting of royalties in the imposition of the MRRT. If all royalties are credited, this is unlikely to be an issue, but if they are not, it could be argued that this would constitute a prohibited discrimination between the states.[18] A possibility examined below is that the federal government will limit the credit to the rates that were imposed on 2 May 2010, the date the government reached agreement with the larger miners on the terms of the MRRT. If a state raised its royalties above those rates and the increase was not credited under the MRRT, there would be an argument that this was discriminatory, particularly if the state was only raising its rates to match the levels of higher charging states.[19]

Section 118 of the Constitution raises a further problem. It requires the federal government to give 'full faith and credit' to the laws of the states. While the states would still be able to receive royalties, the impact of the states' royalty laws on mining companies would be neutralised by the full crediting of royalties against the MRRT. From the mining companies' perspective their operations, once profitable, would effectively be subject to tax at rates determined purely by income tax and MRRT rates. The companies would still pay royalties to the states but because these are credited against MRRT they would generally be rendered irrelevant in after tax profit calculations. The only situation in which this would not be the case would be if a state were to impose royalties higher than the effective MRRT rate, an unlikely scenario, or if the federal government imposed limits on the crediting of royalties, a hotly contested possibility. The interaction between royalties and MRRT is considered further in the next section of the chapter.

None of these constitutional issues have yet been determined by a court, but a state government or mining company challenge to the MRRT based on these arguments is widely anticipated.[20]

INTEGRATION BETWEEN ROYALTIES AND THE MRRT

There is heated debate between the federal government and the resource-rich states over the crediting of royalties against the MRRT. Federal government insists that credits be limited to royalties in force on 2 May 2010 while the states (and the mining companies) assert that credits should extend to any future royalty increases. In this, the states have been supported by the federal government's Policy Transition Group (PTG) in its report on resource taxation released on 21 December 2010.[21] The states maintain that they should be free to set their own royalty rates without restriction.[22] While the MRRT does not attempt to preclude states from raising royalties, a quarantining of credits would constrain their freedom to do so because it would raise the total tax payable by mining companies, which can be expected to raise formidable opposition, given their forceful and successful opposition to the RSPT. Allowance of a credit on all royalties, present and future, has important consequences for federal revenues, as it would free resource states to raise their royalties in the knowledge that federal government, rather than the mining companies, will effectively bear the cost.

In its support for full credits, the PTG said

> ... the MRRT should not be used as a mechanism to enable States and Territories to increase inefficient royalties on MRRT taxable commodities. Accordingly the PTG also recommends that Australian, State and Territory Governments put in place arrangements to ensure that State and Territory Governments do not have an incentive to increase royalties on coal and iron ore.[23]

The PTG did not say what these arrangements might be but given the financial dependence of the states on federal funding, one approach, albeit provocative, would be for the federal government to withhold payments to any mining state which raised royalties.

OBSERVATIONS AND CONCLUSION

Throughout the debate and consultation process over the new resource tax there has been no real consideration of environmental objectives. Some thought should have been given to taking express account of environmental damage in the calculation and imposition of the tax.

One possibility would be to calculate the tax on the basis of energy yield (with the lower grades taxed at a higher rate) rather than exclusively on the basis of profits. This would have sent a signal to the market highlighting the environmental damage caused by the burning of coal, imposed a greater impost on the worst polluting ores and generated support for renewable energy sources. This should be a central consideration in the design of all future resource taxes. While it would have produced a more desirable outcome, it is a regrettable reality that in the current Australian economic and political climate it would have been highly problematic. It would first have required a determination of the energy yield of all coal extracted which, while this is done with brown coal in Victoria, would have added a layer of practical complexity and provided more ammunition to the opponents of the tax. Moreover, it could have resulted in a flight from investment in the lower grade ores, particularly brown coal.

Another possibility would have been a pure carbon tax, taxing the coal on its carbon content.[24]

While either of these possibilities would have yielded environmental benefits, it must be recognized that they would have involved economic and political damage. A tax based on energy yield or carbon content would also have drawn attention away from the major and most politically successful argument for the MRRT – that miners are experiencing extraordinary profits which should be shared with the owner of the commodities upon which the profits are generated – the community at large. Given the political sensitivity of the issue, it is an unfortunate truth that an appeal at this time and in this setting to voters' environmental concerns could well have been premature and politically unpalatable.

Less politically sensitive would have been to allocate a meaningful part of the tax revenues raised by the MRRT to environmental protection measures, including the research and development of renewable energy sources and 'clean coal' technology.[25]

The resources tax, as currently designed, has been constructed without regard to environmental issues. Equally regrettable is the absence, throughout the vigorous and highly publicized debate surrounding the resource tax, of any serious discussion of the environmental damage caused by the widespread dependence on coal as an energy source. Unless there is an unexpected and major policy change in the very near future, the story of the Australian mining tax represents a delayed (rather than missed) opportunity to achieve greater public awareness[26] and tangible environmental benefits.

NOTES

1. Australian Coal Association, NewGen Coal, 'Our energy security', available at: www.newgencoal.com.au/coal-in-australia.aspx.
2. Coal accounts for 25 per cent of Australia's export earnings. See MBendi Information Services, 'Coal mining in Australia – overview', available at: www.mbendi.com/indy/ming/coal/au/au/p0005.htm.
3. Australian Coal Association, *supra* note 1.
4. Pew Centre on Global Climate Change, 'Coal and climate change facts', available at: www.pewclimate.org/global-warming-basics/coalfacts.cfm.
5. Table source: Bowie, Craig (2010), *A review of mining royalties in Australia*, MinterEllison Lawyers, available at: www.minterellison.com/public/connect/Internet/Home/Legal+Insights/Newsletters/Previous+Newsletters/A-ERU3+mining+royalties+overview. Tasmania imposes a composite royalty, capped at 5 per cent, which is a combination of an *ad valorem* royalty and a profit tax.

6. For discussion of Pigouvian economics, see Milne, J. (2003), 'Environmental Taxation: Why Theory Matters', in Janet Milne, Kurt Deketelaere, Larry Kreiser and Hope Ashiabor (eds) *Volume 1 Critical Issues in Environmental Taxation: International and Comparative Perspectives,* Richmond Law and Tax Publishing (UK).

7. They also normally take no account of environmental damage. The New South Wales distinction between open cut mining, underground mining and deep underground mining is not typical.

8. Commonwealth of Australia (2010) *Australia's Future Tax Review Final Report – Detailed Analysis,* p. 230.

9. Commonwealth of Australia, Policy Transition Group (2010), *New Resource Taxation Arrangements,* p. 57.

10. The economists' term for such windfall profits.

11. *Supra* note 8, p. 237.

12. Commonwealth of Australia (2010), *Tax Policy Statement Stronger Fairer Simpler – A Tax Plan For Our Future,* p. iii.

13. In this way, the RSPT is a form of modified 'Brown' tax. The Brown tax is named after a paper by American economist E. Cary Brown, 'Business income and investment incentives', in Lloyd Metzler (ed.), *Income, Employment and Public Policy: Essays in Honor of Alvin H Hansen,* 1948, New York, W.W. Norton & Co., which at its simplest involves the government sharing with investors in profitable periods through taxation and in unprofitable periods through refunds.

14. Thornton, H. (2010), ''Super-profit tax will damage Australia's safe for business reputation, *The Australian,* 21 May, available at: www.theaustralian.com.au/business/opinion/super-profit-tax-will-damage-australias-safe-for-business-reputation/story-e6frg9ix-1225869601896.

15. Managan, M. (2010), 'That's it – the RSPT is dead', *Business Spectator,* 24 June, available at: www.businessspectator.com.au/bs.nsf/Article/Thats-it-the-RSPT-is-dead-pd20100624–6PTN8?OpenDocument&src=blb.

16. Commonwealth of Australia (2010), 'Fact Sheet – a new resource taxation regime', 2 July, p. 3.

17. *Ibid.*, p. 4.

18. The restriction against discriminating against the states is implied in the Constitution: *Queensland Electricity Commission* v. *Commonwealth* (1985) 159 CLR 192. Arguably, a form of discrimination already exists because different states impose different rates of royalties, which are currently deductible to the mining companies against their (federal) assessable income, but since *all* royalties are deductible it has never been suggested that this is unconstitutional.

19. As shown in Table 14.1 *supra,* royalty rates are not uniform across the states.

20. ABC News (2010), 'Mining tax legal challenge ' "highly likely"', 3 July, available at: www.abc.net.au/news/stories/2010/07/02/2943832.htm3.

21. Commonwealth of Australia, Policy Transition Group (2010), *supra* note 9, p. 57.

22. Keho, Je and R. Kerr (2010), 'Swan mulls tax breaks for miners', *Australian Financial Review,* 22 December, available at: www.afr.com/p/national/swan_mulls_tax_break_for_miners_0DDPNDpzmueYYIZxxo6NGN. The primary resource states are Western Australia and Queensland.

23. Commonwealth of Australia, Policy Transition Group (2010), *supra* note 9, p. 57.

24. Milne, J (2007), 'Green taxes and climate change theory and reality', in CESifo DICE Report 4/2007, 9, available at: at www.cesifo-group.de/portal/page/portal/DocBase_Content/ZS/ZS-CESifo_DICE_Report/zs-dice-2007/zs-dice-2007–4/dicereport407-forum2.pdf.

25. The Australian government currently operates a $5.1 billion Clean Energy Initiative, consisting of the $1.9 billion Carbon Capture and Storage (CCS) Flagships Program, the $1.5 billion Solar Flagships Program, the $150 million Australian Solar Institute and the Australian Centre for Renewable Energy. See www.ret.gov.au/ENERGY/ENERGY%20PROGRAMS/CEI/Pages/default.aspx.

26. See Pigou, A. (1932), *The Economics of Welfare*, 4th edn, London, Macmillan, pp. 113–14 contending that education on environmental prudence has long-term benefits through its impact on future generations.

Index